David

Good luck ... leadership wher you are and whatever you do.

Warm Regards

Jonathan

Jan 2015

inspiring
LEADERSHIP

Leadership Lessons from my Life

Jonathan Perks MBE

Fisher King Publishing

Inspiring Leadership
Published by
Fisher King Publishing
The Studio
Arthington Lane
Pool-in-Wharfedale
LS21 1JZ
England

ISBN 978-1-906377-86-1

Edited by Mary-Ellen Wyard
Illustrated by Jake Shepherd
Photography by Bill Prentice
Cover design by Sam Richardson

Dedicated to generations past:
My parents Paul and Tricia Perks.
You continue to inspire
our today and tomorrow.

Also to my family
Bridget, Harriet and Bryony
and my brothers Graeme and David

CONTENTS

ACKNOWLEDGMENTS

The most powerful encouragement for me to write this book came from my wife Bridget, who for the last six years has believed in my ability to write it and patiently encouraged me to begin. She has been my constant companion through the shaping and editing process over the past twelve months. I am grateful to Nancy Kline and Reuven Bar-On for their personal examples and inspiration. I am indebted to Reuven Bar-On who reviewed two previous drafts of the manuscript and suggested the idea of the eight-point compass.

Rick Armstrong the owner of Fisher King Publishing gave me further encouragement and the publishing support to enable me to produce this book. I also appreciate the creative branding skills of Jake Shepherd of MSDC and photographic genius of Bill Prentice. My colleagues in Penna Consulting, in particular my friends in the board and executive coaching team have also supported me and over the years have taught me a lot about leadership.

Life is full of feedback and if you are prepared to listen it is a true gift. I appreciate the help of close friends and colleagues who painstakingly read my first draft which has changed into this significantly different book. Finally my gratitude goes to the many leaders I have come across in my life so far who have been my role models. Thanks to their example I have been able to develop this philosophy of "Inspiring Leadership".

FOREWORD

Nancy Kline
Author of *Time to Think*
and *More Time to Think*

We have needed this book for a long time. We have needed to hear unequivocally that the finest acts of leadership are acts of inspiration and love. Not acts of fluff. Not of seduction. Not of sentiment. But acts of respect, of feeling, of humility, of presence, of listening, of being-with, of letting go. We have needed to hear from the world of hard-results that the finest leaders actually lead with humanity, inspiration and hope.

This message would be bold enough coming from the life of a leadership developer, an executive coach, a builder of corporate teams. Jonathan is all of these. But this message is profound coming also from a military officer, decorated for his leadership brilliance and his success in the organisation that hardly anyone associates with the softer people skills. It turns out that inspiration is crucial when leading soldiers. As a pacifist, I have been moved to learn through this book about the complex peace-making that is the expertise of military officers. I have been encouraged about the ways they make a difference in the world through their inspiration and about why this inspiration defines their leadership.

Jonathan's message surprised me. Stereotypes, including military ones, suck their way through your skin. So when I discovered, after knowing Jonathan for three years, that he had been an army officer for twenty, I had to tear out every tentacled assumption about the military, and let this gentle, attentive, connected, congruent, emotionally intelligent, deeply-thinking man be also a retired military officer.

Jonathan's message also did not surprise me. My twin brother had flown the C-41 transport plane in the US Air Force, also a commended military officer. And he was inspired. I knew that. But I had assumed he set aside his humanity to lead soldiers.

And our friend Charles Bremner, Colonel in the Welsh Guards, I had known always as a deeply caring, empowering person. Now I realise how important inspiring leadership was to him and those who followed him.

It turns out that great leadership depends on inspiration. Even in preparation for battle. Even in corporate teams. Even in boardrooms. It is when inspiration is missing in any of those sectors (or anywhere) that trouble starts. When inspiration and integrity leave, the important things: aligning action with values, asking hard questions, facing the truth, finding the better answer, building on strengths, igniting new thinking, also leave.

Jonathan tells us exactly what this leadership, this inspiration, is. He is concrete. He is factual. He is accurately theoretical. But he also shows us how to do this inspiring leadership by showing us people who have done it.

Most compellingly for me, he asks us questions. And he is serious about our answering them. He wants us to think. Actually, he wants us to re-think – just about everything: our dreams, who we are, what we most want, how we want to change the world, what we want to leave behind, what we care about most and how we express that with our lives and our relationships, not just our rhetoric.

And throughout he gets to the heart of leadership by speaking from his heart. He leads us, too, by inspiring us to stretch our thinking and our acts of personal leadership.

If we took to our hearts what Jonathan says, really absorbed and applied it systematically, many things would change, some fundamentally. I think we would find ourselves with new structures of economics, governance, learning and healing. I think, in fact, that if all leadership were to become inspiring leadership we would find ourselves at last in a world driven by meaning, and yes, ultimately, by peace.

My Parents: Tricia and Paul Perks

ONE

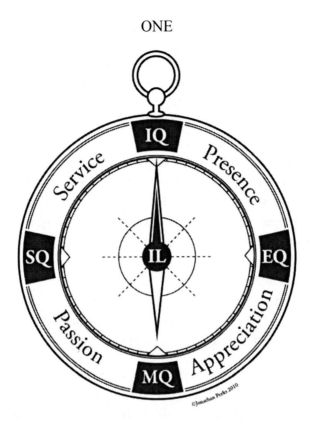

The Calling

"When soldiers know their leaders care for them as they care for their own children, then the soldiers love their leaders as they do their own fathers."

Liu Ji (1310-1375), Lessons of War

Inspiring Leadership

Changi, Singapore. 26th November 1964. Thursday. The day began with great promise as Lieutenant Commander Paul Perks climbed confidently into the cockpit of his Mark 1 Buccaneer aircraft. He grinned and gave a thumbs-up to his Senior Observer, Bill White. The shimmering heat was rising from the tarmac on the runway of RAF Tengah and the water sparkled across the bay where their aircraft carrier lay. Paul was Commanding Officer (CO) of 801 Naval Air Squadron flying the latest Buccaneer strike aircraft on board HMS Victorious. He had been the CO and inspiring leader for just seven months. This was a job he loved passionately: leading his fellow pilots with courage and calmness. To keep below the enemy radar, he had a reputation of flying so low that other pilots following him were afraid they would hit the sea. He featured in a famous Royal Navy recruitment advert, where he was filmed skimming across the sea with his own commentary: "There we were at fifteen feet with nothing on the clock but the maker's name!"

The Squadron's highly classified role was to strike at enemy ships and as a last resort to deliver nuclear bombs against the Soviet fleet. The Buccaneer was a brand new aircraft for HMS Victorious. As part of the aircraft sea trials Paul and Bill, being the most experienced pilots, stepped forward to test fly and check out the engines of every single aircraft. On that fateful day they were testing the 4th Buccaneer when an unexpected fault redirected the engine flame against the side of the aircraft. Inside the cockpit alarms were going off and red hazard lights were flashing right across the dashboard. A vicious fire took hold of the aircraft and Paul calmly outlined the critical situation to the control tower. He explained that he intended to bring the aircraft back in to be examined, so that the fault could be rectified so the other aircraft would be made safe for his pilots to fly.

Paul's last words were: "I'm bringing it in". He instructed Bill to eject immediately which he did successfully for the second time in his career. The ground crew watched helplessly as bright flames and billowing smoke trailed the aircraft while Paul continue to wrestle with the controls and fly back towards the runway. At the last moment when the flames were engulfing the aircraft, Paul himself ejected. The power of rockets that fire off the ejector seat are known to be so forceful they can permanently compress a man's spine. In this case the ejector rockets misfired and sent Paul at top speed into the tailfin and he was killed instantly. The aircraft ploughed into the sea and his body was washed up and identified two days later.

About this book

It is rare that a person's untimely death has positive benefits. My father's death has proved to be both a traumatic family disaster and an inspiration. My mother Tricia never fully overcame her deep sense of loss and grief. However this loss has also been an incredibly powerful motivation for me. It has been the cause of my search for other people who show the inspiring leadership traits which my father displayed. I continually aim to model the qualities of an inspiring leader myself. It has been a tough journey full of disappointment, anxiety and fear, as well as success. This book has been written to explain why, among all the different leadership styles, I identified inspiring leadership as a particularly successful way of leading people. It is a philosophy and an approach, which I have used while mentoring and coaching leaders, and it resonates strongly with them. I hope you experience the same benefits as you incorporate these ideas into your life.

This chapter is named "The Calling"; for that is what my father answered when he joined the Royal Navy as a teenager to serve his country. He later died leading his people, which was a calling he was passionate about. In my own way I answered a similar calling when I joined the British Army. By writing this book about the best leadership qualities I have identified from my experience in the army and from studying people I admire in business, I am fulfilling my life's purpose.

For this book to emerge I had to write an autobiography and this informed and clarified my philosophy of inspiring leadership. Only after my life story had been critically analysed, could I create this book. My aspiration is to share the hard earned lessons that I have accumulated from my own experience of different leadership styles, throughout my career. I have also drawn observations from the lives of the leaders that I have been privileged to work with. These leaders are inspiring and have changed lives for the better both within the military and in global businesses. They have much to teach each other. I have also garnered many ideas from working with misguided and ineffective managers. My views have been fundamentally shaped both by my own mistakes and the mistakes of others, as well as the triumphs. The core theme of this book is to encourage, and perhaps to teach you about excellence in leadership. Its mission is to inspire people in authority to care deeply about those for whom they are responsible. My call to arms is for people to develop inspiring leadership abilities underpinned by kindness rather than cruelty.

To adopt an inspiring leadership approach is a personal choice. We have to choose this approach every day and every hour. Leadership does not come as a right, simply from holding a position in an organisational chart; it has to be learned. This book contains autobiographical stories and is unashamedly personal. I have tried to make it practical and it is all about people. Inspiring leadership requires intimacy and people need to make rapid connections with others on a deep and emotional level. I encourage you to connect to others with both your head and your heart. I liken my message to the phrase used by Mary Beth O'Neill:[1] to lead "with backbone and heart". My twenty years as an Army Officer have taught me that leadership success is not simply about being a rough and tough warrior (although that is needed at times), it is more about nurturing and caring for those you are privileged to lead. Inspiring leadership is a style of leadership that anyone can develop and continually improve upon, once the principles are fully understood and absorbed. This book therefore is a message of hope.

Why read this book?

How will this book benefit you? Do you consider yourself to be a successful leader, or do you aspire to be so? If so then this book is for you. Do you wish to lead your teams in the most effective and energising way?

Are you a follower seeking to be well led? Are you in the business of helping others to improve their performance? If you answer yes to any of these questions then you'll find much to help you in these pages. From my own practical experience, from my observation of other leaders and from my wide research I have found that people who have become highly respected usually display the eight characteristics I espouse within the inspiring leadership philosophy. Employing these qualities is how they manage to get others to follow them willingly. You could do the same. A coaching client, Sarah Jane Mills, who critically reviewed a draft of my book, described the benefits as follows:

"This is a fresh approach to leadership and it is named perfectly. It brings together a wealth of different ideas and concepts under a very clear and simple set of 8 principles. This is about leadership based on relationship. It gives people permission to be inspiring leaders. You can analyse your own strengths, weaknesses, opportunities and threats using the compass and you will be given a set of tools to develop your skill so you become a better inspiring leader. If you focus on these principles you will affect others in a highly positive way."

Who is this book for?

This book has been written for leaders, and for those in the business of helping others to develop. Our value as a leader is based on our ability to inspire and bring out the best in the people we lead. Whether you are a CEO, a Partner, a Managing Director, a senior executive, a team leader, or a potential leader, you will occasionally find yourself in difficult and challenging situations. At such key moments, your ability to handle people effectively is critical to the outcome. It is our humility and humanity that are at the foundation of the philosophy about which I speak.

As a leader you might recognise some of the scenarios described in this book. I hope you find the key points and questions at the end of each chapter useful when you encounter awkward moments. The ideas in this book are exemplified using real events, so you might empathise with the qualities of good leadership, and use them as a foundation from which to generate your own "best thinking". I would like to convince you of the power of following the inspiring leadership model, which has been developed from my study of many real life stories supported by arguments from academic research and theoretical logic. I hope that you find these stories, advice and anecdotes in this book of direct practical help.

Call to action, my key messages

From my life experience I have accumulated a set of 8 principles which define what I call "inspiring leadership". Examples of good and poor leadership attitudes and behaviour show how top quality leaders and high performing teams differentiate themselves. I have found that leadership coaching clarifies and improves both. Coaching helps leaders develop clear business and personal goals, which in turn enable them to become more successful. You might like to think about how you could use the ideas in this book to enhance your own leadership style, and provide a focus for coaching sessions.

One of the charities I support is **Help for Heroes** (H4H) and a donation will be made from the proceeds of each Inspiring Leadership book that is sold. H4H highlights the principles discussed in this book. Inspiring leadership is all about courage, vulnerability, serving to lead, appreciation, respect and purpose. The vulnerability and sensitivity of the true warrior is highlighted in the work that H4H does.

My call to action is for you to lead in a different and healthier way. Many of those reviewing this book have been clear about the fact that inspiring leadership is a philosophy whose time has come and that it is needed in business and in our lives today. I would be honoured to support your journey towards becoming a truly inspiring leader.

Strength through vulnerability

It is usually only strong leaders who have the confidence to show vulnerability and share personal details about themselves. When they do, they enable others to find the courage to do the same. This revealed humanity allows inspiring leadership to flourish and it creates a powerful, more trusting work environment. Dropping your work mask and being truly seen for whom you are, builds greater respect. This behaviour is unusual, although I have found that most people quietly admire such leaders. My intention is to be deliberately open throughout this book, although sharing so much about myself, my upbringing and my career in leadership positions is exposing. My doubts, fears, anxieties and feelings of inadequacy, as well as my triumphs are described. You will therefore have a measure of my own vulnerability. This is a high-risk strategy, but is a price I consider worth paying to demonstrate the message of inspiring leadership. I hope that you too have the strength to be vulnerable and develop your personal culture of inspiring leadership.

How to get the most out of the book

You could read straight through the book as a practical philosophy and leadership guide. Equally you can dip into the 8 core chapters (one for each principle) that capture your interest. This book contains a mixture of pragmatic leadership concepts, personal stories (from both the military and business) and case studies. I have found far more inspiring leaders in the military than business and the amount of stories reflect that. My calling is to ignite more inspiring leadership in business to rectify this perceived imbalance. These case studies are about real leaders who role model inspiring leadership in a wide variety of different situations. The studies are supported by practical tips and questions for you to follow, at the end of each chapter. I refer to leaders in general as "him" throughout the book, but as you will see from many of the case studies, good leadership is just as often to be demonstrated by women and I could equally well have made my "leaders" female.

About the author

My role is to act as a CEO's Global Leadership Coach. I focus on high performance leaders and teams with a focus on CEOs, Partners and Managing Directors. I work in the corporate, financial services and professional services sectors; bringing commercial acumen and leadership advice from my time in PwC Consulting, IBM and as British Army Officer. I was Assistant to the Head of the British Army, Chief of Staff of the Army's largest Brigade and Commanded my Company on 3 operational tours. Drawing on six years as a PLC Managing Director I encourage clients also to lead by example, have courageous conversations and give inspirational feedback. I run my own coaching business.

As an entrepreneur, motivational speaker and passionate leader, I have been sought after for comments in publications such as Reuters, CIO, The FT, The Mail on Sunday, and The Times. I have coached and spoken at: HSBC, KPMG, Asda, Goldman Sachs, Cambridge University, Barclays, UPS, RBS, Eversheds, HP, Accenture, Morgan Stanley, Booze, Macquarie Bank, E&Y, DWP, Scottish Power, ICI, BP, Centrica, Astra Zeneca, Northern Foods, PwC, Ulster Bank, McDonalds, Pearl & IBM.

HM the Queen awarded me the MBE for my services to leadership in addition to my MA and MBA. To find out more about what I do, to experience my leadership coaching style and to hear me speak about inspiring leadership, please visit www.jonathanperks.com.

About you and your impact

I wish you every success on your journey towards inspiring leadership. I would appreciate hearing which principles particularly resonate with you, as you think about your own life. What question does this book raise for you? Hearing how you enhance your leadership qualities as a result of reading this book, would be of great interest to me. This is the first edition of Inspiring Leadership. Please e-mail me at: jp@jonathanperks.com and share your stories about how you have applied inspiring leadership to your businesses and lives. Undoubtedly you may have been applying some of the eight principles already and perhaps this book finally makes meaning of your own leadership style. With your permission, the lessons you share with me will become the material for the second edition of Inspiring Leadership. Thus in your own way you will become a leader who develops and motivates other leaders. Allow me to help you create a positive legacy within your lifetime.

Warm regards

Jonathan Perks

Lieutenant Commander Paul Perks, Fleet Air Arm, Royal Navy

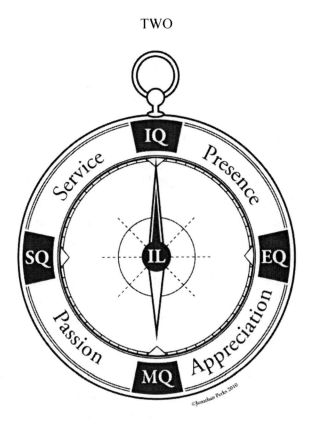

TWO

Inspiration

"No one lives long enough to learn everything they need to learn starting from scratch. To be successful, we absolutely, positively have to find people who have already paid the price to learn the things that we need to learn to achieve our goals."

Brian Tracy: Personal and business training author

My personal inspiration

My father Paul Perks was killed violently and tragically at the age of 33. He paid the ultimate price trying to enable others to learn from his experience. He was just starting his married life and left behind his wife with a very young family. His highly promising career came to an abrupt and unexpectedly early close. We have all missed him desperately and have only learned about him through the stories from our mother Tricia and his Royal Navy colleagues. My brothers Graeme, David and I were individually brought to tears on different occasions, recounting to our future wives the feelings of loss at not having a father to guide us as we grew up. My father's attitude to life has been my ultimate driver for inspiring leadership. He was described by his fellow naval officers as: "Passionate, yet calm, grounded and wise". He served them with pride, loved leading them and inspired them as their role model. He held very strong moral principles, values and beliefs and appreciated the differences and talents of the people he led.

His very last act was one of inspiring leadership for his officers. Knowing the dangers involved, he test flew all the new and unreliable Buccaneer aircraft from their aircraft carrier HMS Victorious. He did this so that any lethal faults could be rectified, before handing the planes over to the pilots under his command in his squadron. He managed to persuade his co-pilot to eject, but he died trying to bring the plane back for examination. His body was washed up 2 days later in Changi Bay near Singapore. From the moment the Royal Navy duty officer appeared in his smart full dress uniform on our doorstep, my mother knew he brought tragic news. Life was never the same for Tricia and the three distraught small boys who clung to her that night.

Twenty five years later, as a leadership instructor at the Royal Military Academy Sandhurst, I invited naval officers who had served with him to have lunch in the officer's mess. I was overwhelmed by their response. When I met the pilot whose faulty aircraft my father was test flying, he said: "Your father bought my ticket and died in my place. If he had not cared so much about his men, he would be here today with you, instead of me." I was completely choked by the guilt this brave man had been carrying all this time. I was almost overwhelmed by my emotion at the sense of loss and the realisation that my father might have been able to see me, his son as an officer too. I asked this ex-pilot to let go of his burden of guilt and I made it clear that I held no resentment about the decision that my father made, to protect his officers. Recalling that poignant moment still brings me close to tears.

My father's legacy is that I am choosing to carry his baton as I navigate through my life. I aspire to live in a way that he would respect and understand. This has culminated with the development of my 8 factor inspiring leadership model. Throughout my life I have looked for leaders who have the drive and qualities that exemplify the finest styles of leadership. Such people make a positive impact in both their organisation and the wider world. My father has been the inspiration for my own life purpose, which is continually evolving. Currently my life purpose is: "Inspiring leaders by supporting and challenging them, so together we make a positive impact in the world."

This book is a journey from school through the military into the corporate world. Inspiring leadership is a compass that you can use as you navigate through your own life. You can overlay this 8-point compass onto your own map to make meaning out of the terrain you are travelling through.

Definition of inspiring

I am grateful to Oliver Johnson for the definition of the word inspiring. It is an explanation that he has developed from his considerable research:

Inspire: drawing in of breath, infuse thought or feeling into (The Oxford Illustrated Dictionary)
Inspire: from Latin *Inspīrāre* - to breathe upon or into *Spiritus* - breath, breathing, life, spirit.

What does this mean when used to describe leadership? In the context of leadership, inspiring may best be understood as 'breathing life or spirit into'. If you have had the good fortune to work with an inspiring leader you will know what it feels like to be encouraged, to soar like an eagle in the updrafts and to have your spirit lifted in the downdrafts. Inspiring leaders enable us to recognise our true capability and to release it.

Imagine inflating a balloon by breathing into it. As you do so its characteristics change from being lifeless and deflated to being light and full of energy. Release an inflated balloon without tying a knot in the end and you will see the result of inspiration in action through the energy released. Inspiring leaders know that in order to inspire others they must first be inspired themselves. When blowing up a balloon you need to inhale deeply before transferring that breath to the balloon.

The opposite of **inspire** is **expire** - 'to draw breath or spirit from'. If you have had the misfortune to work for an "expirational leader" you will know what it feels like to have your spirit drawn from you.

Being inspirational is not the same as having charisma. Charisma is centred on the cult of the individual. It relies on personal magnetism and the ability to arouse fervent personal devotion in others. To rely on your own charisma for leadership purposes, you have to have quite an inflated ego.' To be an inspirational leader relies on a more down-to-earth and realistic self-assessment. Inspiring leaders understand that, in reality, they do not actually inspire others. Rather, they create an environment in which others can find their own inspiration.

Three key questions for leaders remain:

1. Am I inspired?

2. Do I create an inspiring environment for others?

3. Do I truly enable others to release their full potential?

It seems to me that you cannot be a little bit inspirational. You are either an inspiring leader or an expiring leader. The choice, my friend, is yours.

What is Inspiring leadership?

Inspiring leadership is a healthy way of interacting with the people with whom you work. It is an effective approach that enhances the growth and development of people in your team. Inspiring leaders deal in the truth and consequently engender high levels of trustworthiness. They have a thirst for connection with the people they lead. They find ways to listen, have time to be curious and ask thought provoking questions. They have an ability to enlighten, energise and inspire their team. They are comfortable themselves; knowing their own strengths and limitations. They do not need to "act big", or pretend to be important. Humanity and humility are their foundations. They know that people do their best thinking, and are most innovative, when they feel that they are in an environment of appreciation. Such leaders know and value their colleagues' real strengths and talents. When there is blame directed at their team, they take its full force. When there is praise to be given out for successes and achievements, they direct it to the people who deserve to receive it. The ripple effect of their inspiring leadership behaviour and positive intention, creates waves that wash up on shores long after they were initiated, far away from the where they began. Never underestimate the positive impact of this way of being in the world.

I am aware as I write that some people may have conflicting and critical views. Indeed for many this model is a highly challenging and revolutionary philosophy which threatens their traditional way of managing and leading others. The word inspiring has great depth, power and is highly emotive. Those leaders who use inspiration appropriately do things deliberately for the benefit of others, sometimes at a considerable personal cost. Taking an abundant attitude they realise that the more they give, the more they get back. It is often the case that the benefits that you later receive are rarely from the person you helped. Good leaders combine a positive state of mind with the ability to learn lessons. They have the power to forgive and the ability to move on from setbacks, grievances and disappointments. Inspiring leadership sits easily with humility, for as Ogden Nash once said: "Whenever you're wrong, admit it; whenever you're right, shut up".

Inspiring leadership is a style that can be learned and embedded by everyone. It will be easier for some and more of a struggle for others. Applying this philosophy has proved to be effective numerous times in my life. The evidence that this style of leadership works in business became apparent in one significant case. An executive who made a conscious effort to change and become more of an inspiring leader made an additional £198M profit for his company in the following twelve months. That is too big a number to ignore. In my experience there are only a few exceptional leaders who display all 8 qualities of this style of leadership. There are however, a large number that have learnt to lead using just some of the characteristics. To identify exactly what it is that differentiates the most successful and admirable leaders from the rest, I have reviewed the last thirty years of my experience working with impressive and distinctive leaders. Equally valuable, have been my studies and observation of poor leaders. They have taught me many raw, painful but useful lessons about how not to behave.

Future research

Reuven Bar-On and I intend to develop a variety of semi-structured series of interviews and psychometric instruments to help people assess their level of inspiring leadership qualities. This will most likely include various different formats of self-reports and 360^0 feedback questionnaires that will be specifically designed to assess the comprehensive nature of inspiring leadership. I would like to encourage feedback from you, and I suggest that this First Edition of Inspiring Leadership is what I believe this model should look like at present. Future research and experience will put this theory under more scrutiny, and this may change and enhance the model.

What inspiring leadership is not

Inspiring leadership is not soft and fluffy. It encompasses an honest and courageous approach to dealing with people. The focus is always to value and be highly appreciative of others, but it is not about hugging people, being insincere or sycophantic. Such attitudes merely serve to repulse, alienate, or disempower others. It is not about weakness since at times inspiring leaders also need to be tough. People at work need to achieve some severe, challenging, financial bottom-line results so this is not about avoiding difficult financial facts and reality. Instead it involves getting disparate groups of people to work together to achieve challenging goals. Such leaders motivate their teams to feel good while they are achieving these tasks. It is not about meekly pleasing others. Rather it encourages people to identify the heart of the problem and call out the truth. Doing that is tough, especially when it can threaten your career.

Poor performance can be tackled by asking challenging questions. One such question is: "You are responsible for your own life and therefore you are responsible for your under-performance. What exactly are you going to do about it?" Challenging colleagues is not a soft option, nor an easy way out, and a leader often has to travel a very lonely road. It is far easier and highly tempting to lower your own standards and drop your values to merge into the grey mass of average managers. Meanwhile the cynics sit back in judgement with their arms folded, observing you with disdain. Setting and maintaining high personal standards is one of the keys to good leadership.

The "inspiring" word that I choose to use is also about caring for others in genuine, sincere and appropriate ways. Boundaries are respected between the leader and those they lead, but there should be a special emotional connection, which encourages others to go the extra mile for their leader. Followers willingly give their all to achieve a successful outcome. In the military this means soldiers are prepared to die for their country and the cause they follow. Inspiration galvanises normal people to achieve incredible results, because of the special way they are led. This philosophy is for people who are passionate about leading other people.

My story: seeking inspiring leadership role models

On reflection, the death of my father when I was aged three served as a catalyst for me as I grew up. It drove me to find other male and female role models to fill the gap in my life. I found people who exhibited similar inspiring leadership qualities to the ones I thought my father exemplified. You may say it is unrealistic to expect to find people who could live up to such highly idealistic standards. I disagree. The business of leadership is too important a task in which to set low standards. What is encouraging is that the highly inspiring role models that I was searching for do exist. Like my father, these people are remain human and have their faults yet their skill in developing high levels of self-regard and emotional self-awareness means that they are able to understand themselves. They respect their own capabilities and limitations and appreciate themselves as they really are. They have their shortcomings, their faults, yet are wise enough to find ways to compensate for them. Consequently they select a great team of people to work with them to mitigate such human failings.

At first as I grew up my mother rarely talked about my father. His photographs in our drawing room showed a handsome, dashing pilot akin to the characters in the Hollywood film *Top Gun*. I naturally got to know the fathers of my friends, and was acutely aware that my brothers and I did not have such a figure in our family. As I grew older I craved an inspiring male role model. I dug out photographs of him and once tried on his old naval officer's cap. It fitted me comfortably. I even took my mother on holiday to Texas where she had first met my father completing his flying training with the US Navy. I learned from my mother that my parents had had a whirlwind, rather fairy-tale romance. They were deeply happy in their short marriage. Their fascinating story is captured in the book *America* by Patricia Bowman. This account my brother David lovingly collated, edited and published privately a couple of years ago.

The more I learned, the more I felt sad and I became aware of a void in my life which I ached to fill. I wrote to the Fleet Air Arm Officer's Association. They were very helpful and replied with letters from retired and serving officers all over the world. My request was simple: "If anyone served with Lieutenant Commander Paul Perks Royal Navy who was killed in Singapore in 1964 would they please write to his son, Captain Jonathan Perks. I wish to learn more about the father I never knew." I was overwhelmed by the letters which people wrote in response. They spoke of Paul's modesty, his dry sense of humour, impish fun and passion for leading others. What I knew with a burning passion then, was that while I did not have an interest for the sea or flying, I definitely wanted to be a leader. I wished to emulate the very best of my father's qualities which others admired and spoke of in these letters. The inspiring leadership flame had been lit and still burns fiercely today.

I remember the advice given to me from one of my first mentor-coaches. Like my father before me, I was working in America and was being guided by a retired US 4 star General. His sage words still ring in my ears: "Son, you have not got time to make as many mistakes as I have made in my seventy years of life. Let me give you some advice by asking you some questions." He said that experienced leaders had already been in some of the minefields and pits that I could blunder into. They had usually stepped on the anti-personnel mines and consequently had the proverbial battle scars on their backs. By sharing his experience, he said he did not promise me a risk-free journey through life, because he knew that I would find problems that no one could ever imagine, but I would avoid a few difficulties. He assured me that by listening and watching how others go about their business, I'd learn and become a better leader.

With that advice in mind I have been on a passionate journey to gain experience, knowledge and qualifications, by studying the actions of others and reading their advice. As a leader of a team myself and as an executive coach to CEOs and other leaders, I have identified excellence in leadership many times. During my twenty years as an Army officer, in London where I now work, in Yorkshire where I live, and in the last ten years as a leadership coach, I have seen the beginnings of this style of leadership in many people. I have found it in a huge variety of business environments. These include: government departments, global investment banks, energy companies, professional service firms, global retail businesses, the police and universities. In spite of their humility and modesty it is time for these people to share their stories. Inspiring leaders are by their nature abundant and I find that there is enormous truth in the adage that: "Everyone has something to teach you; if only you would have the humility to listen."

While I'm not a deeply religious person, both my wife Bridget and my friend Reuven Bar-On have reminded me of my rich family background of Quakerism. My wife and daughters are the 5th and 6th generations of my family to go to The Mount School York which was founded by Yorkshire Quakers in 1831. Working quietly and softly in the background, their set of values and beliefs will inevitably have had an influence in developing my philosophy of inspiring leadership. It may explain why I believe that integrity, values and beliefs, which are a part of what some refer to as "moral intelligence" (MQ), are so important. It is interesting for me to note the impact on inspiring leadership of the Quakers' approach of: reflection and self-awareness; integrity; being truthful to oneself; simplicity; the importance of community and equality in interpersonal relationships.

If you decide to adopt these 8 principles you may become more successful in your life with less effort. Very few of us need to work any harder. As leaders in the UK, America and other developed countries we are already working some of the longest hours in the world. The consequences are that we do not spend sufficient time looking after our families, friends, or ourselves. Inspiring leadership is not about working physically harder, it is about integrating the use of your mind, heart and soul. Building relationships that allow you to lead in a smarter and more effective way will create a synergy within your team which can make the apparently unremarkable people achieve outstanding results.

Inspiring leadership is not just about accumulating qualifications, certificates and degrees. What really matters is how people show up in life. The way we behave, and how we interact in our relationships with other people, will help us all become more effective with less effort. Unfortunately, most of us take much longer to become wise than we do to become old. Before I continue with my life story and the lessons that come from other leaders here is the essence of the model. You can reflect upon these principles as you read the rest of the account.

The eight principle components of an inspiring leader

Here are what I consider to be the top eight principle components of the model:

1. **IQ** – Cognitive Intelligence & wisdom
2. **Presence** – Personal Power
3. **EQ** – Emotional and Social Intelligence
4. **Appreciation** – of others and self
5. **MQ** - Moral Intelligence, Values and Beliefs
6. **Passion** – Love and inspiration
7. **SQ** – Spiritual Intelligence, Meaning and Purpose
8. **Service**- Serve to lead

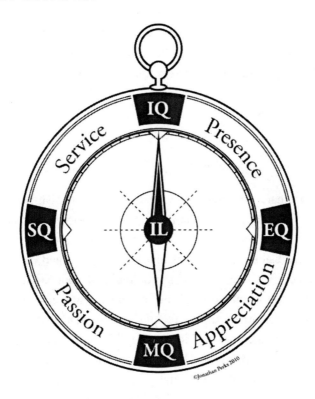

(1) IQ and wisdom

Cognitive intelligence (IQ) and wisdom are the foundation to inspiring leadership. When you are in charge you have to wrestle with complexity, select the "least bad" option and then encourage other people to follow you and achieve extraordinary results. Wisdom comes from experience, but can be developed more quickly by using the coach-approach to leadership in order to make visible what was previously invisible to you. Continually learning from others and seeking their advice is another way to enhance your wisdom.

Cognitive intelligence provides the basis for doing the **correct thing** (in this specific leadership context), while wisdom, which is based on experience, provides the foundation for doing the **wise thing**. The distinction between IQ, wisdom and moral intelligence (MQ) is that MQ provides the basis for doing the **right thing**. Combining all three provides you with the ability to do the correct, wise and right thing. That is a vital foundation for leaders in business today. Its absence creates the "disintegrated leader" who have the potential to bring down firms and economies.

(2) Presence and personal power

When you are naturally yourself, you step into your own personal power and radiate confidence. This honesty has a positive impact upon the behaviour of those around you. To be completely present with those to whom you are listening is a talent that has to be learned, and being fully present is a key factor in the success you make of your life. High levels of personal power also enable inspiring leaders to cope effectively with the politics within an organisation. People can influence others to achieve positive, healthy outcomes and to resolve difficult situations successfully. Developing personal power and presence enhances people's natural ability to connect genuinely with individuals and truly to understand any person. In the Nepalese, Navajo Indian and Zulu cultures people look deeply into another's eyes and say to them in their own way: "I am here to be seen" and the standard reply is: "I see you". To be fully present is to see the other person properly. People are liberated when you recognise and accept their talents and this enables your own ability to be recognised. It becomes a virtuous cycle.

(3) EQ – Emotional and Social Intelligence

High levels of EQ allow inspiring leaders to cope proactively with life's demands and challenges without caving in. People with high EQ are able to thrive and even thrive whilst under pressure. They are able to build collaborative, supportive and rewarding relationships with others. With high EQ it is easier to set and achieve personal and professional goals that are compatible with what is best for you and others. High EQ enables you to understand others before explaining your own viewpoint. You can be sufficiently assertive and act with authority when making difficult and courageous decisions. By developing high levels of EQ people become realistically optimistic about achieving their potential. They are also able to understand, manage and draw the most out of others.

(4) Appreciation

To appreciate and value others' strengths and talents and acknowledge what is working well is something we often forget to do. Having said that, people also need to be prepared to have courageous conversations about what could be even better. Appreciation is closely aligned with an attitude of gratitude. This is the ability to value and be grateful for everyone's gifts and talents. Nurturing appreciation and gratitude creates a happy working environment. Happiness can be defined as "wanting what you already have". Making a point of catching your colleagues doing things right and naming what is working well is a fundamental part of the inspiring leadership model.

(5) MQ – Strong Values and Beliefs

Moral intelligence (MQ) focuses on how people live and enables people to identify a set of explicit values which they believe in. A strong desire to give the best you have, combined with a powerful self-belief is attractive. Hold high, positive expectations of those you lead and your team will rise to the challenge. Integrity and trust, in my view, are two of the most highly prized values and have a direct impact on the emergence of top performing teams. Applying strong values to your life requires immense courage, stamina and personal discipline.

A personal compass that is pointing towards north is the sign of a fully functioning inspiring leader. In this model, north is doing the correct thing, while south is doing the right thing. A fully functioning compass points both north and south simultaneously and such an inspiring leader does the correct and the right thing.

(6) Passion – Love and Inspiration

Passion is the most overt quality possessed by any leader and requires an ability both to give love and inspiration to those being lead, and to receive it in return. This inspiration and support exchanged enables team members to believe in the cause or undertaking, and to give their full energy to it. They know that in adversity their leader will look after them and not leave them exposed. Inspiration is the ability to breathe life, energy and passion into an individual, or group. Consequently the team is able to undertake even the most difficult, or unpleasant task. Maintaining personal integrity, looking like a leader and releasing personal charisma means people will want to follow you even more. When people commit to leading others with passion then instinctively others willingly give their full commitment to follow.

(7) SQ – Meaning and Purpose

Spiritual intelligence (SQ) is based on a clear sense of purpose, or life calling, and shapes all that a leader does. SQ is what inspires followers to commit their discretionary life energy willingly to support the leader. The leader becomes someone they publicly acknowledge, respect and recognise. When faced with moments of crisis, either at work, or in their personal life, someone with high levels of SQ is able to refer back and assess their actions against their life purpose. Such a clear focus defines what people attract to them, or consciously decline, as they go through life.

(8) Service

British military training emphasises the philosophy of "serving to lead". This ensures that no one is asked to do a job by the leader that he would not be prepared to do himself. Servant leadership highlights the paradox of "humble excellence" which is shown by someone who has a modest confidence, combined with genuine expertise. This engenders trust and an ability to build a team where the other members' abilities complement your expertise and this fact is acknowledged.

A brief outline of my life journey so far

In the following chapters I will be drawing from experiences in my life, my study of the subject of leadership and my observation of leaders I have worked with in both the military and business. Since these experiences are selected to match and explain what I mean by the 8 principles, they will not be in chronological order. In order to set the context for what follows I am going to outline below my life history so far:

1. After my father's death my mother brought up her three boys in Halifax, Yorkshire, England.

2. I was educated at St Olaves School, York and Crossley & Porter Grammar School, Halifax.

3. Welbeck Sixth Form College became my introduction to the Army.

4. The Royal Military Academy Sandhurst (RMAS) gave me some amazing leadership insights and I became a member of the cadet government.

5. I was commissioned as a Second Lieutenant into The Royal Corps of Signals and served at the Apprentice College at Harrogate and then with 22 Armoured Brigade HQ in Germany.

6. My lucky break came when I was selected to be a Platoon Commander with the 2nd Battalion Scots Guards in Cyprus, just after they returned with experience from the Falklands war.

7. At 5 Airborne Brigade I passed parachute selection training (P Company) and completed my parachute jump course to earn my coveted red beret and parachute wings.

8. 14 Signal Regiment (Electronic Warfare) gave me experience in leading very intelligent linguists who intercepted and interpreted the movements of Soviet and East German forces.

9. As Adjutant I became responsible for discipline in our Regiment and was the right-hand man to the Commanding Officer of 2nd Division HQ & Signal Regiment in my favourite city, York.

10. I met and married Bridget, who was a fellow officer, in a whirlwind romance at York. I moved to be a platoon commander instructor at RMAS and Bridget was posted to be Assistant Adjutant at 2nd Gurkha Rifles.

11. I arranged to transfer to the prestigious Green Howards Infantry Regiment, and served in 24 Airmobile Brigade as an acting Major Company Commander.

12. Next I was selected to attend the "Junior General's course" and complete a two year MA degree at the Royal Military College of Science and the Army Staff College. Our daughters Harriet and Bryony were born and added a wonderful dimension to our lives.

13. As a Major in the Green Howards I experienced counter-terrorist operations in Northern Ireland and Armoured Infantry peacekeeping operations in Canada and Bosnia.

14. The role of Chief of Staff of 15 (NE) Brigade in York was my dream job and we took the talented HQ team on two successful deployments to Australia and France for which I was awarded an MBE.

15. For my transition into business, whilst Chief of Staff, I took my two year MBA and then worked for the Army Management Consultancy Services.

16. On leaving the army I was immensely proud to become a senior management consultant with PricewaterhouseCoopers (PwC) and developed an interest in leadership coaching.

17. After IBM's acquisition of PwC's consulting arm I moved with my colleagues into IBM Business Consulting and gained deeper consulting and coaching experience.

18. Time working with the $10 billion US consultancy – Science Application International Corporation (SAIC) was cut short when I was invited to run Penna's Board and Executive Coaching business.

19. I had a very happy six years as Managing Director of Board Coaching in Penna Consulting gaining experience on a PLC executive board with P&L responsibilities.

20. Finally I achieved my aspiration of setting up my own private leadership coaching practice and I now deliver global leadership coaching to CEOs, Partners, MDs and their top teams.

4 Key Points:

- My father's life and attitude has always been my ultimate drive for inspiring leadership.

- Inspiring leadership is a practical and energising approach that allows the best talents of the people with whom you work to emerge.

- The highly motivational inspiring leadership role models that I was searching for do exist. Like my father, these people are very human and have their faults.

- In future chapters I will be drawing on lessons from my life, my study of the subject and my observation of other leaders in both the military and business.

4 Questions:

1. Who is the most inspirational role model in your life?

2. What have your own leadership framework and principles been so far in your life?

3. On what do you base your leadership principles?

4. Which of the 8 Inspiring Leadership principles resonates most with you?

Major Jonathan Perks, Warrior Company Commander

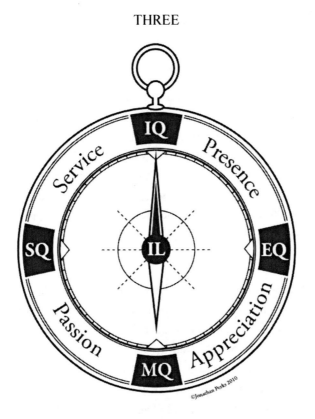

THREE

IQ – Wisdom & Judgement

"Consult your friend on all things, especially on those which respect yourself. His counsel may then be useful where your own self-love might impair your judgment."

Seneca (3 BC – 65 AD) Roman Stoic, Philosopher and Statesman

My leadership induction, gaining wisdom from a mentor

You only get one chance to make a good first impression. That moment for me was on day one, hour one and minute one at the Army Apprentice College at Harrogate. My new uniform was neatly pressed, I was very nervous and my heart was pounding. I marched into the office of an impressive leader (respectfully known as Captain Commando) Captain Ian Buckley Royal Signals, who was to be my first "boss". I halted, saluted and nervously stuttered: "Second Lieutenant Perks reporting for duty sir. I have just come from officer training at Sandhurst but I realise that I know very little about the real Army and am hoping you might be able to teach me."

One brilliantly simple tip that I had learnt in training was that "time spent in preparation and reconnaissance is never ever wasted". I now always research into the people I am going to meet. Today social networks like Facebook, Linked-in and Google give me lots of pre-meeting information. In those days information came in the form of advice from friends. As a consequence, I knew that Captain Ian Buckley was a legend in his own lifetime. He had risen at speed through every rank from private soldier to Captain, via Regimental Sergeant Major. He had served with distinction in the Royal Marine Commandos, been on operations in the Far East, was a top level Army squash player and was described by his men as being as fit as a butcher's dog. He lived life to the full, had a wicked sense of humour and did not suffer fools gladly, especially officers who came out of training with overblown confidence.

There was a pause, while he scrutinised me closely and remarked fiercely that luckily I had said the right thing! He was expecting me to be some arrogant, stuck up, know-it-all novice from Sandhurst, who would be about as useful as a chocolate teapot. He said it appeared as if I had the right attitude and therefore he agreed to help me. He then proceeded to share his wisdom and gave me the rules that I should follow to become a successful leader. These were: to identify the best leaders quickly, whatever rank they may be, then to make a point of listening and learning from them; to ask questions in private and absorb the answer first time. He remarked bluntly that to ask the same question twice shows that either you did not listen properly to the answer or that you are stupid. He said that people do not willingly follow uncaring, or unintelligent leaders. Men find ways of getting rid of them, or moving them on. I was informed that followers make rapid judgments on first impressions of their leaders. Consequently I should always appear on time, be immaculately dressed and be fully prepared for whatever task I had to deliver.

He went on to say that I should master my leadership profession and earn the respect of my followers. As an Army Officer I had to be physically and mentally fit, have stamina, know what I was talking about and surround myself with "an army of giants". These would be experts in the areas where I needed advice. He said leadership is a choice people make. It is not a name badge on a door, or officer's pips on your shoulders. Leading by example was crucial, as was making wise, fair decisions. A leader's judgement is critical. In his view people could not hide behind rank, or their position, for very long.

I could not have asked for a finer induction into my very first job as a leader. It would be good if there were more wise leadership advice for new managers in business today, from leaders with equally strong values and beliefs. For the next twelve months Ian acted as my mentor and trusted advisor and became a great personal friend. I learned to respect the wisdom that he had accumulated, often as a result of unintended mistakes that he and others had made. He had had twenty years of experience interacting with a wide variety of officers of varying quality; what he called the heroes and zeros. Captain Buckley Royal Signals exhibited many fine qualities, especially the love and inspiration he elicited in the officers and people under his command.

The legacy of any great leadership mentor is that their protégé remembers their tips and words of wisdom years afterwards and are able to pass on the advice themselves. I remain impressed when working for bright leaders who can see to the heart of difficult issues under pressure and I have therefore selected IQ and wisdom as the first of my eight principles. Leaders with high IQ stand out because of their ability to use their knowledge and experience to great effect. In addition they usually have the humility to draw on the learning of mentors with far greater experience. High IQ is not in itself enough to make someone into a good leader. It has to be combined with wisdom which comes from being grounded in reality, for it to be effective in a leader.

Definition of Intelligence Quotient and Wisdom

IQ or intelligence quotient is a measure of cognitive intelligence determined by a standardised test[2]. In simple terms IQ is the ability to learn new things, to use that which one has learned, to think logically and solve problems. There are many ways of defining different types of intelligence, such as Howard Gardner's definition of multiple intelligences[3]. In the work place IQ is closely associated with technical business intelligence and the ability to learn and absorb new information quickly. In the inspiring leadership model I have linked IQ to wisdom and judgement, since I have found that it is the wisdom that marks out the most successful leaders based on their innate intelligence. There is a wealth of writing on the definition of wisdom in all books of the major religions and by many famous philosophers. It is found in both the Old and New Testament teaching, in Islam, Buddhism, Taoism and the teaching of Confucius, Aristotle and Plato. The simplest definition of it is the application of knowledge based on experience. Wisdom involves discernment between what is right and wrong, and making judgements from a wealth of information and conflicting facts. Often there is incomplete information. Consequently a leader has to call upon their previous experience in conjunction with their learned theoretical knowledge, to weigh up the evidence and make decisions. We must not confuse wisdom and discernment with being judgemental which has a negative and critical connotation based on superiority. Being judgemental is not a principle of inspiring leadership. Instead you are looking to unlock the best qualities from those you lead and meet.

I concur with the following advice from Field Marshal Harding[4] on the value of judgement:

"You have got to be able to assess values, and assess them quickly and under difficult circumstances, and that calls for judgement, and judgement is only learned by experience and practice. You will never learn to judge and to assess value if you are afraid of making mistakes, never. So do not be afraid of making mistakes.

On occasion the principles of war conflict with each other in problems with which you may be faced. You can be forced to weigh up the situation and decide which in is the more important of the principles in that particular circumstance - which you can stick to, which you can discard - and that requires judgement. That judgement stems from knowledge, practice and experience."

Consequences of a lack of wisdom in a leader

Sadly, too many of us have had bad experiences of working for a leader who lacks wisdom or has limited IQ. Some people would probably describe such a person as stupid, crass, ignorant and their decisions and actions as pure folly. Professor Norman Dixon[5] wrote an excellent book called *On the Psychology of Military Incompetence*. It was compulsory reading at the British Army's Royal Military Academy Sandhurst and contains many lessons about the pitfalls of being an authoritarian leader in both the military and business settings. My coaching clients have on occasions worked for leaders in business that had limited intelligence and inadequate wisdom. Just like the incompetent Generals that Dixon writes about, these business leaders manage to delete, ignore or distort the information that they have been given.

They are often driven by an intense fear of failure, especially if they are slightly aware of their inadequacy, and their lack of wisdom can cause them to act impulsively. They often refuse to rectify their errors and then stubbornly resist changing their viewpoint. These fearful leaders often believe that strong leaders stick to their original decision, despite conflicting information which can emerge later. Meanwhile their team and their organisation blunder on towards obvious disaster. More than anything it is a fragile ego which prevents leaders from admitting that they either do not know what the answer is, or have made a mistake and may need help from other people.

The consequences of a lack of wisdom in a leader are significant for a team and an organisation. I recently came across a bullying leader in business that on occasion had reduced some of his staff to tears. He so terrified his subordinates that they would never dare to challenge his highly questionable decisions. These were decisions that were made impulsively, with incomplete information. When queried he defended his crass decisions ferociously because he felt it was his authority that was being challenged.

How can wisdom help you as a leader?

High IQ is common amongst many of the most effective leaders that I have met. Those who are described as "very intelligent" are often admired and respected by their followers because they are perceived to make fair and balanced decisions. Life as a leader is often fraught with problems and can be highly stressful. Good leadership requires the ability to stay calm under pressure and to be grounded so clear thinking can occur.

The best conclusions are often reached by using your own experience and knowledge alongside the combined wisdom of a team of advisers, coaches and friends. While IQ is believed to be almost fixed after the age of eighteen, fortunately your wisdom can continually grow and develop. Experience is guaranteed but learning from it is optional. Acquiring wisdom is a personal choice. You can seek shrewd "mentors" from whom you can learn.

If you surround yourself with people who have experience and wisdom in areas where you do not, you will be more able to make quick but good decisions under pressure. In Greek mythology Mentor was the loyal friend and advisor of Odysseus, and teacher to his son Telemachus. A wise leader knows the limitations of his own knowledge and where to go to find missing information. My advice for you is to be highly discerning when identifying your own mentor or team of mentors in various business and leadership disciplines.

Wise leaders make decisions based not only on their knowledge and experience but also keep themselves in line with their integrity, values and beliefs (about which I shall speak later as part of moral intelligence - MQ). There is a close connection between wisdom and intuition which is an instinctive application of knowledge based on previous experience using rapid mental calculations. Leaders who use intuition or gut feeling, do so with a sixth sense of what feels innately right. Such intuition comprises of the four main types of intelligence that are part of the inspiring leadership model: IQ, EQ, MQ and SQ.

Lessons from the military

Wisdom drawn from military history

At Sandhurst I heard and remembered many stories and anecdotes that have served me well as a leadership coach. Winston Churchill said: "Those who fail to learn from history are doomed to repeat it". I am passionate about history and enjoy stories of disaster that eventually turn into success. I find it fascinating to understand how leaders overcome many failures eventually to break through to success. Stories and anecdotes stick with me far more effectively than any collection of business school theories. One story that lands powerfully with business leaders is interpreted below:

During one of Wellington's campaigns he was observing the start of a battle. He was on a hilltop vantage point accompanied by a collection of Generals on horseback. One of his newly promoted Generals had risen rapidly through the ranks because he was a very bright and technically skilled officer in the Artillery. Rather than observe the battle from Wellington's hill which gave a strategic overview, this new artillery General rode down to his guns in the valley below. This was his comfort zone. No one knew as much as he did about the technical deployment of artillery guns.

Very quickly the artillery General jumped from his horse and pushed the Captain of the guns to one side. He started barking orders to the four guns and their crews. The view of him by those on the hills was quickly obliterated by the smoke of the guns. His own battlefield vision reduced to a mere 200 metres. While the Captain stood idly by watching in frustration, the General passed cannon balls and got involved in the short-term tactical battle in this small part of the battlefield. Wellington realised the strategic battle was going wrong due to a lack of guidance from his artillery General. He therefore sent his assistant to bring the General back to the hilltop. He forcefully reminded the General that he was promoted and paid to make the few key strategic decisions that would win the battle. The artillery General could see the whole battlefield from this strategic vantage point, gave one command which mobilised a complete Allied Brigade and prevented the French Division from outmanoeuvring the guns in the valley where he had previously been. This contributed decisively towards Wellington's victory.

This story is highly relevant to many business leaders who are tempted to "go back to the guns" and do what they know well and had done skilfully in their previous roles. In doing so they mistakenly think they are "serving to lead". They are proud to be "rolling up their sleeves and getting stuck in". Actually they are unwise and risk getting caught up in reacting to short-term needs. Instead they should be setting the longer-term strategic vision and goals. The more senior you are, the longer your time horizon needs to be (six, twelve, or twenty four months). This is still relevant even in our chaotic time of uncertainty. While the Prussian General advised that "no plan survives the first meeting with the enemy" you must still plan ahead. Failing to plan is definitely planning to fail! Serving to lead means you understand the challenges of others' roles, yet you do not demotivate your subordinates by actually doing their jobs for them.

Wisdom acquired from the Borneo jungle

At the age of nineteen while still at Sandhurst, I was most fortunate to learn some amazing lessons in wisdom. I trained with an eccentric and courageous SAS Captain called Nigel Farley who took fifteen cadets including me on an expedition deep into the Borneo jungle. He exuded the essence of serve to lead. In the short lulls between operations, when the Army did not have a full-scale conflict or war, officers were encouraged to plan and undertake daring and risky adventure training expeditions. Hence I found myself abseiling in full jungle equipment, out of the side of a Scout helicopter 150 feet down through the canopy of the steamy Borneo jungle into a very small clearing hundreds of miles from civilisation.

Understanding how to survive in the jungle was a steep learning curve. Through necessity we were taught to build shelters in a tropical rainstorm, fight off snakes and poisonous insects and pick leeches off our legs and bodies. We once swam unwittingly with piranha fish under a waterfall and tracked and trapped animals with the guidance of a local Eban tribesman. The tribesman struck me as a man with a deep sense of wisdom and calmness. This was built on his knowledge of the jungle and his years of experience in dealing with the obstacles it throws up. He responded instinctively to our traumatic difficulties. With hindsight his actions have made me wonder whether, as we become more civilised, we lose sight of our own innate wisdom. In many cases in our manic business lives I fear we do. I have been able to help leaders tap into their in-built wisdom and judgement. The coaching we do together encourages them to create a strategic thinking environment and reconnect with their personal power and presence.

That expedition made a deep impact on me and I developed a love of adventurous training expeditions and led a number of them myself during my twenty years of Army career. Each expedition stretched and challenged me. I learned to value camaraderie, and to appreciate other people's strengths. The importance of trusting people with specific roles and responsibilities and to watch out for other members of the team also became embedded in my approach to running the exercises. These expeditions imparted many valuable leadership lessons.

Wisdom gained from working for the Head of the British Army

Later in my career I was posted into a very different and far more conservative and controlled world of Civil Servants, Ministers and Senior

Officers. IQ, wisdom and judgment were still all highly valued in this environment. This was a place for the brightest and best many of whom had been educated at Oxford and Cambridge Universities. I worked as an assistant to the head of the British Army, General Sir Peter Inge (now Field Marshal the Lord Inge). My title was rather grand: Aide de Camp to the Chief of the General Staff. This was abbreviated in true military style with two three-letter abbreviations into ADC to CGS. The year that I worked for the General was a high-speed existence and an incredible experience. I was privileged to be party to many fascinating discussions as a fly on the wall. It was also a humbling experience. The General ensured that I learned as much as I could about the art and science of leadership, manners and diplomacy. He was a formal disciplinarian and ensured that I kept my feet firmly on the floor. He insisted that I remain modest and humble and was fully aware of the importance of judgment and getting things right. He was very clear on the political implications and the dire consequences of making even the most minor slip in attention to detail.

It was too easy in such an environment to think that I was someone important as I followed in the wake of the General. On the few occasions when I made that mistake, the General firmly and quickly brought me down to earth. Working for the General was a high-octane twelve months. It also contained very high risks. As my Sandhurst instructor had said years before: "As an Army officer you will never be a rich man; yet at times you will live the life of a rich man. Whilst on operations around the world you will also suffer hardship; live in shared squalor with your men; see injury, death and depravation. That will keep your feet firmly on the floor and stop you becoming stuck-up and arrogant."

Coping with the fear of failure

On reflection I do not think I was particularly suited to the role I was given as the General's assistant. I was not good at attention to detail, nor was I politically savvy enough. I did not like being firmly controlled and did not enjoy the need to be servile. There were multiple leadership lessons for me to learn in this role. The greatest challenge of all was to work in a somewhat critical, anxiety inducing and intimidating environment. Appreciation and praise were a scarce commodity. Because of the serious consequences of even the slightest mistake, the fear of failure for me was very high. After all, I had clear evidence of what happened to those who failed. Both my predecessors had been removed from post early by the General and later were made redundant from the Army.

While I felt very excited to be involved in such an interesting role, paradoxically I was quite frightened and intimidated by the repercussions of making minor mistakes. I empathised with a previously successful assistant who shared his anxieties while he was in this role. He did not sleep too well. He kept a notebook by his bed, so when he was not sleeping he could write down tasks the General had given him to do and that he had forgotten to action the previous day. I personally found my fear of failure was highly debilitating. I did not perform at my best or feel particularly good about myself.

To date I sometimes see a similarly constraining environment in some of the macho, highly driven business environments where I coach leaders. I can make more sense of what happened now that I have learned more about neuroscience and SCARF: a brain-based model for collaborating with and influencing others[6]. This is a fascinating model which in simple terms is founded on our basic survival instincts. It explains the development of a human response of "*approaching*" when you are rewarded, or "*avoiding*" when you are coping with a threat.

David Rock and his researchers found that an approach response is connected to many factors. He said: "An approach response is synonymous with the idea of engagement. Engagement is a state of being and a willingness to do difficult things, to take risks, to think deeply about issues and develop new solutions. An approach state is also closely linked to positive emotions. This state is one of increased dopamine levels; important for interest and learning." On the other hand the researchers identified that when a human is threatened, for example by his boss, adrenaline floods the system. Consequently we have less oxygen and glucose available for brain functioning which in turn affects our working memory. Other research identifies that IQ drops by approximately 20% in such a threatening situation. It becomes harder to find smart answers and we do not pick up the more subtle signals. Instead we generalise more, tend to err on the safe side and avoid opportunities, since we perceive them to be dangerous in such a threatening environment. I realise now that I was developing an avoiding response when working for the General in the Ministry of Defence.

The SCARF model has five domains: status, certainty, autonomy, relatedness and fairness. These are directly linked to a human's response to either threat or reward. I will connect the model to the situation I found myself in at that time working as the General's assistant. It is also highly relevant for many situations that I have since come across in business and which have caused leaders untold problems. This is especially intense when levels of stress have badly affected their health. In a couple of cases it almost killed them.

Status

David Rock's research indicates that your relative position in the pecking order, your seniority and the respect with which you are treated is a trigger. It produces increased dopamine when you are given the sense that you are "better than" others. Equally critical is when you find that you are demoted, excluded from a group or treated with disdain. Then the activity in the brain is triggered in the same way as when you experience pain. While working for the General I underwent a roller coaster of emotions. At times I found myself amazed and flattered to be in the company of royalty and VIPs. At other times I was required to perform very menial tasks and was informally excluded. I found that demoralising and hard to understand. A further recent example of a dramatic change in status involved one of my business clients. He was a Managing Director of a high profile business and was demoted abruptly as a result of an internal restructuring. Since it had nothing to do with his performance and his division was far above their planned profit target, he found this to be a very painful experience which badly damaged his health and he spent a time in hospital.

Certainty

When you find yourself in an environment of constant threat, change and moment-to-moment uncertainty, then life becomes highly stressful. The research found that it is debilitating not to know your boss's expectation of you, or whether your job is secure. My experience working for the General and with clients since, has taught me that the resultant stress can have a serious negative impact. In some cases this syndrome has led to my clients becoming depressed, seeking comfort in drink and needing considerable time off work. On the other hand, when you can create certainty and people do meet expectations, then they are rewarded with increased dopamine levels and the feel-good factor. This neuroscience explains why there is value in creating detailed project plans, structure and frameworks when you work in an environment of constant change and uncertainty. We must be realistic and it is healthier to let go of some issues by accepting that we cannot control everything.

Autonomy

The belief that you have choices both in your life and how you handle the job has a major positive impact on your success and reduces stress. Personally I value having high levels of autonomy and being able to select from a range of options as to how I will perform my job and live my life. In situations where I have been told exactly what to do, how to do it and then have been micromanaged in the way I do it, I have become highly stressed. That is why I welcomed the Army's approach to what they call "mission command". You are given the resources to do the job and are told what the expected outcome is and what the end result should be. Then you are left to get on with the job using your wisdom to make your own decisions as to how best to achieve success. Mission command is a philosophy that could be of great benefit to business too. Like me, many military officers teach that philosophy to CEOs in a variety of forms and produce highly successful results for task achievement, teams and individuals.

Relatedness

David Rock said: "Relatedness involves deciding whether others are in or out of a social group; whether someone is a friend, or foe. Relatedness is a driver of behaviour in many types of teams or organisations: people naturally like to form tribes where they experience a sense of belonging." When we meet someone we decide within a fraction of a second whether they are a friend or a foe. If our brain perceives that we're in competition with the new person, then we are less able to empathise with them. The positive connection hormone oxytocin is produced naturally in the brain when we believe we are amongst "people like us" who are friendly. The oxytocin hormone is a chemical. The hormone acts as a neurotransmitter, reducing the stress hormone cortisol and facilitating bonding. It may be called the "feel good hormone" since it can make the brain perceive greater happiness, while stress levels decline.

My work with teams highlights the enormous value of trust. Where there is threat or competition from peers the natural response is for people to withdraw from the team. I now realise that the wide variety of exercises used to build collaboration and trust will also be generating increased levels of oxytocin. My alternating inclusion, then exclusion by the General was another source of stress for me.

Fairness

The need for fair and equitable treatment for you and your colleagues is a big driver. Fairness affects many aspects of life. For example in my various clients' employee engagement surveys I have frequently seen a major issue being the perception that people are not paid fairly for the work they do in comparison to their colleagues. In pay and reward situations which are open, transparent and equitable, high levels of engagement and motivation can be generated. That is why it is crucial to be explicit and inclusive when designing the success criteria on which you will judge someone's performance. Then it is crucial to measure and reward them against those particular criteria.

Understanding the five components of the SCARF model has helped me come to terms with the challenges I had at that time working for the General and I recognise the challenges faced by fellow leaders today.

Attracting wise and bright talent

Another technique that I observed in senior leaders is that they surround themselves with bright and talented leaders. The two Military Assistants (MAs) that the General selected, in their turn became successive Generals in charge of London District some years later. Sebastian Roberts and Bill Cubitt were both respected as the brightest officers of their generations. While fully utilising their talents, the General acted as their relentless and demanding mentor. This was a deliberate policy on the General's part to develop their wisdom, judgement and prepare them for the day when they too would become very senior leaders, responsible for the lives of many people. The General had a wide network of other top-quality leaders in the military, in politics and across the upper echelons of society. He drew on their expertise at appropriate moments. He also expected and encouraged his MAs to develop and use their own networks of business associates and develop their own team of talented people. This was all focused towards making things happen successfully behind the scenes. Peter Inge was a leader who developed other leaders.

Mentors

The value of seeking wise counsel was evident from the Generals I observed. They all sought the advice of others, often by asking retired Generals to act as mentors. Sadly too few business leaders tap into such a wealth of knowledge and experience. In a previous posting General Sir Peter Inge had worked for Major General Desmond Gordon, another highly talented Green Howards officer. I learned to be prepared for General Desmond's occasional phone calls inviting CGS to lunch with him at their club, for what were essentially mentor sessions. One day General Desmond surprised me by inviting me to have one of these lunch time mentor sessions at the club, instead of the General. I was deeply flattered. Yet it was with some awe and trepidation that I agreed to meet the only man who earned the deep respect of CGS, and who in his turn unsettled almost everyone else, and certainly me.

For some inexplicable reason on the day of General Desmond's lunch invitation, I became totally immersed in another task. I completely forgot to go to his club for our lunch meeting. I was reminded later of my missed engagement, by an anxious officer who had spotted the General sitting alone at the club. He had asked him where I was. Feeling mortified I had to take immediate action to make amends and survive my blunder. I wrote a speedy letter of apology and then instantly rang General Desmond's home to apologise and in his absence spoke to his wife. I cringed at her honest reply: "Oh dear, you are in trouble!" Realising the enormity of the faux pas that I had committed, I knew the next thing I had to do was to confess my mistake personally to CGS, before he heard from General Desmond. I realised that my offence would be considered a great enough blunder for CGS to terminate my time as his assistant and sack me, as he had done many others. I decided that honesty was the best approach and so confessed my error.

When I admitted that I had made a stupid blunder, the General calmly replied that he did not expect it was as bad as I thought and asked me what I'd done. I quietly mentioned that I had completely forgotten to have lunch with General Desmond. At this point my General went rather whiter than normal and said: "Oh my God!" In reply to his questions, I confirmed that I had indeed both written and had rung to apologise. I escaped with relief from his office, to live another day by the skin of my teeth. Understandably my credibility with CGS was severely eroded.

Two weeks later, I received another phone call from General Desmond. He invited me once again for lunch alone at his club. I thanked him profusely and assured him this time I would not forget. There was a gentle pause and he mildly replied: "I know". The lunch itself was fascinating and was an enormous education. He was a fabulous host, who quickly put me completely at my ease and I learned many wise tips about leadership. He reminded me how every situation, especially mistakes, could be used as lessons. Here are a few that have stuck with me:

1. Appreciate your own and other people's finest qualities

2. Always have the humility to remember you might be wrong

3. If a leader develops your talent, then "pay it forward" and bring on another leader in the future

4. Personal power and presence emanates from the quietest, most attentive leaders

5. Listen and learn from every mistake

6. Check your diary at the start of each day and also look a week ahead

I still feel privileged that such a wise man was prepared to meet me and take the time to mentor me.

Lessons from Business

Learning from my transition into business

My last Army job was at AMCS (the Army Management Consultancy Services) and this enabled me to gain a little knowledge of business issues. It turned out to be a perfect opportunity for me to utilise my recently acquired MBA skills fully. I became a management consultant and widened my horizons beyond the Army. It was a small organisation containing an equal mix of civil servants and Army officers. We conducted surveys, completed analysis and management consultancy reviews on behalf of the senior echelons of the Army. At AMCS and the Civil Service College I trained to become a certified management consultant. I learned about the technical aspects of management and leadership as well as kindling an interest in management consulting and leadership coaching. I became good friends with a bright and creative, "fast stream" civil servant called Richard Leach. Together we studied and then applied our newly learned management consulting skills. Some ideas were well received by our clients around the Ministry of Defence. Sadly other reports and recommendations we made may still be gathering dust on a shelf somewhere.

My time at AMCS was also a great time for reflection on the forthcoming transition into life in "Civvy Street" that I was contemplating. This idea had begun to formulate when working for the head of the Army. At that time I had looked around the senior members of the Army Board and asked myself three fundamental questions. Firstly I asked: "Was I dedicated enough to the Army to become one of them?", then: "Did I aspire to be one of them?" Finally I asked myself: "Did I really fit into the Army mould?" The answer to all three of them had been a resounding "no". Consequently it was at that point in my career that I began mulling over other options and so I began to study for my MBA and work at AMCS.

Fortunately I had a good experience and very smooth transition between the military and my life as a civilian management consultant. Based on that experience I recommend that others who want to make similar career changes apply the following four principles. Plan well in advance, research thoroughly, gain necessary qualifications, and learn all you can about your new career whilst still in your current organisation. This ensures that you have looked at all the options available from every perspective. My career change was planned in detail as if it were my last and what I considered to be my finest military operation. I spent a lot of time meeting with, listening to and accumulating wisdom from other mentors and leaders who had left the military and were successful in business. It was essential to have the full support and active encouragement of my wife Bridget, my family and friends.

When people change anything significant, they often seek to move away from the pain of the situation that they are deeply unhappy about. Alternatively they are attracted towards a potentially pleasurable situation. In my situation I was hugely attracted to the profession of management consulting and leadership development. It felt that while I had learnt much in the Army, I had completed that chapter of my life. Everything I had learnt had now prepared me for the next life step. I left the Army with absolutely no regrets, on very good terms with all my friends and contacts in the Army. While I still enjoy going to annual reunion dinners with other Green Howards officers, I have always been very pleased that I made that decision to leave the Army.

The wisdom that comes from setbacks and failures

In my job hunting as I transitioned from the Army into business, I followed a number of dead ends and had a couple of unsuccessful interviews. One of my unsuccessful interviews was with McKinsey & Co. and in my view they are one of the top global consulting firms. I respect this company for the high quality of leadership amongst its senior employees and strong culture. Not being selected was a great disappointment at that time. Despite getting through various stages in their recruitment process, my undoing was my poor showing in the mental maths tests. I realise now that my strengths are more in interpersonal skills, rather than mathematical and analytical skills. In another management consulting firm, despite having a good start in their selection process, I was the architect of my own downfall. In the later part of the selection process I became too self-satisfied and rather flippant. This did not go down well with the highly analytical, attention to detail needs of the Partner running that particular selection day.

With the wisdom of hindsight, it is fortunate for me that I did not join either of those organisations. I would not have been a good fit in their culture. I probably would have struggled and might have been unhappy in those roles. All my work in self-profiling, researching and using the feedback from these interviews, helped me to focus my job search onto just four Management Consultancies. PricewaterhouseCoopers Consulting (PwC Consulting) was my particular favourite. In my final crunch interview the PwC Consulting Partner asked: "So what happens if McKinsey offered you double the salary we might offer?" Without a pause, I replied: "I would feel undervalued by you." The Partner smiled, chuckled and gave me my ideal job in PwC Consulting.

Developing wisdom and selecting your leadership coach or mentor

Over the last few years as I have met business leaders, a recurring question has arisen from them when they contemplate enhancing their leadership abilities. Which qualities should you as a leader look for in the coaches you are selecting to support you? In my view the job of your leadership coach is to act as a catalyst for the changes that you wish to make. You need a coach to bridge the gap between where you are now, and your future goals. You have to select someone who will motivate and stretch you so you are able to make significant and sustainable changes. Many of the changes you will make are deep and lasting mental and behavioural shifts. Your coach needs to be able to see the end goal and help you get there. They need to be wise. I strongly believe that as a coach I also need to improve my own skills continually, and accordingly I have also sought the finest coaches to inspire me to develop my ability further.

What is it that makes a great coach? From my point of view you need to be supported by someone who is an inspiring leader themselves. You should look for someone who has wisdom with "humble excellence", a curiosity about what you as their client are thinking, and someone who can be utterly present and attentive to what you are saying. You can benefit from working with a coach who can make themselves almost invisible when required. The coaching session is then focused totally on you as the leader and is not about the coach or their personal opinion.

I also find there are times when I am asked to be a mentor. In those circumstances I willingly share the experience I have accumulated from other leadership situations. You should expect the coach or mentor to have a wealth of leadership experience, business acumen, coaching training and to have undertaken a considerable amount of personal development. It is worth studying the coach or mentor's CV before your "personal chemistry" meeting. If it does not feel right, then change your coach immediately. The choice is totally yours. In my experience, the most authentic coaches have undergone significant life changes themselves. They have had to stand in front of their own metaphorical mirror and look both at who they are being and what they have been doing. When you look in your own leadership mirror do you like what you see?

It is easy to tell whether you're in the presence of a coach who is completely at ease with whom they are. They are genuinely curious about you and fascinated by your potential and your future performance. A poor coach tends to try too hard to please you. They may be motivated by their own agenda and can be distracted by anxiety about their own performance. Often it is quite hard to put your finger on exactly what it is that differentiates good from great coaches. It depends how stretched and challenged you wish to be. Personally I provide a lot of support, and later challenge to inspire leaders to value their strengths and then raise their game. How much challenge can you take? Recommendations from other CEOs count for a lot. Intuitively you notice which coach feels more congruent, at ease and is fully present with you.

Leadership by example
Ian Stuart
President, Hallmark Cards International

Hallmark is the leading UK greeting cards publisher. Ian Stuart's international division is responsible for all markets outside North America with regional offices in UK, Europe, Australia and Japan. He is in my opinion a leader with sound wisdom, judgement and yet humility. He leads 4,500 employees who create and produce approximately two billion cards per year. When I recently interviewed Ian, he described his inspiring leadership style is a follows:

"My style has been influenced by the experience of being a leader from the age of twenty seven when I was a country manager and then leader within a small company. My leadership grounding was overseas in places like Thailand and Japan. It made me realise that you are very dependent on your people; if you can't speak the language, do not understand the culture, or the business practices, then you will be sensitive to the need to build a strong team and encourage, motivate, direct them and look after them in order to earn their loyalty. The importance of working through your team is vital. When I came back to the UK I had the benefit of speaking the language, knowing the market and culture and yet still the importance of the team applies.

My strengths and where I spend my time are: on selecting the right people, getting on with them and motivating them. I have a casual and relaxed style, not a command and control one.

I do like to socialise with my team, I try not to be scary, I have an open door and do not mind being interrupted. I think my team respect me, not because I have a big stick, but because I know what I'm doing; I'm friendly and I let them get on with it. If I have a weakness it is not laying down the law, only coming to a decision after I have enabled all the debate, not getting the team members to shut up and accept that this is a decision and I mean it!"

4 Key Points:

- Apply the motto "time spent in preparation and reconnaissance is never ever wasted".

- High IQ is not in itself enough to make someone into a good leader. It has to be combined with good judgement and wisdom which come from being grounded in reality.

- The best conclusions are often reached by using your own experience and knowledge alongside the combined judgement and wisdom of a team of advisers, coaches and friends.

- Inspiring leaders create safe and supportive environments where team members do their most innovative thinking and work. Places of fear, criticism and ridicule reduce effectiveness.

4 Questions:

1. How do you learn from your setbacks and failures?

2. Who will you select as your leadership mentor from the business world?

3. What development areas would you discuss with your coach, if you had one?

4. What lessons of wisdom and judgement have you learnt from your best leader?

Airborne Forces – Para Selection Course

FOUR

Presence & Personal Power

"The key is to keep company only with people who uplift you, whose presence calls forth your best."

Epictetus (AD 55- 135) Greek Stoic Philosopher

Being awarded an MBE by HM The Queen

Collecting an award from Her Majesty The Queen at Buckingham Palace is an unforgettable experience. Our Brigade HQ team had provided a significant amount of support for the Australians before they deployed to East Timor to prevent the bloodshed between factions. I was awarded the MBE for the work that I had done pulling together and leading this cross UK team as well as my role as Chief of Staff for three years. The Most Excellent Order of the British Empire is an order of chivalry established on 4th June 1917 by George V of the United Kingdom. The gathering at my investiture was made up of a mixture of people, including some who are famous but mainly people who could be your next door neighbour. Looking around at the world famous TV personalities and Olympic gold medallists, I accepted that I was firmly in the latter group. However everything about that day made me feel special; putting on my military uniform for the last time, driving my wife Bridget and daughters through the front gates of Buckingham Palace and parking in the impressive quadrangle. Harriet and Bryony were seven and six years old. They loved seeing soldiers on parade, clapping as I received my award and talked with Her Majesty The Queen, and having a family photograph afterwards.

Undoubtedly the people gathered that day gained a great deal of satisfaction and motivation from being recognised for both our own achievements and for those of the people we led. For in many cases the teams we had been part of had been the main contribution to our success. As Warren Bennis[7] said the capacity to build great teams is a key leadership skill. Great achievements are rarely a solo effort. There is nearly always a vital support team in the background. There have been many things in my life which I have strived for and not quite achieved, yet that one moment made up for any earlier disappointment. I was particularly struck by the ability of Her Majesty The Queen to be utterly attentive and connected with me in the precious two minutes that I had talking to her while receiving my award. She had real presence and an impressive memory (from her brief) about who I was and what I had achieved. Hers was a rare talent and she made me feel like I was the only person in the room who mattered at the moment that she clipped the medal onto my chest.

It was interesting to work later for an organisation which had a policy of not including post-nominals on business cards. Somehow it is "un-British" to enjoy success and stature, since it can cause resentment in others. Recognition in many different forms still remains a strong motivator for many people. Never underestimate the lasting positive impact that you as a leader can have on other people. The natural ability of some people to influence and persuade others to follow their directives is the reason I chose presence and personal power as the second principle of inspiring leadership. It is a powerful and irresistible force that motivates and energises people and teams to achieve goals and exceed targets.

Definition of presence and personal power

Someone with leadership presence appears self-confident, self-assured and gives total attention to the person with whom they are speaking. Presence is often, but not exclusively, found in people of great stature, rank and position within an organisation. Leaders who have considerable personal power and authority emit a sense of presence by their attitude and the way they treat other people[8] and by the way people react to them. They are able to have a dignified, calm and grounded way of being and are able to be comfortable and at ease in moments of silence during conversations. They use their inner ease and self-esteem to calm people around them.

George Fox[9] the Quaker leader encouraged us to "be still and cool in your own mind and spirit". Some senior military officers and CEOs have a bearing, carriage and an air of quiet authority. Presence is an invisible emotional and spiritual force field around a person which has a highly positive impact on others. When we describe someone as having "presence of mind" we imply that they think and act calmly and effectively in a crisis. I recommend the book by Eckhart Tolle[10] called *The Power of Now* which speaks at length about the benefit of being in the moment and present; "in the here and now". It is more challenging yet still possible to develop this personal presence and power without having a position of authority.

Consequences of a lack of presence in a leader

The lack of attention, care, or interest in another person is symptomatic of the absence of presence. Anxiety, stress and depression can also be triggered in others and themselves by a lack of presence on the part of the leader. I've had numerous poor experiences with military and business leaders who were anxious about the future, or were worrying about what had happened in the past. It was very clear from their lack of eye contact, agitation, fast speaking and movements that they were neither calm nor grounded. Such manic behaviour is infectious. It can unsettle a team or individuals in moments of high stress and emergency. The consequences of the ensuing fear and anxiety are cumulative and frequently lead to poor decisions and so failure to achieve goals and objectives.

Leaders who constrain or shrink their personal power are highly ineffective in meetings and public speaking. Some leaders give away their personal power by failing to look the part of the leader. Neither do some people act, behave, or speak as a leader. As a result they diminish their personal authority and are not taken seriously. With a lack of personal connection they fail to develop sufficient rapport with their audience. They find they have to compete to be heard or noticed. By acting in this way they further undermine their own credibility and their behaviour serves to irritate rather than inspire.

In addition when leaders attempt to multi-task by sending messages on their Blackberry or laptop at the same time that someone is speaking to them, they fail to do either task well. They leave an indelible impression on the person to whom they are speaking half-heartedly, that they really do not care about them, and are not interested in them. Many leaders have said to me that they are too busy and have not got time to stop and be fully present with those they lead. That comment is like saying you're too busy driving in the fast lane on the motorway to stop and fill up with petrol. Both situations cause "collateral damage".

The clients I have coached face numerous moments of truth each day. These involve intense periods of stress where the stakes are high and everyone looks to them for decisions. When stressed they admit that it constrains their thinking. They acknowledge that stress also stunts the ability of their teams to innovate and find solutions to the immediate problems. I'm aware of critical moments on military operations where a lack of presence by the leader and the onset of fear and anxiety have been disastrous. In such situations, basic instincts take over and human reason and logic can be completely lost. Film footage of riots and the breakdown of order between the rioters and police provide ample examples of this. Equally, accounts of the demise of famous global companies in moments of financial crisis point very clearly to their leaders. It was at these moments of truth that they lost all sense of presence, were overtaken by fear and anxiety and made disastrous decisions.

How can presence help you as a leader?

Being totally present with one of your business colleagues has beneficial results. First it is energising and inspiring for someone to have the complete and undivided attention of their leader. Second the sense of calmness, ease and attention paradoxically allows both people to do their best thinking in the shortest possible time. The saying "more haste less speed" is most apt. Making eye contact and really "seeing" another person is highly uplifting and engaging. Consequently the recipient will more willingly give commitment and energy to that leader and the organisation.

If leaders slow down and calmly give time to those they lead, it sends a powerful message. It says: "I care about you and you matter to me and our team". The time invested by the leader in making such personal connections produces a return which pays back many times over. The result is increased dedication, loyalty and enthusiasm. A small commitment of time and authentic interest in one of your team members leaves a lasting positive impression for days if not weeks. I can still remember times when I conversed, probably for no more than a couple of minutes, with powerful leaders. They had the knack of being giving me their full attention and created a disproportionate feel-good factor.

My advice to you when you're in a meeting is, be in the meeting. Mentally do not be in your last meeting or be preparing for your next meeting. Be in the moment, in the here and now. In that way you will have a much more successful outcome and could finish each meeting quicker. That in turn might produce spare time for you to prepare for the next meeting. You could even leave work at a reasonable hour to be at a crucial event for family or friends. The people we lead are bright and astute. They can tell when we are not listening. If we pretend and say that we really are listening, when we are clearly not, then we will further erode our level of trustworthiness with them.

When you are seeking to connect with an audience, you need to prepare yourself so that you are calm, grounded and present. Use techniques that ensure you are thinking positively and you can minimise your anxiety and stress. The best speakers have a passion and interest in their subject and hence become completely "in the flow". Using visualisation and deep breathing techniques can help you become at ease. People believe in you when you make eye contact with members of your audience throughout your talk, and smile genuinely where appropriate. Allowing calmness to emanate from you especially with the appropriate use of pauses and silences gives an air of authority.

Lessons from the Military

I learned from several different scenarios and experiences that there are many other ways to develop your personal power and presence. There are many aspects to these characteristics and I will mention a few that can be highlighted by my military experiences below.

Electronic Warfare Troop Commander

Working in the world of Electronic Warfare (EW) was a fascinating and highly secretive world. The experience provided me with some lasting leadership lessons especially about personal power and presence. During my two years as an EW Troop commander I learned in detail about communication information gathering. Our role was to scan communication channels to intercept, analyse and discern the enemy's strategic intentions. Using sophisticated equipment we pinpointed exactly where the enemy was. It was a stimulating role providing access to top-secret information, enabling me to work with some of the brightest and best people in this field from all parts of NATO. One quirky coincidence for me occurred when I was on a two week NATO EW course in Bavaria. I stopped in a corridor and looked at a photograph of a NATO "Cosmic top secret" course from 1958. There to my astonishment, I saw the photograph of my father Lieutenant Commander Paul Perks RN. My curiosity piqued, I investigated his role further and eventually established the fact that my father had commanded an elite Royal Navy squadron, whose role was to deliver nuclear bombs against the Russian fleet, should World War III have erupted.

We played a dangerous game of cat and mouse in EW, gathering intelligence from the Russians, East Germans and various Middle Eastern countries. I was based in a covert site very close to the East - West German border at the height of the Cold War. We operated twenty four hours a day scanning, intercepting, analysing and direction-finding the most important elements of the Warsaw Pact forces. Our EW Regiment formed part of the UK's eyes and ears to establish the seriousness of any military threat. Our role was to give the thousands of troops behind us maximum warning of an impending offensive, should we ever get to the brink of war. Undoubtedly such action would have saved many lives and impacted on the war. As a consequence EW units were seen by the Warsaw Pact as a direct threat to be crushed. Our own intelligence warned us that our listening posts would be destroyed by a massive artillery bombardment in the first five minutes before any offensive began.

Indeed one day we were listening to, and interpreting a massive live and simulated artillery exercise by the Russians and East Germans. It was taking place 8 kilometres away across the border on the Magdeburg training area. Suddenly something we heard put the fear of God into us. When my analyst decoded the grid reference of the location where their artillery was targeted against it was the exact grid reference of our own (supposedly covert) EW base. We replayed the recording three times and each time it was clearly our grid reference. Undoubtedly the Russians intended to let us know that they knew where we were and that they could destroy us at any minute. Perhaps they had a sense of humour, but it was not one we shared at that moment in time!

Communicating your presence

From this unique EW job I realised that as leaders what we communicate leaves a lasting impression. Even the smallest, apparently insignificant comment or act can have consequences. Once spoken, a comment you make can never be unsaid. It is always captured by someone somewhere and later will be played back to you, or worse still to somebody else. I realised that people need to be very clear about the intention behind their communication. Our intention and the way people interpret what we say are often badly disconnected. As Rudyard Kipling said our words can often "be twisted by knaves to make a trap for fools". We must ensure that we correctly utilise our personal power and presence to communicate our meaning clearly and check that the correct message has been received. Just saying something is never enough.

I learned also that you need to communicate via a variety of media. Someone somewhere will collate your information to form a picture of you, your organisation and your brand. This is especially pertinent now, since we have a range of "social networks" such as Twitter, blogs, YouTube, podcasts, Linked-in and Facebook. We have to learn to shape our environment and enhance our "virtual presence". We can do this by taking proactive action to design and manage our own brand, simultaneously communicating it through multiple channels. The danger is that if you do not take the initiative, somebody else will. Your own brand will be shaped by their intentions, judgments and desires. We must be very clear about our personal goals and how we communicate them, otherwise we are destined to live our lives achieving somebody else's goals. The communication that exists in the world about you shows more about your personal brand than most people realise.

As EW specialists we were of intense interest to the Russians and were classified alongside the SAS, pilots and other Special Forces as "prone-to-capture troops". We therefore trained in escape and evasion, resistance to interrogation and survival techniques. My Commanding Officer was Lieutenant Colonel John Stokoe. He is a motivational man who, I now realise with hindsight, lived the values of an inspiring leader. He was later to rise to the top of the Army and become Major General John Stokoe, Deputy Commander in Chief Land Command, before successfully moving into senior leadership roles in business. I will tell you more about him later in a case study.

John led by personal example. He kept fit and encouraged others by his love of leading from the front and motivating his Regiment. He worked hard to train junior leaders to reach their full potential. He was also a talented orienteer. Fortunately for me he acted as an unofficial mentor and role model, which continues to this day. I cannot over emphasise the importance of having a powerful role model or mentor. When done well, the positive and lasting impact can be a powerful force for good in your life and business. Without the leadership opportunities John gave me, my life would not have taken the exciting course it has.

Personal power and presence

My mentor John Stokoe sent me to complete the specialist long range reconnaissance patrol (LRRP) course and later sent me to complete the battlefield survival course in Bavaria. We were taught by SAS and Special Forces experts. They provided me with specific skills and knowledge to organise and run combat survival, escape and evasion and resistance to interrogation exercises for all 600 members of the Regiment. In this enlightening training I learned how to look after myself and the others that I was leading, as we escaped through hostile territory filled with an armed and equipped enemy hunter force. This force we were told was determined to capture us and then interrogate us to establish what we knew about the enemy through our EW work.

I spent a lot of time "on the run" lying in unpleasantly wet and dirty conditions and feeling very hungry. Our senses were heightened like herd animals fearful of predators which could attack us from any angle. Sometimes I smile at myself in hostile business environments since I have noticed on occasion the same feeling developing. My senses have become alert to the potential dangers presented by some supposed "colleagues" who have become competitors with Machiavellian tactics. There are always going to be key moments in life when you or even organisations are "on the run" having to respond to crisis situations. Then the ability to encourage others can depend solely on your personal presence. BP, for example had such a situation in 2010 when an oil rig in the Gulf of Mexico exploded, killing eleven people and causing one of the world's most publicised and contentious environmental disasters. Strong inspiring leaders with personal presence might have been more able to overcome the justified hostility to the company and to motivate the BP teams through the crisis. Business can definitely be like a battlefield.

The other business leadership lesson that I took away from this severe training ordeal was that the time spent in gathering knowledge about your profession, your competitors and your own people is invaluable. On this battlefield survival course, we were stripped of everything and were given some new basic uniform. We were then sent "on the run" to escape back through enemy lines to our own troops. Meanwhile the enemy tried to hunt us down. When you are stripped of all your files, laptops, assistants and rulebooks, you have to rely on what is in your head and your heart. In the same way in business settings you are often put on the spot and can be asked awkward questions. It is at those moments, without a pause, that your team expect you to answer with a calm confidence. You have to do so without researching things, or looking to others for their advice and guidance. You are required to be an expert and speak with authority.

When I was on the run from the enemy and leading a small group of determined men, we felt a mixture of fear and excitement. The fear came from anxiety at potentially not achieving the ultimate goal. The excitement came from the realisation that as a team we had the freedom to do almost anything we wished within the Army Officer's strict code of ethics and integrity. Sadly I am a realist and accept that not everyone has such a code in business. It was simply a contest between my team, the environment and the enemy. As I think about it now, there were many connections to business. As the leader I learned that to do my job properly I had to stay healthy, fit and rested so that I could make the best decisions for the whole team under stress and pressure. I therefore had to trust and empower my team.

I had to make use of all their talents, since it would have been foolish and impossible to over-control and attempt to do everything myself. I see too many managers in business who are not able to do this and they micro-manage their teams. With the right encouragement I found it stimulating to see how often my team met and exceeded my high standards and expectations. We were able to achieve extraordinary results as people whom others had previously considered to be unexceptional and quite ordinary. I also found that in harsh conditions when all is stripped away, you can only be yourself. I learned that genuine personal relationships counted for everything.

Resistance to interrogation

The training that we organised after completing this course was unusual in its scale and challenge. Members of the Regiment were first captured and transported to a barbed wire concentration camp deep in the German forest, manned by our Russian-speaking guards. We had to create battlefield conditions rapidly. So after three days of rigorous physical activity, no sleep, and a minimal amount of gruel-like porridge, different trucks transported the camp inmates to new locations. En route they were ambushed by friendly partisans. The "prisoners" were set free with a basic map and instructions to escape 120 miles to the west and cross the border. If members of the hunter force recaptured them, they were taken to a fully equipped and carefully controlled interrogation centre, complete with video recording devices, doctors and medics. This was vital training to help us in the event of war and eventually it was to prove invaluable as highlighted by Special Forces friends who were involved in the first Iraq war.

It is eerie to see people in business employing the kind of mind games that I experienced under my training for resistance to interrogation. This is a misuse of power. One example is the male and female combination of tough man, nice woman. I know of a pair of executives on the Main Board of a Company who use this tactic. The CFO plays the tough man, who takes no prisoners and insists on slash and burn tactics with significant cost cutting. He uses a "deep dive" strategy to interrogate the various team leaders and question any financial data, sales figures and profit projection. He viciously pulls apart the executive's arguments to weaken and belittle any opposition to his approach. His colleague the CEO uses her female guile and strong emotional intelligence to build consensus and apologise for her tough CFO. She wins over the shell-shocked executive. Consequently the executives open up completely and feel understood and trusted. She can then compromise a bit but still make huge progress and get the outcome she has earlier agreed with the CFO. That is a brief example of psychological interrogation techniques in business. In my view these actions are underhand, unsustainable and this method of managing people involves a cynical abuse of power. Developing personal presence so that people willingly work towards the goals you set has to be a far better way to operate.

Presence - The King of Norway and Royalty

When working for the General in charge of the British Army I was fortunate to meet the King and Queen of Norway. The General and I flew by private jet from London to meet the King. En route to the airport in the General's staff car, I broke into a cold sweat, when I realised I had remembered the General's passport, but had forgotten my own. This could have been another "red card" moment where I might have been sacked. While the General was definitely unimpressed, my frankness and honesty in admitting my error gave me a reprieve. By being polite and respectful to the Royal Air Force, I managed to get the necessary paperwork to fly to Norway without my passport.

Thereafter the visit went extremely well. King Harald had an easy manner and he accepted the General's proposition to become Colonel of the Green Howards Regiment. Two months later we hosted him and his beautiful wife Queen Sonja at a state banquet in the Royal Hospital Chelsea. It was a splendid affair with full silver service. We had rehearsed every last aspect of the evening and had attended to the smallest of details. The General took a keen interest and showed an ability to switch between major decisions on war fighting in Bosnia one minute to the fine detail of a State Banquet the next. I will remember it as an example of how to do things with true "form" and style.

The following day I arrived at the Norwegian embassy in London with the Regimental tailors to advise the King on the first fitting of his Green Howards Colonel's uniform. It was quite surreal being in a room as personal advisor to a King! The tailors were in awe of him and extremely anxious to make a good impression. There was an awkward moment where I made a joke about a pair of trousers that did not fit the King well. The tailors tried to apologise for what I said, but the King just roared with laughter and continued to make a joke at his own expense. It was clear then that he would easily connect and earn great respect when later talking to our pragmatic and down to earth Yorkshire soldiers. From my perspective he displayed great emotional intelligence and true humility. He had fantastic personal power, because he was able to communicate easily with everyone in that room despite his position in life. I have since wondered how the most successful members of royalty managed to exhibit the qualities of inspiring leadership, without appearing to be too arrogant and supercilious. I think the greatest quality is that of showing real presence by being completely focused on the person to whom you are speaking.

Her Majesty The Queen Mother was another iconic personality whom I met through this role as assistant to the head of the Army. On one special occasion we were hosting her at a formal lunch at the King's Troop, Royal

Horse Artillery. I was struck by her gentle manner. Armed with a gin and tonic she listened intently to whoever she met, asking insightful questions and making each person feel like their point of view was fascinating to her. Perhaps it was. In a leader this total focus on individuals is an act of love and caring for those for whom you are responsible. It inspires those being led to go the extra mile, because they feel special and genuinely believe that their leader cares specifically about them. When as a business leader you do the same, remember it has to be genuine. Often people can sense if you are pretending to be interested in them, when you are clearly bored. Everyone has a story to tell and something to teach us if only we would listen. Be with people in that moment. It will leave a lasting positive impression and is the beginning of the creation of your own personal power and presence.

Presence - first impressions on anti-terrorist operations

Later when I was a Company Commander I deployed on very high risk anti-terrorist operations in Northern Ireland. It became apparent to me that the physical appearance of a leader is very important to many of those who follow them. When a good image is combined with attributes of inspiring leadership such as presence it enhances the respect given to the leader. In my many years leading and learning from leaders, there were probably only a handful of leaders whom I and others respected who were scruffy, unkempt and chaotic. In those cases, I know it was deliberately cultivated as part of their unorthodox, alternative Special Forces style. This observation is backed by studies of human behaviour which attribute a significant amount of people's success in communicating their message, to the initial positive physical impression they give.

During my months on anti-terrorist operations whatever the time of day or night, however tired I was surviving on three to five hours sleep each night, I always made an effort to look smart. My aim was to appear well-organised and in control. Internally I had my moments of stress, anxiety and self-doubt. Somehow a smart image helped members of my Company to have the necessary confidence in me, and this enabled us all react as a team to the chaotic and frightening situations we faced. My deduction was that when everything around me was uncertain and I was feeling pressurised and stressed, looking smart and appearing outwardly collected helped me give an impression of calm and feel more in control. When you are calm and at ease within yourself, then that sense of personal power and presence acts as a positive influence on those around you, who in turn are also steadier. Every move you make as a leader is observed and deductions are drawn from them.

Looking immaculate and unflustered, gives a significant psychological advantage to maintaining the edge and authority over your opponent. When trying to maintain a sense of calm on peacekeeping operations, in highly stressful conflict situations, or at times when leaders need people to have confidence in them to carry out their request, having such an appearance is crucial. There will always be people who maintain a poor outward image, yet who are admired for their intellectual ability. I would argue that these people still give away some of their personal power and the respect they could have received. Inspiring leadership includes the need for followers to be motivated and encouraged by someone who looks and intuitively feels like a leader.

Bosnia - using personal power whilst saving face

Of all the leadership challenges that we faced while we were on Peacekeeping Operations in Bosnia, the one that I remember most vividly was when the Bosnian Serb General tested us by flexing his muscles. On that particular day, all three of my Platoon Commanders were spread to the far-flung corners of our territory. My storeman and his driver were travelling in their Land Rover past the huge Bosnian Serb barracks. Just then three of the General's trigger-happy Bosnian Serb militiamen ambushed my men's vehicle and held them up at gunpoint with Kalashnikov automatic weapons. Luckily for my timid and very passive storeman, by pure coincidence, a Challenger 2 tank happened to pass by two minutes later. The militiamen, who were shocked at this (completely coincidental) rapid response by the British, dropped their weapons and ran back into their barracks. I realised that I had to respond quickly. The challenge was to nip this seemingly minor breach of the peace accord in the bud before their General thought he could escalate such infringements. This was a situation that could easily have spiralled out of control.

As leaders we had been taught to know our potential enemies well. My Bosnian Serb interpreter had therefore briefed me about this general. I knew he had a large ego, a reputation for machismo, was prone to posturing and cared about "saving face". I decided to keep a low, non-confrontational profile when meeting him to discuss the breach of the Dayton Peace Accord rules. I arrived at the gates of his massive barracks in my low key, deliberately vulnerable Land Rover. I wore my beret, rather than a steel helmet, keeping my pistol in its holster having left my automatic rifle behind. I walked confidently to the front gate accompanied by my interpreter. I looked the sentry straight in the eye and said: "I would like to see the General." The sentry shrugged, glowered at me in a surly way and said in Serbian: "He is not here." I understood his blatant and disrespectful body language.

I know that many people from different nations (and the Serbs especially) respect power, force and superior might. Therefore I gave the pre-arranged signal and called up a couple of my waiting Warrior armoured fighting vehicles (AFVs). With a menacing roar they sped from their hiding place around the corner. They came to a shuddering halt in a cloud of dust, two feet away from the camp gates and pointed their barrels directly at the sentry. This produced the required result. The General appeared calmly a minute later and invited me and my interpreter warmly into his barracks to talk in his office.

The interpreter had previously explained to me the importance of allowing the General to "save face". So, as advised, I began with small talk about various topics. Our discussion ranged from the winter weather, boar hunting, to the Sarajevo Winter Olympics. As a sign of machismo, the General tried to get us both to drink at least five glasses of his lethal, neat alcohol called Slivovitch (plum brandy). Luckily a couple of my glasses could be tipped subtly into a conveniently placed plant pot. Eventually, I chose my moment and raised the issue of his men ambushing one of my Landrovers with weapons outside the camp. He feigned complete surprise about the whole incident. I pretended to be completely relaxed. This I was definitely not, despite the Slivovitch. I said I looked forward to seeing the three men in his jail, when I returned for a follow-up the next week.

He assured me that it would not be a problem and he would have everything sorted out by then. I managed to get out of the barracks before the alcohol took effect and my Company Sergeant-Major took command of the company in the afternoon. Meanwhile I slept off the effects of my unusually high-level UN negotiations! Luckily on my visit the following week, the three were in his jail. I sometimes wonder what I would have done if they had not been arrested. I was lucky to have called his bluff before he called mine! Who knows, perhaps they were only in jail for the duration of my return visit. Allowing people to save face, preparing for difficult meetings and giving a relaxed and confident impression are all ways I believe we can increase our personal power.

Lessons from Business

Presence built on congruence and authenticity

Being truly yourself and congruent, is a vital component of inspiring leadership and creates a powerful sense of presence. In my business coaching I have found that the most authentic people live in a very similar way both at work and home. They are consistent in the way they "show up" and treat other people. The most successful, effective and contented leaders bring their "whole self" to work; not just a part of themselves. This is in contrast to some less effective leaders, with whom I have worked. They assume that everyone has a work persona and a completely different way of being at home. Such tension is unsustainable and eventually the cracks begin to show. As I have observed this results in leaders coming off the rails and in some cases having breakdowns, or experiencing varying degrees of depression. If a leader is fully congruent, they live lives which have close alignment between their personal values, the way they treat others and the work they do. These people survive the challenges at their workplace and in their personal lives. They also thrive because they are behaving naturally and become utterly comfortable with whom they are as individuals. This authenticity shines through when they are with you and they emit a powerful yet quiet confidence that makes them attractive leaders. I like the following quote by Lao Tzu, father of Taoism:

"When you are content to be simply yourself and do not compare or compete, everybody will respect you."

Being a role model to others is a considerable burden to carry. Whether people seek it or not, when others look on a leader as a role model of the best qualities of leadership, that leader becomes open to accusations of hypocrisy should they fail to live up to the high standards expected of them. The British have a perverse pleasure in seeing great leaders fall off their pedestals. Personally I'm well aware, that by writing about inspiring leadership, I am exposing myself to scrutiny. I am in no doubt that there will be many people who are able to describe occasions when I have personally fallen short of the clear principles and values which I am espousing. To make mistakes is a very human trait. I can think of no leaders who have lived an authentic life of perfection. When I make mistakes, I now reflect on what happened. I listen to feedback, no matter how brutal. I consider what my intention had been at the time and then look at how my actions had been interpreted. From that analysis I decide what I should do next time to change the poor perception that others may have taken of my leadership.

Being a consistent inspiring leader involves travelling a long road, and you will never get to the final destination. Instead a better goal to have is making a pattern of healthy behaviour and leaving a legacy that survives long after you have left a room, or an organisation.

Personal power or potency - the leader sets the tone

I have always found that it is leaders, in particular the CEO, or most senior leader, who set the culture of an organisation. After all, an organisation's culture is nothing more than a collection of acceptable behaviours that are rewarded and encouraged by the most powerful and influential people within that organisation. It is their personal power and presence which can be a force for inspiration to the team of talented people they lead. The law of attraction works strongly on the culture of an organisation. Leaders attract, develop and inspire people throughout the organisation to behave in similar ways to them. If inspiring leadership has previously not been the dominant culture and style of the organisation, then when such a leader arrives, there will be a period of turbulence. During this time, individuals will adjust their behaviour and attitude to align with the new leader and what is considered acceptable, or choose to leave.

In cases where the previous leader had a very potent, dominant, controlling and perhaps bullying style, some of the old guard will continue to behave as before under the new leader. Despite this no longer being acceptable they are often unable, or unwilling to change. Sometimes such individuals cannot change, even with the support and inspiration of an experienced leadership coach. If this is the case they need to leave the organisation and seek out a different culture that rewards their particular style and attitude. The finest leaders are authentic and ensure that other people in the organisation also lead by example with deeds that align with what the overall leader considers acceptable.

I have experienced alternative situations where it was tragic to watch value being destroyed. For example the culture in one particular team was engaged, energised and was highly performing. It all changed the moment when the inspiring leader was replaced by an over-controlling, task focused manager. Sadly much of the good work of the previous inspiring leader was undone, since the new manager disenfranchised, undermined and micro-managed their subordinates overlaying a blanket of fear and control. In such difficult situations the solution may involve coaching this new manager and the consequences of their behaviour need to be explained clearly. If little is done, as in this case, talented individuals will leave the organisation.

How our manic business pace destroys presence

A couple of years ago I ran two separate self-awareness workshops for twenty senior leaders in a top global professional services firm. After a very long day a couple of the leaders wanted to stay behind to discuss their profiles with me in more depth. Even though I was tired, I agreed to delay dinner and stay on with one leader and give him my undivided attention to help him. We found a coaching room and he began to outline the problem and consequences to his team of his lack of presence. After five minutes his Blackberry rang.

Without thinking he instinctively reached across to answer it until I stopped him dead in his tracks. "Stop! Do not answer that!" I challenged him. He looked shocked and offended. "Do you know who that is, and are you expecting a critical business call?" I asked. No he confessed, he had absolutely no idea who it was. No, he admitted, he was not expecting a critically important call. I asked him did he know what message his action was sending to himself. Also did he know how his behaviour made me feel? Again he was lost for words and had a complete blank and vacant response. I explained that he had asked for us to have a vital life changing conversation about his leadership and his team. Instead he had just signalled that the phone call from an unknown stranger was more important than him or me. He finally realised what it meant to be present with the people he was talking to.

This links to an article I wrote recently in the FT [11] about the importance of being present with significant people in our lives and having down time to unwind and relax with our families. The challenge is to be present with our families and friends when not at work. The point is that "work" is an activity, not a time or a place. Now with the tyranny of our i-phones, i-pads and Blackberries, the more senior we become as leaders, the longer we are "at work" every day. For many our work consumes over eighteen hours per day, weekends and holidays.

Far too many senior leaders are "always on", checking emails just before bed (using the phone as an alarm clock) and when they first wake up. That little symbol says "you have mail" and it can be exciting or sometimes anxious-making. If the messages are something new then we feel obliged to respond to in milli-seconds. "Responding quickly to an e-mail or writing one late at night will show them how efficient and hardworking I am," you think. Wrong, that is not good leadership, it is enslavement. Here is an interesting experiment for you. In the morning, when you are next in the office check the time when you received emails from others, aside from those from global colleagues in different time zones. I bet some are sent after 10pm and before 6am.

The feeling that a leader needs to be constantly available is often unnecessary. Apart from duty officers and doctors on call, this is often self-imposed pain and stress. Stress like this without relaxation leads to physical illness and mental breakdown. Yet the catch, and the lure, is that it gives some leaders an inflated feeling of self-importance. One leader said to their partner: "I am working these long hours for you darling so we have a good living and can pay for the children's education." But when the leader returned home late from work and continued to communicate with work colleagues through the evening, they were not actually present with their partner. They were not "with them", because they were at work in their minds and checking texts and emails.

Beware the "always on" addiction – it catches many of us. I have been guilty of feeding such an addictive habit too. The solution is to have time-bound periods purely checking your multi-media communications and then switch them off. You can then make uninterrupted time to be present and relax with the most important people in your life. Of course, some leaders are workaholics and live to work, rather than work to live. I find Tennessee Williams quote inspiring: Life is all memory, except for the one present moment that goes by you so quickly you hardly catch it going.

Leadership by example
Deanna Oppenheimer
CEO of Barclays UK Retail Bank

Deanna Oppenheimer is the CEO of Barclays Retail Bank. If you were to ask a cross section of her very large number of staff, they would describe her as perfectly fitting the profile of an inspiring leader. She has immense personal power and presence and can positively influence a large meeting with a few choice comments. Her challenge when she was given the role was to inject a culture of inspiration and high performance into Barclays Retail Bank. Her personal example and impressive reputation amongst those I coached made me learn more about her leadership style. When I spent some time with Deanna recently, she shared her thoughts on what shaped and motivated her:

"The reason I am a CEO is that I never aspired to be a CEO. I always wanted to contribute and to make a difference. I was selected for this job because I had the skill set and track record in retail banking. My eight-year-old son said: 'All you seem to do is eat cookies everyday' because that was what he saw when he visited my office. As a leader it is vital to get buy-in; you need both influencing and directed skills.

You have to be nimble and flexible. I was lucky enough to be in a company that expanded rapidly and I recommend you experience a growth story, where you have to perform. By the age of twenty nine, I was on the Group Executive Committee as the first woman and the youngest member of the board. I learned a lot about sitting back and listening. I realised it was important to do my homework, be prepared and not arrogant. The skill was to listen, yet be assertive without being over aggressive. You have to know how to manage people who work to live, rather than live to work. This is quite hard to accept for some 'Type A' personalities.

On the subject of surrounding yourself with an army of giants, I believe that A players attract A talent, while B players attract B and C talent. You have to surround yourself with the best of class. Leadership is not dependent on a title; some of our great leaders are cashiers and people in our branches, who have the ability to lead and advise from behind. Leaders make tough decisions. Your legacy as a leader is your people. An example of this legacy came when colleagues e-mailed me after I had left to say: 'You provided advice about my future career, I took it and I'm now in that role - thank you'.

On the theme of who inspired me, I would say I was lucky to have great parents. This allows you to get a jump ahead; they encourage you but do not break you."

In both her reputation and from my experience of Deanna, there were specific qualities of inspiring leadership which stood out for me and others. The first was her wisdom and obvious ability which she had accumulated from an early age. The second was her strength of personal power and charisma. The third her high level of emotional intelligence comprising strong interpersonal skills, which meant people wanted to work with and for her.

4 Key Points:

- Her Majesty The Queen has real presence, an impressive memory about who you are and what you have achieved. She also has the ability to make you feel like you are the only person in the room who matters at that moment.

- Leaders with presence have a dignified, calm and grounded way of being and are able to be comfortable and at ease in moments of silence during conversations.

- The lack of attention, care, or interest in another person is symptomatic of the absence of presence.

- Being truly yourself and congruent, is a vital component of inspiring leadership and creates a powerful sense of presence.

4 Questions:

1. What is your philosophy to both work and life?

2. How can you be more present and attentive with those you really care about?

3. Who is the leader with the most sense of presence and personal power you know?

4. Which matters more, the mobile phone or the person who you are with?

Army Chief of Staff earns MBE

by Richard Edwards

AN ARMY Chief of Staff turned worldwide recruitment consultant has brought an MBE back to his home city of York.

Jonathan Perks, who recently left the army after 19 years, was decorated for work he did as Chief of Staff of the 15th North East Brigade.

Much of the brigade's work is currently taken up by emergency planning, as it is involved with slaughter and disposal of foot and mouth culled animals and was last year involved with flood relief work.

Mr Perks helped co-ordinate two major deployments of the brigade, one in Australia to help prepare for a UN peacekeeping mission into East Timor, the other in France to help strengthen Anglo-French military relations.

Mr Perks, of Sutton-on-the-Forest, began his career in the services as a second lieutenant in the Royal Signals.

During that time, he was part of a three-man team who broke the record for running a marathon up – and down – Mount Troodos in Cyprus. The task is to navigate up one day and back down the next, with the record breakers completing the task in a mere eight hours and nine minutes.

From 1990 he served as a major in the Green Howards, before enjoying a spell as assistant to the Head of the Army, Field Marshal the Lord Inge.

During that time, he travelled the world and described it as "a very interesting year indeed."

Mr Perks, 39, now works at the Pricewaterhouse Coopers Government and Defence branch in Leeds.

He said: "I am a York lad. I went to school here, the place has always felt like home. It is a real honour to be able to bring an MBE to York."

Mr Perks is married to Bridget and has two daughters, Harriet, eight and Bryony, seven.

They all made the trip to Buckingham Palace, which was a dream come true for Bryony.

"She has always wanted to go to the palace and meet the Queen," Mr Perks added. "It was a great day. The whole family are thrilled about it."

Jonathan Perks with his wife, Bridget, at Buckingham Palace

Press article on award of MBE

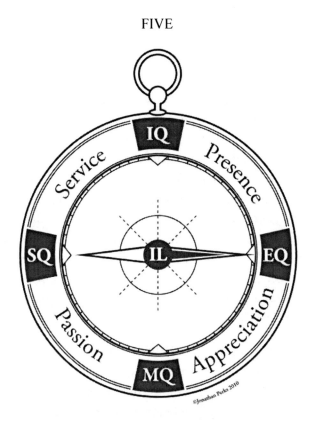

FIVE

EQ - Emotional & Social Intelligence

"There is only one corner of the universe you can be certain of improving.....and that's your own self."

Aldous Huxley - Author of Brave New World

When people buy you

I've known George Griffin since he was fourteen years old. I worked as Adjutant to his father Lieutenant Colonel John Griffin of whom I will speak later. George served with distinction in the Green Howards Regiment of the British Army some years after my time with the Battalion. What is unusual about George is the ease with which he makes incredibly intimate and trusting connections that he makes with people. When he was the Operations Officer on an anti-terrorist tour in Northern Ireland, he had an unusual and wide collection of contacts. During his six months there, George became friends with a number of the local farmers, with influential people in both the Protestant and Catholic communities and with senior officers in the police service of Northern Ireland (PSNI). Some of the people with whom he built trust and rapport were not necessarily the type of people who would have traditionally warmed to a British Army Officer!

George has always said that his father remains a great role model for him. His father displayed strong values, beliefs and a positive, can-do attitude. His mother is also a powerful character and has been very influential in shaping George's attitude of humble excellence. A few years ago, I returned to a more peaceful Northern Ireland with him and his father John on a holiday. What was noticeable was that George was greeted like a long-lost friend by a range of different people who regaled us with hilarious stories and anecdotes about him. They were all prepared to help George and had huge respect and admiration for him. For them he had a highly attractive character and the ability to handle whatever life threw at him. This encapsulates for me the essence of emotional intelligence (EQ).

When my colleagues in Penna Consulting were looking for a top financial services salesman to work in the City of London, I recommended that they consider George among the many other applicants. The selection panel were wary, since he had not been in a similar sales role before, had not worked in financial services and had spent most of his career as an Army officer. I suggested that they test the level of George's emotional intelligence and that of the other applicants. The results I believed might show that George was worth hiring as a risk. I predicted that if they hired him he would be the top selling salesman. My reason was because clients would believe him and he would not need to sell too hard. I stepped back and let the selection panel make their own decision. In the tests they found that George's emotional intelligence levels came out significantly higher than the other applicants. He also performed extremely well in interviews by building great rapport with all members of the panel and acknowledged both his strengths and areas that he wished to develop further.

Within eighteen months George became the top billing salesman within Penna Consulting. He remained in that top position for three years until he was promoted to the new role of Director of Management Development and Coaching. In aiming to understand what specifically made George so successful, I asked a senior financial services client. He replied: "We completely trust George because he gets to know what we really want. He listens to us and then brings in the right people to deliver what we've asked for. He has also become a business advisor with whom I share a lot of confidential information to help solve our business challenges."

Social responsibility is a key component of EQ and George recently raised a lot of money for charity. He competed in the gruelling Marathon des Sables (MdS) which is a 151 mile running race across the Sahara. With the exception of a tent, competitors have to carry everything they need for the duration of the race. This includes food, clothes, medical kit and sleeping bags. The MdS is recognised as one of the hardest endurance races in the World. The terrain over which the course is set, consists of sand and rock and competitors are expected to endure heat and exhaustion. As well as carrying all they need, all competitors must manage to run each section of the race within a given time scale in order to ensure they are not disqualified from the event. George raised a huge amount of money for the charity "Facing Africa" to help victims of the NOMA disease.

Emotional intelligence is the differentiating quality of leaders. People with high EQ know themselves and others, and possess sufficient emotional literacy to read situations and connect with people to get the most successful outcomes with the least amount of damage elsewhere. This is why I chose it as the third principle of inspiring leadership.

Definition of Emotional & Social Intelligence

According to Bar-On model of emotional intelligence[12]: "Emotional-social intelligence is an array of interrelated emotional and social competencies and skills that determine how effectively we understand and express ourselves, understand others and relate with them, and cope with daily demands and challenges"[13]. According to Reuven Bar-On, most descriptions, definitions, measures and models of emotional intelligence have included one, or more of the following key components: (a) the ability to recognise and understand emotions and to express feelings; (b) the ability to understand how others feel and to relate with them; (c) the ability to manage and control emotions; (d) the ability to manage change, adapt and solve problems of a personal and interpersonal nature; and (e) the ability to generate a positive mood and be self-motivated. In the context of the inspiring leadership model, EQ can be simply defined as a leader's ability to cope with life thereby becoming more successful with less effort.

Consequences of a lack of EQ in a leader

I have used the emotional intelligence assessment tool designed by Reuven Bar-On extensively over the last ten years to help 650 leaders get to know themselves better. Watching leaders in action, hearing 360° feedback from those they work with and helping leaders develop their EQ further I have noticed some key themes. The vast majority of senior leaders have very high IQ and deep technical knowledge of their specialist area. What is often noticeably absent and underdeveloped are various aspects of EQ in particular empathy and social interaction (people skills). This is usually a consequence of their training and earlier career experience where organisations value an obsessive focus on the task, technical process and results more highly than the ability to build strong inter-personal relationships.

As people step up into more senior roles greater emphasis is placed on "stakeholder management". This involves the need to handle a web of complex relationships and conflicting agendas. A low level of EQ can be disastrous when trying to persuade, influence and cajole peers and other senior leaders over whom there is no direct authority. I have also noticed that frequently low levels of self-regard, happiness and optimism are hidden behind a façade of activity. This is often accompanied by an aggressive drive to achieve results, gain bonuses and further promotion. If not properly addressed, then I have seen this cause leaders to become depressed and "derail". Leaders then leave, or are encouraged to leave their organisation. At the other end of the spectrum, some elements of EQ can become a weakness if overdone. For example if assertiveness and independence are extremely high, then the person displaying these traits may be perceived as someone who is aggressive and a loner or even a bully.

There are many different permutations of EQ profiles. Someone who has low impulse control, for example may demonstrate a frequent loss of temper. This may also indicate an impulsive and impatient decision making style which, as discussed in an earlier chapter, can have significant consequences for colleagues. The paradox is that leaders with low impulse control often can also be very effective in getting things done, by not taking too long to consider all the options and possible consequences. In some circumstances caution can save the company from significant financial loss, yet in others hesitating too long may make people miss the business opportunity that is presented for a fleeting moment. In any event, impulsiveness needs to be balanced with good reality testing, social responsibility, stress tolerance as well as other stabilising aspects of emotional intelligence.

A low level of reality testing might indicate difficulty in reading what's going on politically in an organisation, an inability to put things into the correct perspective and even creates poor judgement in more extreme cases. As a result of deficiencies in this aspect of emotional intelligence, some people may make the wrong decisions by totally misreading it.

Self-actualisation can also be measured and this is closely associated with SQ which is described later. Low levels of self-actualisation can indicate that the person is not clear where they are going in life, is not getting a real sense of fulfilment from their work or does not have the drive to set and accomplish personal goals. These people are usually under-performing, lacking in self-motivation and can possibly demotivate those around them.

On the other hand, there is also a potential danger from extremely high levels of self-actualisation, because these individuals (the "alpha males" and "alpha females") may exhibit an insatiable drive to achieve goals regardless of the cost to themselves and others. An alpha male or alpha female is the individual in the community to whom the others defer. The alpha is normally the most successful male or female leader. In top global companies, there can be a deliberate policy of recruiting high numbers of alpha leaders to put them in competition with each other. In the majority of cases, this drives up standards. The down side can be that many of these leaders may show lower levels of EQ, specifically in the area of empathy. The resulting competition encourages selfishness, greed and turf wars in which leaders and their followers compete in underhanded ways.

How can EQ help you as a leader?

For those needing to understand the value of EQ leadership, there is some good advice, in Goleman's 1998 book[14] *on the hard case for soft skills*, where he summarises one of the most important findings from an extensive data analysis conducted by Hay/McBer:

"Emotional and social competencies were found to be twice as important in contributing to excellence as pure intellect and expertise; emotional competence is particularly central to leadership, a role whose essence is to get others to do their jobs more effectively."

For those who need additional evidence that hiring emotionally and socially intelligent leaders can help their business be more profitable, and get staff to be more motivated, productive and willing to work, review the Gallup findings[15]. The researchers, who conducted this study, concluded by suggesting that: "people join great organisations and leave poor managers!" There is additional empirical evidence supporting the benefits of hiring emotionally and socially intelligent leaders in the chapter that Reuven Bar-On and I wrote in the Association for Coaching's book *Leadership Coaching*[16]. This chapter concludes that successful leadership is a function of making the most of your strengths whilst strengthening your weaknesses in emotional intelligence. This chapter suggests that coaching should focus, in particular, on self-awareness, managing and controlling emotions, flexibility, and relating responsibly and cooperatively with others. I recommend that you complete the online EQ-i questionnaire with a qualified coach, benchmark yourself against other leaders and focus on improving those emotional intelligence factors that impact most on your leadership.

Lessons from the Military

Using EQ when leading technical experts: The Royal Corps of Signals

The first ten years of my career as an Army officer were spent in The Royal Corps of Signals. I was required to lead very intelligent men and women who had deep technical knowledge about communications systems that were often on the cutting edge of technology. My training in this mass of very complex technology was only superficial due to limited time. Our role was to set up mobile communications systems in the harshest of climates and physical conditions, even before mobile phone technology was used widely in civilian businesses. In such situations I had to rely on my emotional and social intelligence plus common sense, rather than just my IQ to persuade talented technicians to follow me willingly as their appointed leader.

My pragmatic answer to "what is leadership?" is that it involves: "Persuading people willingly to do what they did not originally want to do and encourage them to feel good about it". I started to learn that there is more than one way to influence and persuade people to your point of view. You can win people over by your powers of reason and logic, or you can listen to their viewpoint and draw them towards yours. You can also share common ground and inspire them with a joint future vision. Whichever approach I used, it took every ounce of skill and leadership acumen. These intelligent experts believed in a more egalitarian and meritocratic system of management than that which is common in the army. To use the famous quote from the comedy film Monty Python and the Holy Grail, you could almost hear them thinking: "I did not vote for you!"

I see very similar parallels with those who are leading individuals with deep technical knowledge in professional services firms and investment banks. Such academically brilliant and proud individuals need the finest leadership. They will verbally shred and intellectually destroy any leader who is not displaying the values of inspiring leadership and sound common sense. Leading talented Royal Signals soldiers was an experience which has served me well as a leadership coach. I now work with other technical experts, in a wide variety of businesses especially banking. One of my most frequent challenges is to help technically adept individuals to achieve promotion. To do this they have to develop their EQ and learn how to manage people with technical and intellectual capabilities as good as their own.

Counter-Terrorist Company Commander

Later in my career I was recalled to my Green Howards Battalion for a second stimulating tour as a Company Commander on active counter-terrorist operations in Northern Ireland. If I had developed a higher level of emotional and social intelligence at that time then I would have better handled the challenges which life was throwing me. The pace of this job was very fast and furious. There was no room for error, moments of high stress and anxiety, very little sleep and lots of pressure. We rushed in and out of our base trying to anticipate every move of our opponents, but often having to be highly reactive to them. It was interesting to compare and find that life was in many ways similar for my wife Bridget with two very small babies back in England!

I spent much of my life on this six-month operational tour in a variety of helicopters. This was normally at the dead of night being dropped with my troops into remote fields in South Armagh. We attempted to outmanoeuvre phantom-like members of the IRA Active Service Units. They were respected rightly, as some of the most deadly and professional terrorists in the world. I was conscious that many of my long serving infantry peers had already been on multiple tours of anti-terrorist operations and I was a comparative novice. As a leader I had to learn extremely fast. My competence and capability to make rapid and wise decisions was a matter of life or death for the people I led. It also had severe implications for others in the local community who could be affected by a shooting, or bombing. I went through many moments of anxiety and indecision during my time as a company commander, since making a mistake could prove fatal for me and the people for whom I was responsible.

Trust is crucial in leadership and is asymmetrical. It takes a long time to build up and can be lost in seconds. Those whom I led on this operational tour expected to be treated with integrity, fairness and honesty. They needed to know quickly that I was competent, fit, able to lead by example and delegate wisely. In order to be able to trust others, a leader has to know his people really well. Much relies on a leader's ability to be emotionally intelligent in coping with such pressures. They have to appreciate others strengths and talents and interests, as well as their vulnerabilities and areas that they need to develop further. In particular it was crucial to project my own personal power and be fully present with those I led and met. Trust has to be built on a foundation of mutual respect and when it breaks down, it can be terminal. Luckily I had a very good advisor in the form of my Company Sergeant Major (CSM). In those dark moments of uncertainty and self-doubt, I was able to use him as a mentor. We talked about various options and scenarios, before I decided and acted. Ultimately we both knew that the responsibility rested solely with me.

I was taught a powerful lesson about getting priorities right and how insensitive some leaders can be. My wife was very ill at one stage during my time in Northern Ireland. I knew instantly that I needed to be back with her to help share the burden of two children under the age of two while she recovered. Our operations were so all-consuming that the Commanding Officer made me feel especially bad for requesting permission to be back in the UK for a week to help my family at this critical moment. Neither he nor I were particularly emotionally intelligent at that time, and we did not handle the conflict well. I knew then and I know now that it was the right thing for me to do, but I felt his deep resentment and disapproval that I should put my family before military operations.

The value of EQ in 15 (North East) Brigade HQ

After this tour of duty with my Battalion I was able to take on the role to which I had aspired at Staff College. I became the Chief of Staff (COS) of the largest UK Brigade Headquarters. It was a daunting responsibility to lead the HQ staff of seventy people in support of the Brigade Commander, when so young. The Brigade looked after over twenty thousand people in the Northeast of England and had a £103M budget. The Chinese have a saying "beware what you wish for". In this case I rapidly realised that the job was far too big for me to do successfully in the way I had initially begun to tackle it. I had mistakenly thought that as COS, my role was to be the ultimate problem solver. So in response to any problem given to me by the Brigade Commander, or from the Second Divisional Headquarters, my reply initially was "leave it to me". That was a big mistake.

I worked later and later and went into work earlier and earlier. Yet still the paperwork in my in-tray and the mass of e-mails began to accumulate and overload me. My solution was to work even harder and ever longer hours. I got to the point where I felt I could not cope any more. Looking back with the benefit of hindsight, I now understand this situation through a simple analogy which may help you too. I visualised that people walked into my office with a monkey on their back (a large difficult problem). Their aim was to transfer the monkey onto my back in order to free themselves. I willingly took every monkey that people gave me. I then had a veritable zoo and was too overloaded to think straight. I hated this situation and after a mere two months, I thought of asking for another, much easier and lower profile job. Essentially I was considering giving up and resigning from that job.

Unlocking the best in others - coaching to delegate monkeys

When you are deep in the mire it is often so dark that it is difficult to see the solution. At moments like that you need the benefit of an independent person to bring some illumination and challenge your poor thinking by asking incisive questions. You can then make clearer decisions on how to get yourself unstuck. Fortunately for me, my wife Bridget encouraged me to start "coaching" my brigade officers. The aim was to empower them to solve their own problems more easily (keeping their own monkeys). Listening with attention and without interruption followed by one or two powerful questions can liberate another person's best thinking.

An emotionally intelligent "coach-approach" to leadership also allowed me to delegate more of the monkeys that I was given. This was far wiser that trying to do everything myself. There is a fine line between delegation and abrogation. At times people mistakenly believe that by passing on an unpleasant task, which they do not want to do themselves, they are delegating. This is not the case. Leaders need to be completely honest about their intention when sharing out tasks. Delegation often involves allocating the more interesting pieces of work too. In spite of sharing the workload, the responsibility for the outcome must still remain with the leader who was given the initial task. The leader is always ultimately accountable. My military mentor taught me: "Pass on the praise from above to your team and absorb the criticism yourself".

As an early adopter, I tried out this new "leadership coaching" approach. The result was an instant success the next morning with the Finance Director in the Brigade HQ. Using the technique, I helped coach her so that she solved by herself an issue she had intended to pass to me. In addition she also took away, and successfully solved, another financial monkey that I was struggling with. Very soon a culture of coaching became the norm in the Brigade HQ. As a result there was far more empowerment, delegation and accountability amongst the brigade officers. They, after all, were more knowledgeable than me and were the real experts in their own specialism with immense, previously untapped talent.

This is a timely reminder for military and business leaders. It is import to trust others and set high expectations of what your team members can achieve. The problem often rests with some leaders who are not confident enough to let go of control and power. This is closely connected to the difference between the leadership philosophy of abundance and that of scarcity. Those with a scarcity mentality incorrectly believe that if you share an idea, some control, or power then you will have less for yourself. Those with an abundance mentality believe that there are more than enough ideas and power to go around for everyone. If you hang on to everything, then you will either burn yourself out, or block progress. After a few months I had begun to empty my office of all the metaphorical monkeys and so created some strategic thinking space. This enabled me to truly add value and deal with the bigger issues facing the brigade.

Deployments to Australia and France

I had generated a huge amount of extra time by using a culture of coaching and delegating the monkeys. This proved especially important to me one day when I received a career-changing phone call. I now had the strategic thinking time and space to deal with the bigger, higher value opportunities. As I was standing at the window of my office, I received this call asking if I would speak to my Brigadier, Alan Deed. Did the Brigadier want his Brigade HQ to be considered as the one to lead a strategic overseas exercise? The selected Brigade HQ would need to pull together 120 officers from all over the British Army to deploy to Brisbane in Australia.

Intuitively we both knew this would be an amazing opportunity. Within a few days, we had analysed the situation in detail and made a case to be selected. We were successful in being nominated as the UK HQ to work with the Australian, New Zealand, Canadian and American HQ's for a month in Australia. This was a fascinating experience, starting with the challenge of selecting the most appropriate officers for the right roles in a large, brand-new headquarters that was going to work in a multinational setting. We also had the spin-off benefits of global travel and adventurous training in some wonderful parts of Australia as a reward after the intensity of the military exercise.

The Australian Divisional HQ and Brigade HQ were preparing to deploy as a UN Force to East Timor to prevent the continuing massacre and abuse of locals by militia forces. On the surface our exercise seemed to be just a large and very complex simulation. In reality it actually had a crucial purpose; to train the Australians for peacekeeping in East Timor. The simulation required all of the participating nations to pool their peace-enforcing knowledge and experience. We needed to give the Australian team the best possible preparation for their crucial humanitarian task.

There were some parallels with an earlier experience. I was reminded of when I was the Chief of Staff of the staff college team that was deployed to Fort Leavenworth in the USA. I had to identify people's strengths and talents, create a framework and provide structure to make sense out of chaos. In some ways this was an entrepreneurial challenge for me as a leader, and was a memorable learning experience. I packed our UK team with as much talent, knowledge and experience of peacekeeping operations as I could find. My aim was to show just how professional the British Army was. More importantly we aimed to help the Australians prepare as professionally as they could for their life-saving mission. As a team, we needed to use EQ skills to manage our own interactions in a stressful situation, communicate clearly with foreign troops, manage change and stress and be self-motivated.

Organisational terrorists

It took an immense amount of organisation and preparation to pull together a collection of officers and NCOs to make a brand-new HQ. While I was not the most senior officer in our team, as Chief of Staff I was expected to be the leader. The new group had to be welded together into a cohesive, happy and motivated team and start to become high-performing very rapidly. Nearly everyone we selected brought a huge amount of energy, passion, enthusiasm and inspiration to the specific roles that they were asked to fill. This made it a real pleasure to lead the team. Out of the 120 officers and NCOs whom we trained and took with us to Australia, there were just a couple who lacked sufficient EQ. They had a highly critical, destructive and negative attitude to other people. These two displayed the classic characteristics of "organisational terrorists" and the lesson I learned with hindsight was to trust my intuition early. If such team members were not prepared to change their attitude, then I needed to have the courage to challenge that behaviour. If they still persisted, then I knew that I had to act quickly and remove them from the team. Unfortunately I was not firm enough at that time. Consequently I let the metaphorical bad apples stay and turn one or two others against their colleagues and undermine my leadership.

I learned that it is better to focus most of your leadership energy on the top talent who can produce the best results. They deliver the greatest impact with the least effort. If poor performers with negative attitude do not commit themselves, then they should be moved to somewhere where their talents are better suited. Do not waste too much energy on them. It is like spending time with a child who has bad behaviour. They are rewarded by getting your attention and the well behaved children do not get the attention they deserve.

Those disaffected people were however a very small part of an otherwise professional, high-performing team. I found that I was in a position as a leader who was in a position to develop leadership in others. People were keen and eager to learn, improve their skills and collaborate with our multinational colleagues. The leadership tool which worked particularly well was the "bird-table briefing" for the brigade commander. In this process, about twenty five people would gather around the four sides of a tabletop displaying the huge map of our area of operations. Each of us would update Brigadier Alan Deed on our area of responsibility and symbols representing our troops, the militia and terrorists were pushed around the map. The British HQ became a centre for attention of other multinational VIPs who came to listen to our bird table briefing. Being able to move around the edge of the table and look at the situation from physically different perspectives was of great value. Consequently today as a leadership coach, I encourage executives to move their physical position and look at their problem and the people involved from totally different perspectives.

I developed my EQ and learned a lot about working with multinational cultures. This now serves me well when coaching global leaders. The way I communicated at that time was to use the three Ps: pause, pace and power. I paused to research, observe and understand the culture and modus operandi of the foreign armies. Next I found it helped to keep pace with them at the speed with which they spoke and made decisions. Finally I analysed and respected the way they used personal and positional power within their organisations. Every person is different, however, to generalise I found some national traits in the military. I found that the Americans operated at a far faster pace than the French-Canadians. The Australians and New Zealanders, in turn, were less concerned about rank and position than the Americans.

The simulated exercise in Australia was considered to be a great success. This was especially the case when viewed historically from the perspective of how well the Australian HQ and troops enforced peace in East Timor on behalf of the UN. We were invited to deploy our Brigade HQ a year later on a similar multinational exercise with a French division HQ and a number of French Brigade HQs. It was interesting this second time to experience a completely different atmosphere. Again I was able to hand-pick the UK Brigade HQ team. This time I left behind the organisational terrorists; that made all the difference!

There were initially lower levels of trust between British and French forces and correspondingly higher levels of misunderstanding and suspicion were prevalent. This mistrust was mitigated by the large number of French-speaking British officers that we had acting as liaison officers in the various French HQs. Even our Brigadier spoke French and had a French wife. As with the previous exercise in Australia, there was a huge amount of mutual learning. Once levels of trust improved, the speed of our operation correspondingly accelerated. By the end of two weeks, the British and French definitely could have deployed successfully together into a range of trouble spots to tackle any difficult issue involving peacekeeping around the world. In addition, I'm sure the few glasses of wine at a social event helped our multinational collaboration!

As a result of the work I did as Brigade Chief of Staff for three years and especially on these two exercises, I was awarded an MBE. The key feeling for me about this award is that it is not an individual reward. Instead it was because I developed an excellent and a high performing team who supported me and enjoyed the work we were doing. No leader can receive any awards without the total commitment of a great team.

MBA, consulting and coaching

There were many benefits to building my EQ and adopting the coach-approach to leadership. I began to relax more and made better use of my time both for work and my family. I also began a three-year Open University MBA. For this, I have to thank my boss Brigadier Austin Thorp who encouraged me. I shared my dilemma with him as to when might be the best time in my career to complete the MBA that I was interested in studying. He was very robust and supportive in his response and said: "Start it now, for tomorrow is not a slower day and there will never be a good time to begin." The MBA taught me much that was of direct relevance to being a Brigade Chief of Staff, administering a large region of the UK. I learned the theory and practice of financial management, strategy, creativity and innovation, organisational design and human resource management. In addition, I learned the value of quickly building rapport with a cross section of leaders from many diverse backgrounds, businesses and cultures.

Until I took my MBA I was not aware of how many close parallels there were between leadership in the military and business. I frequently applied the business theory from the MBA to lead and manage the

Brigade HQ more effectively. Often this was extremely well received, especially by my far-sighted Brigade Commander. At other times, I was thought of as slightly eccentric in the way I tried out the latest business method. I was one of the first military officers to take the MBA and had a considerable amount of groundbreaking to do. Today, it is common practice, and management consultants and executive coaches with their fresh ideas and concepts can be found throughout the Ministry of Defence.

As I studied business management and finance theory, I applied elements to my day job. As the Chief of Staff I made a point of getting into the heart of the annual budget which was something most officers avoided with an intense loathing. I took the opportunity to apply practical management consulting techniques to run meetings in the Brigade HQ more effectively. I used techniques from the MBA course to generate fresh ideas, with varying degrees of success. In addition I created a network of other MBA officers around the Army and achieved a strong pass in our Investors in People (IIP) accreditation.

A three year part-time MBA (on top of a highly demanding leadership role) took a lot of what would normally be spare time with my family and down-time at weekends, in the holidays and evenings. As with my whole career, this was only possible due to the immense support from Bridget. She fully supported my somewhat self-focused obsession with leadership mastery. She too is a leader who always likes to learn in order to develop and teach others. So when the children were five and six, she joined me by taking her Open University course in a Post Graduate Certificate in Education. For eighteen months our distance learning overlapped, and we could be found together in our converted study-bedroom working into the night. We took turns in making coffee and motivating each other to keep up our stamina. We lived by the motto: "Everything is achievable if you're prepared to pay the price and live with the consequences".

A seminal moment for me was on the MBA summer school. My psychometric results indicated that I was more highly innovative (rather than adaptive at the other end of the scale) than all the other one hundred students from various industries and businesses. My tutor asked me:

"With highly innovative skills like these, what is someone like you doing in the Army? Are you a bit of a misfit?" The simplest questions are often the most powerful life-changing catalysts. This was such a good question and it strongly shaped my next army job. I was being lined up for a challenging job working for a General in the Ministry of Defence and strongly resisted this. Instead I did some research and lobbying and arranged a job for myself with the Army Management Consultancy Services (AMCS). I was told disdainfully by my postings officer and my Regiment that this would not be a good career move. I assured them that it was, and that I knew exactly what I was doing. I was beginning to take ownership of my career, identify my clear life purpose and use both EQ and SQ (which will be described later).

Lessons from Business

Developing Emotional Intelligence

At its simplest level, emotional intelligence means coping successfully with life and its pressures and demands. You can measure, develop and enhance your emotional intelligence to achieve five outcomes: to know and manage your own emotions, to read and manage others' emotions, to handle stress more successfully, to manage change better and to be self-motivated.

I have found that using a tool to measure emotional intelligence has led to some very powerful conversations with business leaders that I have been fortunate to work with. These people have been very successful in their lives so far and usually have been described as having high IQ. My experience is that these leaders get hired for their high IQ. They are fired or "moved on" for their under-developed EQ. One impulsive outburst can end a career. I have frequently had to help leaders cope with the consequences of the fallout from such impulsiveness. Their inability to manage their own emotions or read others' emotions effectively can be damaging. Developing EQ has often been the key to these leaders continuing to flourish.

I find a crucial area for executive development is enhancing trust. This is notably stronger in those teams with leaders with higher EQ. In some cases it takes a catalyst like stark results from the EQ-i for people to realise how much they need to change. Only then do the executives realise that it is not sustainable to carry on blundering around. They cause too much collateral damage as a result of their currently ineffective behaviour. It is at this point that they may initially react negatively to their EQ-i results by casting doubt on its validity. They may project their own shortcomings on the coach and challenge what has been revealed. This is a classic moment on the journey through the dip of the "change curve". Once this stage of denial has been recognised and overcome, then the breakthrough allows a significant amount of change and healthy development to be achieved.

The great news remains that we are not stuck with our current level of emotional intelligence. Research conducted by Reuven Bar-On and my experience support the view that we can develop emotional and social intelligence. When we do, we significantly improve the feedback we receive from others and the business results we achieve. We feel and are more successful as a result.

The successful leaders that I work with often earn significant amounts of money. Sometimes, however, they feel neither successful, nor that they have enough money. Without a sense of proportion they constantly strive for more and more. Rarely do they stop to appreciate or be content with sufficiency. One definition of success is getting what you want. I challenge that and say that happiness is more important and can be defined as wanting what you already have. The development of clear life goals may free you from such feelings of dissatisfaction. They enable you to focus more on developing characteristics that produce feelings of satisfaction and happiness.

I have found that developing my own emotional and social intelligence has helped me to build and sustain higher levels of happiness. I have also become more successful in achieving what I focus my mind and my energy on. It does not prevent me from having moments when things have gone badly, or are not working the way I want them to. However, I find that I can now self-coach and consequently rapidly lift my focus back to a more effective and successful level. Others have also increased their EQ and learned to manage their share of disappointments and setbacks too.

Building emotional and social intelligence for Managing Directors

James was the Managing Director of a successful engineering company in the North of England. It is an independent, specialist engineering company, with over fifty years' experience of providing high reliability, precision instrumentation to customers from a diverse range of markets. James has a thirst for knowledge and is a leader who constantly seeks to stretch and improve himself, which in turn led him to ask me to become his executive coach. He is a leader who believes in serving to lead and he learned hard lessons from working on the shop floor of this family-run business. There he learned to appreciate as many different tasks as he could and understand the complexity of this highly technical engineering business. I spent time with him and his family in both business and social settings and was most impressed by his ability to connect to people, to listen and appreciate others. He took time out to show my daughter Harriet around the company and was able to explain some very complex processes to her so that she was fascinated.

James was aware that he was not as emotionally and socially intelligent as he could be. He knew that this was causing problems in the way he was handling relationships and challenges at work. He has since thrown himself into learning as much as he can about himself as a leader. As a result of his executive coaching he started to read widely about leadership and also sought ways of learning the skills he needs to embed a coaching-style of leadership with the people he leads. He has been very open to 360° feedback on his own emotional intelligence and has adopted ways of being more successful with less effort. James's determination to learn and develop is especially impressive when we reflect on the enhancements he has made in his emotional and social intelligence. In James's words:

"I was very fortunate to have taken the route from the shop floor up; this taught me from an early age that it is people's attitude, skills and dedication that result in exceptional products backed up by the right equipment, rather than the other way round. People are most certainly the biggest asset of any organisation, rather than your largest cost. The latter view is sometimes taught to us now and at business school; immediate action one- cut headcount.

I would consider myself very lucky to have been introduced to my coach – through the coaching process, I saw a massive improvement in my ability to look at things in a variety of ways and therefore have become more able to deal with the multiple challenges facing me then and now.

The coaching was a reminder to engage the full team, not just apply management theory X (the tough 'tell people what to think and do' attitude which is common in many engineering companies) and more actively help build the leadership of the company. We had previously created an environment where people were more likely to fail – we could have been clearer on what was expected of them and we did not highlight, or invest sufficiently in the crucial soft skills in management and leadership.

To have a sustainable future we need to continue to increase the quality of our leadership and consequently two more of our top leaders are now working with Jonathan and his leadership coaches. During my two, six month coaching programmes with him, the company's financial performance improved – that was surely no accident!"

Courageous conversations

I have seen business leaders build EQ and become more assertive. As a result, they then have long overdue, yet successful courageous conversations. The key is to have these conversations in a non-destructive way. When taking on the leadership of an existing team, the most common situation people find is that team members were hired in the mould of the previous leader. They survived by adapting to the previous leader's preferences and leadership style. However, these colleagues are sometimes unable to adapt to new directions. On occasion, you might find you have inherited some team members who you feel are not up to their job and lack EQ. Sometimes, this could be because your predecessor either lacked the courage to tackle their poor performance, or remove them from post. Equally it might have been that they recognised other talents and so deliberately chose to overlook other areas of poor performance, especially interpersonal behaviour.

This is a common shortcoming in leaders, known as the "horns or halo effect", where people can either do no right, or do no wrong. People whom leaders constantly criticise are allocated metaphorical devil-like horns and are normally removed early in their tenure, or leave the team of their own volition. Those, to whom a previous leader gives the angelic halo effect, can do no wrong. If however they are not as good as they seem such people can get away with under-performing for a very long time. These people often use "sophisticated suck-up" strategies to inveigle their way into the leader's affection. It takes a completely new leader, or an independent and objective leadership coach, to challenge the illusion and point out that: "This emperor has no clothes".

As a leader you require an ability to check on reality. You need to continually review the opinions and judgements you hold on your close team members. By creating a sense of intimacy, openness and trust between you and the team members it becomes very hard for a leader to identify and highlight poor behaviour, or poor performance. Many leaders often avoid such a confrontation and mentally filter out any negative traits in their favoured team member. Confronting poor performance or bad behaviour takes courage and is likely to change, or potentially damage the relationship permanently. It is essential that using this reality testing, you look for the authentic strengths and talents in everyone that you inherit in your team. During your first six months as a new leader, you will have ample time to get to know your team and receive feedback from colleagues and clients on their strengths and areas for development.

Many leadership traits can be developed and improved. The key trait to watch for is attitude which will define the altitude to which a person can aspire and their potential level of performance. If a team member's attitude is poor and they lack the will, or desire to improve, then you need to have a courageous conversation and ask them: "What are you going to do to change?" It is healthy to have a diversity of attitudes and backgrounds amongst your team members. That encourages the best kind of thinking and problem-solving. However, if as a leader you find a team member is obviously misaligned to your stated purpose, values or beliefs, then you need to discuss options with them. Perhaps they need to find somewhere else, where they would be better suited to use their own, unique talents. If you do not act on this issue, both of you are living in denial. It will seriously impact the effectiveness of the whole team, the level of trust and everyone's respect for you as a leader.

Leadership by example
Gary Duggan
Managing Director, Barclays Retail Bank

Gary took on a challenge that might have overwhelmed even the most talented managers. He was newly appointed to the role of Managing Director at Barclays Retail Bank. He needed to bring together two under-performing businesses and turn them into a single, profitable division. His business challenge was to rebuild his team and lead two hundred colleagues through rapid change. For this mammoth task, Gary needed high levels of resilience and greater EQ. Without this, the inevitable conflict that he had to manage might have sapped his energy, creating low morale and a failure to inspire colleagues with his vision for change.

Despite the pressure to deliver huge change in a new culture and a new market, Gary knew that he needed clarity of thought to generate a solid strategy and well thought out solutions. To achieve this, he wanted to create thinking time for himself while carrying out a role which threatened to become all-consuming. Understandably his organisation wished to see results from the new division quickly. Gary needed immediate, quick and effective support so he sought out a leadership coach. I was fortunate to have been selected for the task.

At the beginning of the coaching process, I met with Gary to agree a "coaching contract" and create a written document which clearly defined the desired outcomes of the coaching for the Barclays Retail Bank, and for Gary himself. The contract was then reviewed with his managers and both were interviewed to ascertain their view as to what Gary did well and what he could do even better. To understand the culture in which Gary worked, I also spent two days with him and his emerging new team on an "off-site team event". This gave me a clearer understanding of how they operated together. It highlighted levels of trust, how Gary responded to the team and they to Gary.

We both knew that changing a pattern of behaviour is a challenging process. Gary needed to understand his motivation to do this, and I also helped by offering him objective evidence of his current behaviour and the consequences. As part of several two-hour one-to-one coaching sessions, Gary completed a Personal Directions psychometric tool, which enabled him to understand what his motivational drivers were and the values they were built on. He also reviewed his EQ-i results to understand his current level of emotional intelligence better, and I provided suggestions and clarity on those areas of behaviour which were strengths that he could most usefully leverage, or work on to develop.

As well as addressing solutions to the ongoing change process in his organisation, Gary raised "live issues" during his coaching sessions that were having an immediate impact on his work. Through a process of structured questioning, I drew on Gary's own considerable experience and wide range of abilities. This enabled him to find solutions which best suited his own leadership style and strengths. The outcomes and benefits from a twelve-month intervention with Gary were considerable and were publicly recognised by his bosses and across the organisation.

Gary displayed many of the qualities of an inspiring leader, especially humble excellence as he acknowledged that his was a team-generated success. His focus was on developing his EQ which increased by an average of twenty percent. He has gained a fascination for this area and continues to learn, develop and assists others to become more aware of how to be more successful with less effort. Gary believes that the coaching process has already made a "fundamental difference" to his self-belief. He now has the ability to focus on issues that add the most value, offering him both the clarity of thought he needs to build effective strategy and an improved work-life balance.

In reflecting on his coaching programme Gary said:

"Initially, I approached the role in my usual highly driven, impatient, solution giving mode. I applied all my previous experience to drive out some quick wins and was marginally successful. I presented our strategy to the CEO and she liked the approach and we delivered one or two quick wins. I did not feel however as though I was getting the wholehearted support of my colleagues, or delivering a sustainable improvement in performance. This became a very lonely job and my usual charm tactics did not seem to be working this time.

Then I met Jonathan and we started working together to understand how to alleviate this stressful situation and find a way of gaining more support across my network. Using Jonathan's wise counsel, I began to think about the challenges differently, seeking first to understand then to be understood. This approach began to pay dividends very quickly and having adapted my style, I began to gain more support for my plans.

We delivered one of the most successful campaigns in our history and suddenly everyone wanted to be part of our success. I relaxed, realised that I was 'good enough already'. Our sales and profitability results got better and better, I recruited some great talent, who wanted to be part of our transformational story, and suddenly my teams were no longer seen as the two problem children, but were the rising stars of the organisation".

4 Key Points:

- In the context of the inspiring leadership model EQ can be simply defined as a leader's ability to cope with life thereby becoming more successful with less effort.

- Remember "people join great organisations and leave poor managers!" Such poor managers often have under-developed EQ.

- Empty your office of all the metaphorical monkeys, and so create some strategic thinking space. This will enable you to add value genuinely and deal with the firm's bigger issues.

- I have found that developing my own emotional intelligence has helped me to build and sustain higher levels of happiness and success.

4 Questions:

1. How emotionally and socially intelligent are you?

2. What makes you feel successful?

3. Who in your team is under-performing and do you need to ask: "You are responsible for your own life. What are you going to do to change?"

4. Which area of EQ could you personally develop that will add the most leadership value?

Meeting her Majesty The Queen

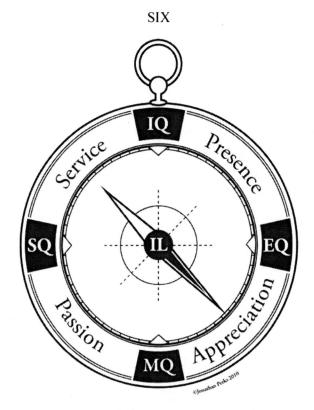

SIX

Appreciation - Valuing Yourself & Others

"Appreciation is a wonderful thing; it makes what is excellent in others belong to us as well."

Voltaire

Leaders who appreciate others

In my opinion Mike Amato is an impressive, inspiring leader with whom I was fortunate to work. He worked as Chief of Products and Distribution in Barclays UK Retail Bank. Mike is an American with a wealth of experience in the USA, UK and globally. He maintains a focus on appreciation of the talents, strengths and skills of his top individuals and teams within the 30,000 people he leads. When I interviewed Mike recently, I asked him how he learned to appreciate other people and as a great story teller he said:

"My very first job was as a janitor in a company. To many people I was utterly invisible. If they did say hello they would not make eye contact with me and they acted as if they considered me insignificant. Ever since that experience, I have made a point of saying hello to people and building a deep connection. When they respond 'fine', I would ask 'why?' and get into a much more honest conversation."

Mike also remembers the lessons his clients taught him about valuing and appreciating everyone he met:

"I remember a time when I was not in a leadership position. I was an investment counsellor and I learned something about people and life that I'll never forget. One of my clients was a very humble old man; he was small in stature, he had a red face and varicose veins. He was very polite and smiley and always brought flowers to the banking cashiers. We did little bit of business together but not much and finally I asked him: 'What did you use to do before you retired? ' He replied simply that: 'I used to drive boats. ' What actually later transpired was that he had been the Captain on board three different US Naval ships in the Second World War. All three had been torpedoed underneath him in the Straits of Gibraltar. He'd always ensured that he was the last person to leave his ship. The first thing I learned from that conversation was humility. The second was to remember what amazing stories people have to tell you, if only we would stop and ask questions."

Mike went on to explain how he now appreciates the people he leads:

"My team of direct reports are very strong leaders and independently minded, so empowerment is crucial. I need to hire the best and brightest people, who are intent on running their portion of the business efficiently. The challenge always remains to get these competitive people to work together, to bring the best out of them and capture their discretionary energy. Coaching allows me as a leader to bring another voice into the team and provides a way of speaking to them not as a peer, or as their line manager, but from another place of appreciation and respect. Team coaching can give members honest messages about their capabilities and show them how to develop their strengths, whilst de-emphasising their less favoured areas. Coaching always comes from an objective viewpoint. I have used coaching very successfully to make tremendous inroads into getting my team to work together, so getting the best out of them as a team as well as individuals."

Top leaders like Mike attract, develop and encourage people to use their best talent or positive energy, while also identifying the negative energy that is preventing them and their teams performing to their optimum level. As a leader, your job is to accentuate the positive energy and minimise the negative. At times this requires courageous discussions about poor behaviour or performance. You also need to have specific conversations about what you appreciate in each individual. The best inspiring leaders, known by some as A players, attract other top talent, so it's no surprise to me to find that Mike Amato worked for Deanna Oppenheimer (about whom I wrote as an example of presence in chapter 4). Probing further, I also found a wealth of other top talent in Mike's team, and in accordance with the law of attraction this talent cascaded down to teams a number of levels below.

In contrast to Mike's style of leadership, I have observed the effect of constant destructive criticism and compared it to situations where individuals and teams are publicly valued and appreciated by their leaders. The difference in performance between the teams is significant and hence my selection of appreciation as the fourth principal.

Definition of Appreciation

In the context of inspiring leadership, I define the principle of appreciation as valuing both your own talents and those of your colleagues. Appreciation is also defined as an expression of gratitude, to acknowledge others and thank them for their contributions to the success of your team. It is a true estimation of the value and worth of another person and the commitment that they've made. What is important is to provide an honest and genuine recognition of another person's actions and tell them verbally or in writing in a measured and focused manner. Recognising exactly what you admire about your colleague and then naming the qualities or results you have specifically observed has a powerful effect on that person. When correctly applied, appreciation raises the sense of value that a person feels about himself. It has to be acknowledged that giving appreciation is a judgment call, but it is a positive one and you are expressing an opinion by way of thanks and gratitude.

There is a close link between this principle, the philosophy of Appreciative Inquiry (AI) and Nancy Kline's work on appreciation which she describes eloquently in her book *Time to Think*[17]. Appreciative Inquiry is based on the assumption that organisations can change in the way they inquire. The principle is that an organisation which inquires into problems or difficult situations will keep finding more problems. On the other hand, an organisation which aspires to appreciate what is best in itself will discover more and more of what is successful[18]. In the simplest form AI encourages leaders to focus their attention and effort on doing more of "what is working well around here?" (WWW). In turn the things that don't work so well diminish. It is highly affirming of individuals and teams.

Consequences of a lack of appreciation in a leader

Within many of the most ambitious and intensely driven leaders that I meet in business and the military, there is a very high critical faculty. These leaders are often, without realising it, far harder on themselves than they are on those they lead. They rarely stop to appreciate their own talents, skills and successes and hardly ever step back and value a job that they've done well. Speaking personally, I know that my mother and many of her generation discouraged us as children from becoming arrogant, getting "swollen heads" or "getting too big for our boots". Modesty and humility were considered to be great virtues. Her generation took this to such an extreme that huge successes were very quickly brushed over or modestly understated in a "British" sort of way. Instead of appreciating our recent successes, we were asked about our next challenge and how we could achieve that. The impetus was to drive ever onwards and upwards without a pause.

As a consequence leaders brought up in such an environment are hardly likely to give praise to other people. Leaders make the incorrect assumption that their followers innately know that they are valued, without actually being told. If a brief compliment is ever provided, then a caveat is often added in the terms of "yes, but" followed by a more critical area in need of improvement. This completely wipes out the beneficial effect of any appreciation and dampens down the feel-good factor. For example I heard one manager say: "You've done a really good job on completing the report, **but** I was expecting it would be longer and more eloquent." My old army Sergeant Major used to say about the negative effects of such two-part compliments: "Anything before the 'but' is baloney! People just remember the negative criticism."

In some of the organisations that I work with, the tendency by managers and leaders is to find people doing things wrong and to correct them. They believe this criticism of their team members will encourage them to perform even better. Instead, many of the recipients find it demoralising and give up. Brian Tracey[19] likens destructive criticism to the "same effect as taking a sledgehammer to a piece of office machinery." Other leaders believe that their staff will be happy with good salaries and bonuses and that too many compliments will give the impression that the organisation is soft, fluffy, and insincere. They imagine such verbal signs of appreciation will be of little value to their team. In an environment driven by fear, intimidation, overt and passive aggression, followers will comply with their leader's orders in order to survive. However, they will never be fully and passionately committed.

Levels of trust and respect will be extremely low, because destructive criticism and a scarcity mentality are accepted as the common currency.

The other aspect of appreciation that does not work is insincerity and false appreciation, otherwise known as flattery. As Dale Carnegie the author of *How to win friends and influence people* wrote: "Flattery is from the teeth out. Sincere appreciation is from the heart out." Flattery is a short-term sop and people are smart enough to smell the insincerity that seeps out from such sugary comments. The result is that they don't trust the leader when they actually do give them genuine praise.

How can you develop an atmosphere of appreciation?

As with the other inspiring leadership qualities, you have to begin to appreciate yourself as a leader. After all you are the only person you can change in a sustainable way. Your own example of how you value yourself may well encourage others to do something similar. I recommend that you spend time looking at the talents, strengths and the qualities that you have. It may be easier to do this with the assistance of your leadership coach since you may find it to be a slightly awkward exercise at first (depending on your nationality and cultural style).

Please do persist as it is a worthwhile and life-enhancing exercise. Sophocles (497 BC- 407 BC) the Greek author said: "Ignorant men don't know what good they hold in their hands until they've flung it away." When you know what talents and gifts you personally have, then you will be able consciously to do more of what is working well. This in turn will have beneficial results for the teams you lead and the clients you work with. Knowing your own strengths well might also help you beat your competitors. Sun Tzu said in his book *The Art of War* (6 BC): "If you know both yourself and your enemy, you can win a hundred battles without a single loss."

Appreciation - know yourself as a leader

The "Johari Window" model is useful as a very simple self-awareness tool. It allows you to acknowledge what everyone knows about you; to find out what others know about you but you don't; to acknowledge what you know about yourself, but others don't and finally to make known the "unknown area"; which neither you, nor others are aware of.

As I have coached business leaders, I have adopted a variety of ways to help people learn about themselves without self-deception, self-criticism, or self-delusion. The first method is to carry out a number of exercises based on your values and beliefs. The second is to have a comprehensive 360° feedback exercise provided by family, friends and work colleagues. In addition there is a wealth of very powerful and effective psychometric tools which pinpoint exactly what motivates you and what your personality preferences are. These can also help you understand the communication styles you use, your emotional literacy, your "dark side" (extremes of your behaviour) and the most suitable areas for you to work in. These tools have a strong credibility and serve as a very useful discussion point to discover what helps you succeed and what is holding you back as a leader.

Once you have learned to appreciate your own abilities, go around your organisation and catch people doing things **right**. Tell them specifically what you appreciate about their work and their qualities as a colleague. I know that people who joined or worked with our board and executive coaching team in Penna Consulting were pleasantly surprised to find such a culture of genuine and honest appreciation of personal qualities and work done. This was frequently not something they had experienced elsewhere in the culture of other firms they had worked for. I saw first-hand that appropriate appreciation given in a timely, heartfelt and precise way has a hugely beneficial and uplifting effect on the person receiving it. People become far more willing to commit themselves to giving additional discretionary effort to you and your colleagues, when they know that their efforts are publicly and privately appreciated and recognised. A cautionary tip is not to be over lavish with the praise or too frequent with it. This can devalue special achievements.

I know leaders that write beautiful ink-penned notes on hard card to thank people for exceptional achievements and these cards are often kept as a special memento. In the world of e-mails, receiving a hand-written letter can be a treasured experience. Other effective approaches I have seen being used by leaders can be personal meetings with, or calls by the CEO to a person voted as employee of the month. Briefings and presentations are also good times to acknowledge publically specific work done and highlight successes achieved by named individuals. Even meetings and interviews can be ended with a moment to state specifically which qualities you appreciate about each other. One of the exercises I do at team offsite events is to form a circle of chairs around a swivel chair. Each member of the team takes it in turn to sit in the swivel chair. They receive feedback on the specific leadership qualities they possess that their colleagues appreciate. It is a popular and affirming exercise and significantly changes the way team members view each other. It bonds the team and can change attitudes away from one of negativity and criticism. With these techniques the culture easily changes within a team to one where people look for what is working well and which highlight talents and strengths of colleagues.

Lessons from the Military

Appreciating differences

There is a wide range of classes, cultures, religions and nationalities amongst the officer cadets at the Royal Military Academy Sandhurst (RMAS). When I was a cadet myself I noticed that people responded to this UN-like environment with a range of attitudes. Some were highly prejudiced, arrogant and superior. I expect this response came from a need to hide personal insecurities. These cadets excluded others from their group of friends, or made people into a source of ridicule. Such behaviour was possibly triggered by a wish to divert criticism away from themselves. More encouragingly, however many officer cadets were warm, welcoming and treated everyone as equals. My friend Rod Thomas appreciated diversity and judged everyone in a meritocratic way. He based his respect on what he thought the other person had intended to do, their abilities and the way they treated other people. It is a question I recommend you frequently to ask yourself: "How do I really think about, and treat, others who are different from me? Do I try to make them look wrong or stupid, in order to make myself feel better?"

I suppose the prejudice I encountered at RMAS was a residue of the old fashioned arrogance that has been present among some British Officers since the time of the Crimea. This arrogance was demonstrated by Lord Cardigan's refusal to listen to advice and this led to the senseless waste of human life. He misdirected his men to attack the wrong Russian guns at the Charge of the Light Brigade. Interestingly his leadership incompetence was covered up at the time and instead the charge was portrayed as a heroic event. Our nation was acting as an apologist for class over ability. This trend is similar to the total defeat of the British Infantry under the command of Lord Chelmsford, by the Zulus at the battle of Islandwana. The slaughter was hushed up and even today most people have never heard about the battle of Islandwana. In contrast at the following battle of Rourke's Drift large numbers of VCs were awarded for that fierce defence and comparatively minor victory (interestingly led by an Engineer "artisan" officer).

As a Quaker by upbringing, my mother Tricia always encouraged me to appreciate diversity of background and culture. Our house was often filled by people with a range of backgrounds, cultures and opinions, so when I encountered the prejudice as a cadet it took me by surprise. I personally developed a mix of friends from the UK and abroad while at RMAS and still meet up with members of the company, most recently Errol Stewart from Jamaica. We had many a scrape together, usually because we were railing against some petty bureaucracy of the military establishment. We also went through great hardship as we "escaped and evaded" together on a memorable exercise. Errol couldn't abide class prejudice, superiority or arrogance based on position above ability. He still today describes one or two officers who retain this sort of attitude in very colourful and frank language.

My wife Bridget also served as a Captain in the Army. She has been a very powerful influence in my life and on the leadership philosophy that I have developed. For female officers to compete in the harsh military environment at that time they had to be as good as, and at times, even better than the male officers. As a young officer in what had previously also been a male-only bastion, she faced prejudice and discrimination. Somehow she and other women like her are managing to break down barriers, so that female officers now are more often seen as equal. Overall the development of greater diversity has brought many positive spin-offs for the style of leadership being developed in the Army today. I still however notice prejudice and informal exclusion in parts of business today. It is sometimes extremely subtle and is hard to pinpoint. Appreciation of others and treating people from all backgrounds with equal respect therefore has become an extension of the appreciation characteristic in my repertoire of inspiringleadership attributes.

Sandhurst provided an excellent two years of leadership training and we even had our own "cadet government". The top five in each platoon of 30 officer cadets were selected to be the leaders of that platoon. We recently had our platoon's 25-year reunion and Rod Thomas, Adrian Baxter and I reminisced about the challenges of being cadet corporals. We were all terribly proud of the responsibility and authority that this first leadership position afforded. At every opportunity we were given "command appointments" to test out our leadership skills under stressful conditions, while being continually observed and assessed. We appreciated good leadership when we experienced it and knew even then how challenging it was to achieve so early in our military lives.

Twenty five years ago it was clear to us even as officer cadets, which people had the potential to be inspiring leaders and which were less caring and trustworthy. At our platoon reunion we observed that people's characters had changed little, unless people had been on a serious journey of self-development. What stood out amongst the weaker leaders was their lower emotional intelligence and inability to appreciate the strengths and qualities in others. These people seemed to have an apparent lack of interest in connecting with others which made them appear superficial.

When you look back on your own experience of leadership you might find it interesting to write down why some people have been more inspirational colleagues and others less so.

Failing to appreciate others - Sandhurst Platoon Commander

Some years later I was honoured to be selected to return to RMAS as an instructor. I was in some trepidation about the responsibility of developing the next generation of leaders. Fortunately in my twenty years as an Army Officer, I was never "fragged" by my own followers for being a terrible leader, as happened in the Vietnam War. Unpopular officers then were injured or killed by "friendly fire" when their disgruntled troops "accidentally" shot them in battle or dropped a fragmentation grenade into their tent or trench. However, I do remember with excruciating embarrassment, how critical my attitude was as a Captain Platoon Commander to the new Officer Cadets I had in my platoon. I was young, naïve and keen to make a memorable impression as a tough instructor. I thought I could make my name, and almost lost it instead. I was under the misapprehension that the seasoned Guards drill instructors knew better than me. Against my better judgement, I took the advice of this Colour Sergeant and made a point of being judgemental and hard on my officer cadets. I looked for faults, rather than appreciating their strengths. This completely overrode my natural leadership inclination to: encourage, appreciate, love, inspire, identify strengths and talents and build people up.

Instead, I became the platoon commander from hell and looked for ways to catch out, criticise, find fault, highlight failure and eject those who didn't come up to standard. For six months I carried on in this way, yet couldn't understand why my platoon did not gel, succeed, or win competitions. Unwisely, my leadership attitude created a culture of backbiting, criticism, selfishness and sycophants. My fellow Platoon Commander was Captain Lewis Bryan of 1 PARA, and his approach was one of inspiring leadership. It was only when I asked him how he treated his officer cadets and heard his replies that I realised the secret to his success. This was a powerful first hand lesson on how to develop inspiring leadership. In addition, I received a big slap in the face. My company commander gave me the only "average" report that I had ever received in my career. It indicated in stark terms that I was a less effective leader than my talented peers, and I had to change my attitude rapidly. With the help of Lewis, I returned to a style of inspiring leadership that more suited me.

As a consequence of the change to an attitude of appreciation and encouragement, my platoon started to bond. The cadets gained in confidence and succeeded in various competitions. Members of the platoon who had survived became good friends of mine, and they saw a human side to me which had previously been missing. We had a far more empowering, adult-to-adult relationship based on appreciation and respect.

It came as such a shock when, before the year ended, Lewis' Platoon lost their inspiring leader. Tragically he was killed in a horrific motorbike accident. I will never forget his funeral which was conducted with full military honours complete with Regimental band. It was probably one of the most harrowing events I have been to. The fact that he was such a passionate and inspiring leader was blatantly apparent in the way that we were all deeply moved by his untimely death. I am not ashamed to say I quietly shed a few tears.

Understanding and appreciating others - US multinational leadership

Cultural divides can sometimes be an issue, and this became apparent to me later in my military career, during a visit from the Army staff college to Fort Leavenworth in the USA. We were collaborating on a simulated multinational exercise for future operations together. While there were many similarities between the two armies, there were also many clear differences. On this prestigious joint exercise, I was given the dubious honour of being the UK Brigade Chief of Staff, responsible for leading and coordinating thirty of my top peers. This was to prove to be a very overt and covert leadership challenge, and at times I felt quite out of my depth. I was in a new role of which I had had no experience, leading highly competitive peers, with very strong personalities and personal power. They knew that their future careers and roles depended on their own performance and whether they could look smarter and more capable than their colleagues.

It was a very high profile two weeks for all of us, with lots of VIP visitors and constant close scrutiny by senior officers of our decision-making and performance. Trying to direct my peers, many of whom had already served with distinction in the Special Forces or had themselves experienced this sort of role before, was like herding cats. Some fellow officers were very supportive, friendly and made really helpful suggestions, based on their previous experience. Sadly one or two others were slightly more scheming, destructively ambitious and prone to behaving as "organisational terrorists".

I have seen organisational terrorists in many leadership and business settings. They are often very bright individuals, who believe they could lead considerably more effectively themselves. In public they say "yes", however in private their attitude and behaviour is "no". They do not appreciate others and instead criticise them. Organisational terrorists have somehow become disengaged and are resentful about the system and are often jealous of the appointed leader. They look for ways to sabotage without being caught. They often stir up colleagues to challenge the leader, whilst sitting back themselves and enjoying the spectacle that they have created. The skill for the leader is to spot these people and to convert these terrorists. When they are reformed, they can become the leader's strongest champions and ambassadors and can genuinely be brought back on side and be re-engaged. If they are not prepared to change, then the leader has to act quickly. Moving them elsewhere so their skills can be utilised more successfully, before such terrorists corrupt and disenchant the whole team is one solution.

I studied a wealth of examples of different leadership approaches on the Staff college course. We visited NATO headquarters, the Navy and the RAF and other nations including Czechoslovakia. I completed a Masters Degree research paper about manoeuvre warfare and in the process of writing it, I studied aspects of leadership, strategy and military history in depth. I found that I was learning an enormous amount about the technical skills of good leadership. However I really wanted to understand more about human psychology, relationships and how to engage others more successfully. I was curious as to what motivated people to do things, and wanted to find out about personality preferences and leadership competencies, especially when under intense stress and danger. That would have to wait until I became a business consultant and coach.

Lessons from Business

Appreciating your talent - PricewaterhouseCoopers (PwC) Consulting

I was immensely proud when I was offered a role in PwC Consulting since it had a reputation for appreciating the quality of its leaders and management consultants. The consultants in this company were, and still remain highly respected in the role they play as advisors to leaders and managers of some of the world's top companies. The change for me from working for the British Army to PwC Consulting was significant, requiring a completely different mindset. The most obvious change was that while my salary had significantly increased, my responsibility as a leader had initially considerably decreased. To begin with, my only accountability was for myself. I knew this honeymoon period would come to an end after about six months. However, I really appreciated the time and development space that the firm gave me. From their perspective, they were helping me to get up to speed and ensuring that I could provide proper assistance to clients and to make sure that their financial investment in me had been worthwhile.

The leadership development and skills training that PwC Consulting provided was some of the finest I have come across in business. Their community of trainers and tutors was extremely high-calibre. This success was built on a culture where we were taught to appreciate our personal strengths and those of others as well as valuing everyone's differences in this diverse global organisation. The trainers were very professional, kept up-to-date with cutting-edge techniques and were able to enthuse and inspire both the "new joiners" and also the longer serving PwC Consultants. The two-week-long management consultants' induction course was of the highest quality. Ten years on, I remain in touch to this day with many people who attended this life-changing course with me from around the world.

The talents, skills, experience and leadership potential of the other people who joined PwC Consulting at the same time as me, were most impressive. We learned from each other on the course about tools and techniques to help clients resolve their problems. Most importantly, everything rested on our attitude, our passion for our profession, having a sense of service and being completely present when working with each client. Since leadership development and training was a particular interest of mine, I made a good connection with the tutors. I was later selected to come back and be a leadership development tutor both within PwC Consulting as well as for our clients.

Shortly after I joined PwC, a deep recession hit Europe. All the management consulting firms stopped recruiting. PwC started to make large numbers of redundancies in a series of waves. This was a tough time for all concerned. My friends who were made redundant experienced a mixture of shock, fear and anxiety. While those of us who remained, coped with the syndrome of "survivor guilt" and a concern over who would be next in a further wave of redundancies. During this time I became friends with a PwC Partner called Roger Wyn-Jones and saw what a tough time he had as a leader in a recession. He was one of a number of People Partners responsible for the redundancy selection procedure, and he had to look people in the eye and tell them they were losing their jobs. To make people redundant these partners had to decide on the selection criteria based on reports, past performance, value to the client and estimates of future fee-earning potential. It is not easy to continue to appreciate people, while sacking them.

It is interesting to look at redundancy from the perspective of the leader; "letting people go". The partners in PwC Consulting went to great lengths to ensure that the redundancy system was fair, beyond reproach, followed the correct HR processes and could not be subject to legal challenge. Once the panel had selected individuals for redundancy, another Partner had to conduct a personal interview to give notice to each consultant warning them that they were "at risk of redundancy". It is tough for leaders who really care about the people they have previously recruited and encouraged to join their teams.

Partners can find this whole process intensely personal and agonisingly painful. Inspiring leaders especially find this process tough, because they usually have made a personal connection with each of the people in their team. These leaders ensure that they know their team's hopes, fears, aspirations, about their lives and their families. Indeed I believe organisations should provide significant mentoring, coaching, or counselling for leaders who have responsibility for making members of their close-knit teams redundant. I've known a number of leaders who have found this role extremely tough and sometimes have become depressed by the redundancy process. I have never found it easy myself to make others redundant. It can feel inhuman and is an emotionally raw time.

At the other extreme, I met a leader in a famous financial services organisation who takes a more brutal approach. He admitted that he never gets to know his people too well, since when he has to make them redundant later, he doesn't find the process too emotionally difficult. Instead he hires them on high salaries and large performance bonuses. If they don't bring in a lot of money within the first six months, then he fires them instantly. He pays them off to prevent them taking legal action. This is a candid and brutal way of treating people. One of the reasons I dislike the term "human resources" is because it allows some managers to view people as objects to be hired and fired at will, regardless of the personal impact.

An audit to identify an appreciative culture

It takes only a day or two in any organisation to get a reasonably reliable impression of what it would be like to work there permanently. Will it be a place where you and others are appreciated and encouraged to be the best you can be? Here are some of the telltale signs that you should look for:

1. How congruent are the words spoken and written by the leader (for example on the website) when compared to the experience of staff and clients?

2. How are you treated by the receptionist and those in support roles?

3. What do people say about fellow members of this organisation when they're not with them? How do they treat their colleagues and speak to each other?

4. What does the atmosphere in which the employees work, feel like? Is it appreciative, warm, open and friendly, or hushed, closed and defensive?

5. Are talented people really encouraged to step forward and lead? How much leadership training and development do individuals receive within the organisation?

6. What values and beliefs do individuals hold about themselves and their organisation?

7. Do the receptionist and people around the office have a clear idea of the purpose of the organisation and a sense of meaning and fulfilment in the work they do?

8. What behaviour do individuals believe is both measured and rewarded?

Penna Consulting, how an appreciative culture enhances profits

The recent story of Penna Consultancy over the three-year period 2006-2009 provides a powerful example of increasing employee engagement and company profitability. This is an indirect result of the cultural tone of appreciation set by the leaders. Prior to this period, Penna had had a difficult journey. Employee engagement, client experience, revenue, profitability, clarity and focus had not previously been considered good enough by either shareholders, or employees. The new CEO and his executive board members firstly set out a clear vision of the future. They communicated it positively through road shows and in day-to-day meetings, and looked to themselves to improve the quality of their own leadership. As a consequence the executive board members each selected their own coach to help them deliver their part of the strategic focus, and provide inspiring leadership of the teams they led. This coaching included the measurement and development of every leader's emotional intelligence. A leadership style and culture which involved far more of a coach-approach and far less of the old style parental, command and control style of management was created.

A programme called "leader as coach", which had previously been successfully used with clients, was provided for all the senior managers across Penna. The programme taught people to use a coaching style to show appreciation of talented individuals and to provide development for them. It also served as a team building opportunity to break down the barriers between the different departments within Penna. Leaders set out to catch people doing things right. They were encouraged to appreciate what was working well and to recognise people in ways which resonated with each individual. Serious attention was paid to the "Penna Pulse" - the employee engagement survey which was run three times a year.

What was especially noticeable was the infectious enthusiasm of the majority of leaders in the organisation and the great feedback that was received from Penna's clients. This, in turn, led naturally to repeat business. Some organisational terrorists within Penna were tackled about their toxic and unhelpful behaviour. This sent out an incredibly powerful positive message, which rippled throughout the organisation. These disenchanted individuals had previously considered it sufficient that they were focused on making money, rather than on inspiring and leading their teams and collaborating with colleagues.

The conversations that took place with such individuals either caused them to leave Penna, or drastically change their approach. A few were "re-recruited" to be a force for good. Successful re-recruiting conversations emerged when leaders listened properly to the dissatisfaction of these disenchanted colleagues. They identified the drivers and motivators for each individual remembering that these individuals did not join their organisation as dissatisfied people. They were asked what or perhaps who had switched off their interest in their job. Switching interest back on can be especially difficult. Often you need to change the manager or enable the individual to work for someone who better understands them.

During this three year period, the employee engagement level rose sharply from 30% to 79%, the profitability of the organisation increased 300%, the share price rose from 50p to £2.50 and the organisation moved steadily from not being in the Sunday Times top 100 best companies to work for, to being one of the six best organisations at the top of this list. The CEO described his fellow leaders on the executive board as the strongest team he had ever worked with. This was achieved by having leaders with a strong passion for their specialist areas and to whom he gave sufficient autonomy to run their teams in the way they knew best.

There is a direct link between a strong leader who creates a sense of appreciation, meaning and purpose, with a clear customer-focused vision, and the increased profitability and share price of a publicly listed company. Keeping this momentum going month after month, year after year is the toughest part. The challenge for leaders is to keep fit by maintaining their stamina in a sustainable way. In other words, to consistently maintain a focus on the autonomy, development, inspiration and passion for those being lead and the job they do. If as leaders you forget any one of these factors, then you will be punished through negative feedback from your staff, lower employee engagement levels, lack of repeat business from your customers and a reduction in both profit and share price. Reuven Bar-On has solid empirical findings from Steve

Langhorn's work at Whitbread/Beefeater that confirm this in the UK He found that there is a significant relationship between managerial EQ, employee satisfaction, customer satisfaction and annual profit growth. He also has similar findings from Kate Cannon's project with financial advisors at American Express in the US. There is no place for complacency in the challenging world of inspiring leadership. You have a psychological contract with your followers which you ignore at your peril.

An attitude of gratitude

When people willingly choose an attitude of appreciation and gratitude, I believe they attain a far more sustainable and long-term happiness, than those who simply chase ever greater financial rewards. Happiness is maximised when you appreciate the things that you already have, rather than living with constant dissatisfaction and a craving for things you do not yet possess. As a consequence of this attitude, inspiring leaders tend to be more contented. When I come across a business leader who has the qualities of serenity and wisdom, I find they tend to know a lot about themselves and have reflected on their purpose in life.

It costs little to appreciate others with sincerity and to be grateful for the simpler things in life. In the crazy, manic, fast-paced world where we live, many people rush through life, focused on the rewards they hope to have in the future. Why not take time, pause, focus on the present moment, look somebody in the eye and specifically acknowledge something which they recently did well? The inner reward of happiness from that sort of conversation and way of life cannot be compared to the reward of a financial bonus; it is a completely different experience.

Choosing your attitude

Every moment in our lives is a moment of choice. People often forget this and instead consider themselves to be victims of the situation, or system in which they work. The way we choose to think affects our emotions, which in turn affects our feelings. Reuven Bar-On said to me that: "Feelings are essentially what we understand, know, think and experience about our emotions. Most people, including psychologists with doctorates, do not understand the difference between emotions and feelings!" If we don't feel happy about a situation, or another person, then we can choose to change the way we think. This in turn, enables us to feel more positive. Ralph Waldo Emerson once said: "A man is what he thinks about all day long." I have a personal example of how choosing to change my attitude had a positive impact on a very difficult situation.

I was due to have a coaching "personal chemistry meeting" with someone who had a reputation as an intimidating bully. I knew that this person had already rejected a couple of other potential coaches. So I had unconsciously chosen a defensive attitude to help me cope with the impending rejection that I was assuming would follow for me too. I was subconsciously choosing an approach that would set me up for failure. These thoughts were not helping me to feel particularly good about myself. I was unwittingly self-sabotaging and was creating a negative attitude which would attract the very rejection that I most feared.

Fortunately five minutes before I went into the meeting I stepped back and noticed the destructive attitude that I was choosing. I mentally recalibrated my mood and chose to visualise a successful meeting in which the executive and I would get on well. I also decided to take the attitude that he was my mental equal and that I could be assertive and robust with him. I chose to look out for his talents and find ways to support, challenge and hopefully to inspire him to be a more successful leader. As a consequence, I approached the meeting with a different attitude. We established great rapport, and the result was that the executive and I both chose to work together.

Time and again, I'm reminded that if we don't like the situation we're in, or the life we are leading, then we can choose a different, more positive and healthy approach. As a consequence the route through life we choose becomes happier. I believe that a combination of realism and a positive attitude is a hallmark of an inspiring leader. The old saying still holds true that: "Your attitude defines your altitude through life." Choose your attitude wisely.

Leadership by example
Siobhan Sheridan
HRD DEFRA

Siobhan is a successful senior leader in a large British government department. She has worked in both the private and public sectors, as an executive coach and has a considerable depth and breadth of experience enhanced by a wealth of qualifications. Her ability to use high levels of emotional intelligence, in particular empathy and assertiveness, has allowed her to have courageous conversations with peers, direct reports and most impressively also with the board members she reports to. While she is sought out by people from across the department and many other organisations for her wisdom, she also is sufficiently humble to recognise the limits of her knowledge and to apologise publicly when she makes mistakes.

Siobhan has a strong set of values and beliefs which act as a moral compass for her and provide the drive to live her life on purpose. She cares deeply for the welfare of the various teams she leads and is guided by a strong sense of inspiring others. When you meet her, you are immediately aware of the personal power and an intensity of presence, as she listens carefully to what you say and then asks the simplest, yet most profound questions. These are the kind of questions that won't go away and they leave you thinking deeply for a long time afterwards. Whilst she has never served in the military, she is imbued with the philosophy of serving others to lead them. She never expects people to undertake a task which she wouldn't be prepared to roll up her sleeves and do herself if required. My final and most important observation of Siobhan is that she exudes a sense of appreciation for the great work which others do. This means people enjoy working on her team and go the extra mile at her side.

4 Key Points:

- The corrosive effect of constant destructive criticism is apparent when compared to beneficial situations where individuals and teams are publicly valued and appreciated by their leaders.

- Appreciation is an expression of gratitude, to acknowledge others and thank them for their contributions to the success of your team.

- Consider the relevance to you of the saying: "Ignorant men don't know what good they hold in their hands until they've flung it away".

- Learn to appreciate others of different nationalities, backgrounds and abilities; they too have their story to tell and talents to employ.

4 Questions:

1. What talents, skills and abilities do you appreciate about yourself?

2. When can you next catch someone doing something right and publicly appreciate them?

3. How can you value others more and show your gratitude?

4. What else could you appreciate?

Parachute Training at Brize Norton

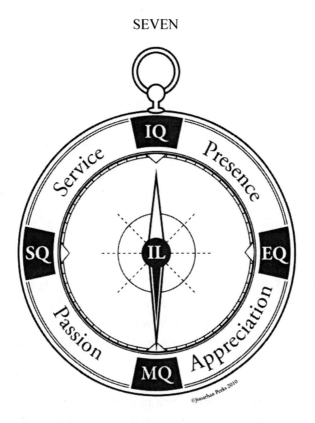

SEVEN

MQ - Moral Intelligence, Values & Beliefs

"In looking for someone to hire, you look for three qualities: integrity, intelligence, and energy. But the most important is integrity, because if they don't have that, the other two qualities, intelligence and energy, are going to kill you."

Warren Buffet, American leadership writer

The Doctor who cared enough, Graeme Perks

Graeme Perks is a Consultant Plastic and Reconstruction Surgeon at City Hospital and The Queen's Medical Centre, Nottingham, UK. He appeared in the British newspaper the Daily Mail in July 2010 described as one of Britain's top 10 surgeons for cancer reconstruction surgery - as voted by the specialists themselves. What stands out clearly about my brother is his strong sense of integrity and the fact that he is unwilling to compromise on his values and beliefs, even if that means he personally suffers as a result. On numerous occasions, he has taken personal risks as a leader. He has stood up against what he thinks are senseless targets and bureaucracy which do not serve the interests of the patients. He once famously asked a member of a hospital management team in a public meeting: "What is the hospital's policy on telling the truth?" He has also campaigned tirelessly for peers whom he has felt were poorly treated by the system. The qualities that his peers highlighted in voting him as one of Britain's top 10 surgeons are that he is, "kind, down-to-earth, self-effacing, and a very good surgeon."

In 2008, Jane Elliott Health a reporter for BBC News[20] wrote an article which highlights the integrity, values and beliefs which he weaves into his work as a plastic surgeon. She said: "When Natasha Wood makes up her mind to do something, she does it. Born with spinal muscular atrophy (SMA) - a neuromuscular disease which inhibits signals from the brain to the muscles - Natasha needs a wheelchair and her arms are so weak that she cannot lift a pint of milk. But when the successful TV producer and actress wanted a better body she was determined to go ahead with cosmetic surgery. Because she has a slightly reduced lung function, she carefully planned each stage with her surgeon to ensure the operation was safe.

Natasha said: 'Graeme gave me back a positive image of my body. With my new and improved look, I felt much more confident in my daily life.' People sometimes imagine me to be this quiet girl in a wheelchair instead of the bawdy, silly, sassy, crazy chick I really am." She and her plastic surgeon have built up such a good relationship over the years that she includes his character in her one- woman autobiographical Charity show, *Rolling with Laughter*, which was a hit at the Edinburgh Festival. Mr Perks, a member of the British Association of Aesthetic Plastic Surgeons (BAAPS) said he had been inspired by dealing with Natasha. 'Natasha's attitude, confidence, determination and incredible outlook on life are an inspiration - she's also a fantastic example of how plastic surgery can have a positive impact on quality of life.'

An even more powerful story is that of Tom who is now 21 years old. Graeme began working with him at the age of 13 when he was first diagnosed with a life threatening cancerous malignant melanoma. The cancer surgery resulted in him having a big bald patch on his head and an uncertain future. Despite wearing a woolly hat, the impact of cancer treatment and surgery are issues for any teenager as they grow up and attempt to build their self-image. Graeme operated on him several times and went far beyond the call of duty in the support he gave to Tom and his mother, sometimes doing surgery for which he was unpaid.

By way of a surprise 18th birthday present, Graeme also arranged for him to have help with his poor eyesight to get the best out of life. His friend Mani Subramanian, an eminent eye surgeon, gave Tom private laser eye surgery and also did it for free. Tom was so grateful with the amazing results that he donated a small amount of his savings to the charity which Mani supported in India. Graeme is most impressed with Tom's relaxed approach to life and his attitude of "take me as you find me". His mother said recently to Graeme: "You can't understand what a difference all this has made to Tom's life."

Choosing MQ as my fifth principle was based on my observation that individuals are galvanised by following people who extol, and live by, a clear set of values and beliefs. When their values and beliefs are aligned with the organisation they work for, then their team members are more inclined to give their all to help the leader and the organisation succeed.

Definition of Moral Intelligence,
value and beliefs

The MQ principle within inspiring leadership highlights the importance of your own integrity, values and beliefs. It is a focus on your irreproachability, character and discernment. It captures what you consider to be right and what is wrong. I'm enjoying the work that is evolving in this area especially by Doug Lennick and Fred Kiel in their book *Moral Intelligence: Enhancing Business Performance and Leadership Success*[21]. Their definition of moral intelligence is: "The mental capacity to determine how universal human principles should be applied to our values, goals and actions." In the simplest terms, moral intelligence is the ability to differentiate right from wrong as defined by universal principles. Universal principles are those beliefs about human conduct that are common to all cultures around the world. Thus we believe they apply to all people, regardless of gender, ethnicity, religious belief, or location on the globe.

I share their view that every leader has their own moral compass. This provides a sense of "True North" which points in the direction of their individual integrity values and beliefs. Doug Lennick and Fred Kiel argue that we are hard-wired to be moral in our behaviour, but often stray from the path. If so, we should pay attention to our moral compass more frequently than we do. A second source of fascinating work is called *Building Moral Intelligence* by Michele Borba[22]. While it is aimed at improving parenting skills as we bring up children it contains many lessons for us as adults. It highlights the key point that MQ is learned and can be developed. Michele Borba writes about the seven core MQ virtues: empathy, conscience, self-control, respect, kindness, tolerance and fairness. I also find that there is a close connection between MQ and the work of Robert Dilts on neurological levels[23] where he speaks specifically of values and beliefs, identity and ultimately mission and purpose (which I shall cover later in SQ).

I share these authors' views that we are not trying to tell people what is right and what is wrong. Nor are we helping people to become perfect.

The most important point is to recognise that we are all imperfect. We often face daily moral struggles, challenges and temptations and a strong MQ helps us make the right decisions. When we have developed skills and capabilities in all 8 areas of inspiring leadership we can describe our leadership as fully integrated. Reuven Bar-On described MQ to me as "being guided by one's moral compass. In its simplest form this will direct us to do what is right and not just what is correct as we navigate through life."

In defining moral intelligence I find great inspiration in the *Values and Standards of the British Army* document supported by General Sir Richard Dannatt the recent British Army Chief of the General Staff (CGS). In the introduction he said:

"The British Army has a worldwide reputation for excellence, a strong reflection of its soldiers and officers. This reputation derives from, and depends upon, unequivocal commitment, self-sacrifice and mutual trust. Our values and standards are vital to operational effectiveness - they are the life blood that sustained the Army.

They have to be more than just words, we must believe in them and live by them. The responsibility of command is to be the heart of this process, it cannot be delegated and I hold you all accountable for it. The values are about character and spirit: the standards define our actions and behaviour."

Consequences of low levels of MQ in leaders

The antithesis of the integrated inspiring leader is the "dis-integrated" one. I'm sure you recall people you have known, who began to lose their leadership ability, once they no longer lived by a clear sense of values, beliefs or integrity. The most obvious consequence of low MQ is the erosion of trust in a leader by their clients and colleagues. This happens when the rhetoric of their claimed values and beliefs are out of kilter with their behaviour. In this situation, their whole life becomes open to scrutiny and doubt. Of the 8 principles, it is MQ more than any other in which personal example is copied by those who literally follow the leader. If the

CEO is perceived to be greedy and to act inappropriately against the stated values of the organisation, then his subordinates will behave in a similar manner. These team members feel that they also have the right to ignore the stated values, beliefs and standards that have been abandoned by the CEO. If any of the employees are stopped and disciplined or cautioned, then they can feel a deep sense of injustice and grievance. They might withdraw their discretionary energy. Their selective effort is often what makes the difference to exceptional client relationships and healthy profit making. The leader's loss of moral compass is a critical moment and can often be the tipping point when a successful, healthy and well-respected company loses its edge.

When individual leaders lose a sense of where True North is on their moral compass, their organisation can drift dangerously too. In my diagram of the inspiring leadership compass the brass housing limits the malign influence of any nearby magnets from diverting the compass from finding "True North".

In one organisation, employees recently quoted George Orwell[24] when referring to their executive board members: "All animals are equal, but some animals are more equal than others". These employees felt angry that the executive board members were feathering their own nest with huge long term incentive payments and were losing touch with the people they were leading. Their perception was that their leaders had forgotten to live by the stated values and beliefs that they had created for the firm. I have found that it is in moments of success or failure that moral competence is most under threat. It was particularly apparent in this organisation, when financial pressures were high that shortcuts were taken and the communal sense of moral intelligence was eroded. At the other extreme, in times of surplus, I have heard reports of individuals who try to use reason to explain their dishonesty. They mentally justified their action based on their belief that: "We're doing very well, we're flush with money and the firm can afford this. No one is getting hurt, or will find out".

In organisations without strong MQ it is processes, data and numbers which become disproportionately important. Managers lose sight of the fact that they are dealing with people and instead focus on data as US General Schwarzkopf observed[25]:

"That summer of 1970, the US Army War College issued a scathing report - commissioned by General William Westmoreland, who was now Chief of Staff - explaining a great deal of what we were seeing. Based on a confidential survey of 415 officers, the report blasted the Army for rewarding the wrong people. It described how the system had been subverted to condone selfish behaviour and tolerate incompetent commanders who sacrificed their subordinates and distorted facts to get ahead. It criticised the Army's obsession with meaningless statistics and was especially damning on the subject of body counts in Vietnam. A young captain had told the investigators a sickening story: he'd been under so much pressure from headquarters to boost his numbers that he'd nearly gotten into a fistfight with a South Vietnamese officer over whose unit would take credit for various enemy body parts. Many officers admitted they had simply inflated their reports to placate headquarters."

How can MQ help you as a leader?

People love working for leaders who have strong values, beliefs and high levels of integrity. Team members consequently know exactly where they stand. They are more trusting of what the leader says and feel that they will be treated fairly and with respect. When I am coaching leaders in preparation for taking up new roles, I encourage them to gather everyone together in the first hour. The dialogue that they then initiate should begin with the leader sharing something about themself. I encourage the leader to share their values and beliefs, who they are, what they stand for and what they will not accept. They could talk about their passions and about what annoys them. It is invaluable to explain what it will be like being led by them. In particular, I advise them to pinpoint the organisational values to which they are attracted. It is particularly important for them to highlight that they as a leader will be nothing without the team to which they're now speaking. It is useful to commit publicly that they will spend individual time with each of the team members in the first two weeks. Their aim is to ascertain every team member's personal values, beliefs, aspirations and hopes for the future so they develop a hugely encouraging ethos.

Leaders with high levels of moral intelligence stand out from the crowd and are respected. I love the encouragement given by the speaker Deepak Chopra: "Live your point of view, don't justify it!" Maintaining high levels of MQ requires courage and persistence and many in society try to undermine and erode your values. I remember a bully at Welbeck College my Sixth Form School, who confessed, in a rare moment of openness, that the reason why he picked on me was that I was "far too nice to other people!" Also when my friend permanently gave up alcohol he found he was pressurised frequently by others who wanted him to have "just the one drink" with them. People who decline to do things because it is against their beliefs or their religion can be ridiculed and pressurised to change their mind. The temptation is to blend in with the crowd and not to stand up for your values. General Thompson[26] captures the challenge of MQ and the courage you need to maintain it when he said it is hard to have:

"The moral courage to do what is right in the face of provocation, threats, bribes and manifest hatred, especially in situations where those making the threats are in overwhelming superiority, and one is junior and far from one's unit."

Lessons from the Military

Airborne Initiative: holding on to your beliefs to overcome adversity

My time training with the Airborne Brigade is seared into my memory. The selection process to become an Officer in the Airborne Forces (Paras) is harsh. I agreed to attempt the course in a moment of bravado. I did not realise that I would not only have to pass the course but during the selection would also have to be a role model to the soldiers on the course with me.

After three weeks of preparatory fitness training, I started the selection course and found myself on a punishing 10-mile march. We all carried 55 pounds of equipment in old steel framed rucksacks, cheap army boots, green nylon socks, rifles and badly fitting helmets. With such poor quality equipment, it was bound to end in tears! We began with fifty in the squad and by the five mile point we had lost a number of people through injuries. Some were unable to keep up with the punishing fast pace of both running and speed marching. The officers on the course were expected to have stronger self-belief than the men they led, with huge self-motivation, drive and an ability to lead under extreme duress by example. The officers were required to run back to pick up the stragglers who had fallen a long way behind and "encourage" or sometimes drag them up to the front of the squad.

One of the Para Corporal Instructors took a particular dislike to me. He said I "spoke posh" and was irritated that I frequently appeared to be in far too good a humour. I believe he wanted to see if I had the heart and backbone to succeed. At one point, with his nose touching mine and eyes bulging, he challenged me with the words: "So ya think yer 'ard do ya?" He sent me back for the fourth time to pick up another straggler. This soldier was so shattered that he was a distant spot a long way back down the muddy track. The instructor's final cruel twist was when the straggling soldier and I had caught up with the rest of the group. He gave me an order to carry this soldier's pack, as well as my own, making my load into a combined weight of 110lbs. The instructor knew this was likely to break me completely. He wanted to see if I would "Jack" (to ask to be put on the back-up truck for stragglers) and therefore fail the selection course. Being pigheaded, I was determined not to be broken. It is amazing just how much further you can go with the right belief and attitude of mind. I took up the challenge and wearing one rucksack on my back, while strapping the soldier's pack onto my front I staggered like a drunk for the last mile into the finish line in Aldershot camp. I had completed that painful ordeal, but I was absolutely shattered and my feet were bloody and covered in deep, painful blisters.

Hard Training: strong values and beliefs

While at the time I found this training very tough and apparently pointless, I must acknowledge that institutional bullying was not to be countenanced in the Army. With hindsight, I now accept that being given a "hard time" both as a team and an individual can be of training value. While speaking recently to John Griffin (a veteran of Para and SAS training) he said: "Combat survival, conduct under capture and resistance to interrogation can all improve if we can minimise the shock of capture. This shock is far worse when you don't know what it is like when someone is brutal and nasty to you. The Turks survived best under capture in Korea, because they were inured to brutality. Therefore they could not be broken as teams. Many Westerners died in captivity, because they had not been trained to know what to expect or how to cope. The enemy had not been trained to respect prisoners."

That endurance march was followed by number of equally Herculean tasks. We jumped on command, without thought or hesitation, from the tops of bridges into a canal 30 feet below. Ironically, other people do this as an act of suicide to end their lives. We bonded in teams in heavy stretcher races. We also carried logs with ropes as a team at breakneck speed up a muddy hill in competition with others. The challenge as a team was to keep replacing each other when our bodies cried "give up!" We also threw ourselves with passion into a whole variety of assault courses. I am amazed to admit it, but I loved most of it. I gained a feeling of elation and huge achievement when I passed each of the stages against all the odds. I learned all about collaboration and supporting colleagues. Selfish individuals failed in very public fashion and were quickly removed. Mixed with my enjoyment were a fear of failure or injury and the disgrace of being "Returned to Unit" (RTU). This was a selection course which required personal drive and inspiration, in a situation where there was a deliberate absence of support.

Another ordeal was called "milling" which for me involved boxing against a man twice my size and weight. This man also seemed to have a strong hatred of officers. I felt I was about to be milled into dust judging by the look on his face as he entered the ring with me. The other soldiers scented blood and the NCOs had subtly encouraged a little bit of "officer baiting". Everyone gathered around the ring to watch my impending humiliation at the hands of my monstrous opponent. Sometimes in business, I see a similar pleasure that people get from watching a colleague get metaphorically beaten up by a tougher opponent around a boardroom table. Reflecting now on my experience in the ring, I believe it is crucial for a strong leader to be sensitive to this sort of intimidation, informal exclusion, or bullying of scapegoats. Such destructive treatment should never be allowed to take place within business teams. Some business leaders consider open competition and intense comparisons between peers to be sport and deliberately encourage such rivalry. Personally, I consider destructive competition to be invidious and to encourage it goes against the values and beliefs that I hold about effective leadership. I call it toxic behaviour and when I experience it in business settings, I highlight it and ask people to change their behaviour. They often seem totally surprised and ashamed to have been caught out.

To pass the Para course, I had to survive five minutes in this ring. Judging by the size the bloodthirsty bruiser I was pitched against, this was going to be no easy task. As my opponent rained blows upon my head and body, I managed to stand my ground. Smack, stagger. Thud, stagger. He then fatally paused for breath. I would like to have said that I felled him with one heroic punch, but that was sadly not true. Instead, I punched him repeatedly in the chest and stomach. He was too tall for me to reach his head, and my attack seemed to inflict no pain. He looked very annoyed that I remained standing and was still bothering him. With a flood of adrenaline through my body, I realised that he had decided it was his turn to batter me to a pulp. Luckily, I was "saved by the bell" which was rung before he finished me off. With relief I realised that I had survived, albeit with a very fuzzy head. Perhaps the fact that I lost a lot of brain cells that day might explain my irrational behaviour ever since! However, my pride remained intact. I was given a round of applause from the totally surprised soldiers. On I staggered to yet another challenge.

I have always been afraid of heights. The next phase of the course was therefore a moment that I had been dreading. We had to run and jump across gaps between planks on scaffolding forty feet above the ground with no harness, or safety net. I am sure the health and safety executive today would not allow this test. However there are no safety nets in war, so this was considered to be necessary preparation at that time. At one point, we were required, on a verbal command, to jump immediately with no hesitation out across a six-foot gap and down four feet. If you missed you would crash forty feet straight down to the ground. Those who refused to jump on their command were given a second chance. Then if you refused a second time, you would have immediately failed the course and be gone from the airborne barracks in 3 hours. I felt physically sick, everything seemed to fall silent and my limbs were like lead as I climbed higher up the scaffolding to my fate.

This was not a moment to suffer from "fear of failure"! It was all about self-belief. I had watched the previous two soldiers seize up with fear, refuse to jump and instantly be removed from the course. I forced myself to use a simple visualisation technique to avoid a similar fate. I convinced myself that the other plank was actually just like leaping across the gym floor, from one bench to another. So when instructed, without pausing to think, or visualise failure I launched myself. In reality, it transpired that the enormity of the gap was a visual illusion. It was not really as far as it looked, and I easily managed to clear it. Using that visualisation technique, in such a terrifying moment, has been something that has served me well many times since then. When doing leadership coaching with CEOs, I have taught them how to use it. It has helped my two daughters to believe in themselves absolutely and visualise their success before upcoming tests or athletics races.

Humble excellence

My next memorable lesson was from what the Paras called "Heartbreak Hill". This was a place where they break weaker officers who don't have the self-belief, resilience and stamina to keep going and inspire the soldiers they are responsible for leading. The process was simple. The

146

instructors ran our squad of fifty around a circuit. It consisted of as many steep, muddy and gravelly hills as they could find. They aimed to establish who had the wherewithal to become an "airborne warrior". When everybody was exhausted, the squad was allowed to collapse and rest at the bottom of the steepest hill. Except for the officers. We were pushed on yet again back up this particular hill, again and again whilst being watched by the rest of the squad. The basic rule remained the same. If we gave up, we were taken off the course immediately. After a while, the instructors decided that "officer's play time" was over. We gratefully staggered back to the camp with the other (rested) members of the squad. Once again, I was only just "hanging in there".

I learned again that day that certain personal values and beliefs are what help leaders through the toughest challenges. These include loyalty, teamwork, flexibility, resilience, dogged determination and fitness. As I learned the hard way with the Scots Guards, you have to have more stamina and be fitter as a leader than those you lead. Equally as a business leader you need to be strong both physically and mentally. When you lose the confidence of colleagues and shareholders, others stop giving discretionary energy as fear spreads throughout the company. Leaders can be ousted by Chairman and shareholders if they are seen to lack stamina to survive the business equivalent of Heartbreak Hill.

On return to barracks while the rest of the squad trudged back to their rooms to shower, I was selected to be the duty officer. My task appeared to be to do whatever took the NCO's fancy. For me, this consisted of sweeping the massive gym floor with a very small brush. Meanwhile, he sat grinning and watching me with his warped sense of humour. He loved his control and power over me. I recalled the words of Eleanor Roosevelt: "No one can make you feel bad, unless you give them permission to do so." I chose humility and got on with sweeping quietly. It is hard to be arrogant, pompous, or superior in such a situation. I was determined in future to stick to my emerging leadership style which treated others with respect, equality and appreciation.

A further lesson that was embedded in my psyche at that time was the value of teamwork, camaraderie and the support given to each other by colleagues. Without willing followers, a leader is redundant. The ordeal of going through such an intense selection course closely bonded squad members together. A team is only as strong as its weakest member. It was at moments of greatest hardship that the finest leaders on the Para selection course showed their true colours. They lived up to the motto "when the going gets tough, the tough get going". The friends I made on the course were friends who I have trusted with my life. One in particular was Dave Hudson who went on to have a very distinguished career in the SAS. You will hear more of his story later. This harsh and brutal Para training was to serve me very well when involved in the battlefield survival training that I have already described that would be a part of my next role. It has also proved invaluable in business and has enabled me, when I've been irritated, to keep everything in proportion.

How values and beliefs brought down the Berlin Wall

I learned much about the power of integrity, value and beliefs as a leader in my role working as Assistant to the Head of the British Army (CGS). In particular, I began to understand the cultural differences between the British, French and German officers and the leaders of their respective Armies. One fascinating trip we took was to Berlin, just after the wall had come down. There was a private lunchtime meeting for CGS with the Heads of the East German Army and East Berlin Police. In the historic discussion between former bitter foes, it became evident how false our beliefs and assumptions had been about other people and nations during the Cold War, which had potentially disastrous consequences. In the discussion, it emerged that the Russians and East Germans had remained on constant high alert for years. They said that they were convinced that NATO was intending to invade within a matter of days. Therefore, they needed their troops and tanks to be fully equipped, bombed up and ready to respond. They believed they might have had to strike first. Who knows how close we were to World War Three, based on deep mistrust and fear of other leaders who simply had a different view to ourselves.

It was also fascinating to know that the historic turning point when the Berlin wall finally came down was influenced by many small acts of kindness. One of these involved the integrity, values and possible indecisive agonies of the then Head of the East Berlin Police. He appeared to be a steely, seasoned and hardy leader. Yet it might have been his conscious decision to disobey the direct orders of Erich Honecker, the leader of the DDR, which precipitated the demise of East Germany. He chose not to pass on Honicker's order for his subordinates to shoot the protesters from West Berlin who had scaled and sat upon the dividing Berlin Wall.

Leadership is indeed a lonely calling, and the decisions an individual makes can have enormous consequences. In this case, the decision not to shoot saved lives, changed a nation, yet lost the Head of East Berlin Police his job. We cannot imagine what agonies he went through as he realised his disobedience would lose him all that he had built up for his family and his privileged position within a communist state. I wonder where he is now and how often he relives that paradoxical act of humanity and defiance based on his beliefs and integrity in not ordering the deaths of innocent civilians. It is my opinion that he is one of life's unsung heroes.

The leadership lesson that I would like to draw from this man's courageous decision is that, sometimes we find that we are battling against the prevailing views and beliefs of colleagues, organisations or society. At such times, we should never underestimate the power of our own values and beliefs that we hold as individuals to make a profound, positive impact. We need to remain true to ourselves and our personal moral compass. We must establish these principles, and then live our lives "on purpose" according to our morals and MQ.

Beliefs values and behavioural drivers for leaders

I have never been short of personal mistakes to learn from, and I pick up lots of tips from experiencing other people's blunders too. Ineffective leadership behaviours probably stem from one of five human behavioural "drivers" described in the Transactional Analysis (TA) model of Ian Stewart and Vann Joines. These drivers are underpinned by our beliefs and self-concepts. They are: try hard, be perfect, be strong, hurry up and please people. It is easy to observe other leaders being too intense and trying too hard. The result is that they make those they lead wary and suspicious of them. Those leaders with a "be strong" driver learn to suppress many of their feelings and emotions. Consequently they harden their hearts and lose the ability to understand and express either their own emotions, or read other people's. This can be useful in the midst of the pain, suffering and bloodshed of war. However it is a disadvantage on peacekeeping operations, or in business. In such environments managing disagreements involving conflicts between two factions requires sensitivity and understanding.

My observations of leaders who overplay the "be perfect" driver are that they can become workaholics. They obsessively drive both themselves and those they lead, in order to get every last detail completely right. There are many occasions where this trait is encouraged and welcomed, for example in a bomb disposal expert. However, being perfect can encourage highly judgmental, negative and often destructively critical leadership behaviours. Such people would often not delegate enough to those they lead, thus they disenfranchise and treat these other colleagues as children. The "please people" driver tends to encourage rather sycophantic behaviour where leaders can be spotted "sucking up" to their superiors. They attempt to curry favour, in the mistaken belief that this would help their career. At times such behaviour can be mildly successful, since many people appreciate compliments. However, when comments of praise and appreciation are identified as being inauthentic, then all the intended benefits are lost.

The fifth driver to "hurry up" is institutionalised within the Army to an obsessive level. This was especially the case at Sandhurst and Staff College, where we frequently had to hurry up to be ready for an event, only to wait for lengthy periods of time. Deadlines were forever being brought forward, as requests were passed down the chain of command, forcing the most junior person to react with urgency. Indeed, I remember during my basic officer training at Sandhurst that we were given "change parades" in which we had to rush up to our rooms, change into a different uniform and run back down again to be on parade. While this reinforced most officers' hurry up drivers, it did have practical benefits. I frequently found during my career that I had less than ten minutes to get out of bed, get dressed and deploy into my Land Rover, warrior or helicopters. I found that the enemy or terrorists are not relaxed gentlemen who are prepared to wait patiently for you.

Any combination of these drivers produces ineffective leadership behaviours if overplayed. People start gossip, or rumours about a rival with the aim of enhancing their own position by undermining another's position. Leaders become inauthentic, saying what they believe others want to hear. People hype up their successes, take the glory and embellish the truth, in an effort to bolster their own ego. As part of MQ, the values we hold and what we believe in turn influence our behaviour.

I remember the one particular officer at Staff College who was highly competitive. He formed a small clique with a couple of other like-minded people. They were critical of other more able officers behind their backs. His stories of his somewhat unbelievable achievements became known as "Jackanory" after the fantasy children's stories told on the BBC. It was also questionable whether his hand-written staff college essays were totally his work. At the time, it seemed as if he had fooled the directing staff into believing that he was more competent than we believed he was. To our disgust, he got the high-powered top job that he desired after the course. However, it was far beyond his abilities, and he struggled in that role and achieved very little further promotion within the army. I understand he has remained in the army and come to terms with what he is most suited to and consequently lowered his ambitions.

Even unhealthy leadership behaviour has much to teach us. I will never fully understand what was happening in this officer's case. However, I assume that he feared failure and his desperate anxiety to do a good job drove much of his critical behaviour. He was especially critical of himself. We know from human psychology that you cannot love or like someone else more than yourself. You are your own limiting factor. I also observed what happened when he was making critical comments about somebody else behind their back. He was not prepared for his comments eventually to reach his target of criticism. I remember on one occasion they did, resulting in a heated argument with the offended officer. I have seen these negative leadership traits and low MQ in all walks of life in both business and the military. The result is that leaders with these characteristics are not trusted.

Re-evaluating your values and beliefs

During my first year at Staff College, the biggest life-changing event for me was the birth of our first daughter, Harriet. As parents, we suddenly understood about minority rule. A small child is never impressed by rank, status or position. Instead, they warm to and relate easily with people who are appreciative, thoughtful, caring and empathetic. Having a growing family also forced me to check whether I lived to work, or worked to live. Quite often, I didn't get my values and priorities right by failing to put my family first. Becoming a workaholic, and hiding in work, in order to avoid family responsibilities is an easy trap to fall into. It is always something for every leader to beware. Stop and think about the bigger picture when you have a life-changing event.

We must review our values, beliefs and priorities and continually reassess what is most important. Having your own children also can make you question what your life purpose really is and what and who you are in service of. Being torn between the demands of a young and growing family and simultaneously developing your career is a paradox that many middle-management leaders have. Mid-career, when people's jobs start to demand the most from them, tends to be the time in people's life when they are also required to give the most support to their family. This family support is needed initially by their young children, and then shortly afterwards it can also be required from aging parents. Getting the balance right requires great MQ.

Nepal expedition

Bridget had been on expedition to Nepal five years before Harriet was born. Her descriptions of Nepal's beautiful countryside and its kind people had captivated me. She had also learnt their language and customs when she had been an officer on attachment with the 1st Battalion of the 2nd Gurkha Rifles (1/2 GR). During my three weeks' summer holiday, in the middle of this intense course, I took the opportunity to travel, led by a Gurkhali speaking fellow officer Major Peter Gillespie, to trek in the Himalayan foothills. The experience of getting into the heart and soul of Nepal was incredible.

The expedition took a lot of planning and preparation. After a long trip from Kathmandu we arrived at the village deep in the Himalayan foothills. The journey itself had been an incredible experience perched on the roof of a rickety bus. As we slid back and forth with our rucksacks on the bus's roof rack, we came perilously close to falling off the sheer drops on that twisty mountain road. The benefit was that we had beautiful unbroken views across the Himalayas towards Mount Everest. Once we arrived at the end of the road in a remote village, we selected a team of porters to help us carry our heavy loads of food and tents.

Whenever we arrived at a small, hidden village, we were greeted with such kindness and generosity. The village elder and his people would go out of their way to share what they could with us and ensure that we were looked after in the spots that we chose to camp. From a capitalist point of view, we saw poverty on a level which I had never seen before. However when we began conversations we realised that despite their lack of money, the Nepalese considered that we were really the poor ones in so many ways. In particular, they were amazed by the limited amount of time that we as parents in the West spend enhancing relationships with our families and our children, especially those of us who tend to be workaholics. I'm very inspired by the campaigning of my friend Oliver Johnson on the topic of "less" and it was highly relevant to my experiences in Nepal. Recently, Oliver has been asking himself three questions fundamental to MQ:

1. Why do I want more than I need?

2. What would happen if I got to like less?

3. Where is true liberation – in more or in less?

At one stage of our Himalayan trek, we finally arrived tired and exhausted in a small mountain village. We were told that there was a collection of wise and courageous men in the village. We went to a small teahouse and met six very old members of the Gurkhas who had all been awarded the Victoria Cross (the highest award possible from the Queen for bravery, often awarded posthumously). We were staggered. It was such a rare gathering of heroic people and being in their presence and experiencing their humility, energy and intensity was a memorable experience. The whole Nepal trip was a reminder to me of the importance of MQ in leaders, yet I list below the other leadership lessons that I absorbed during this memorable trip:

1. I observed the wisdom and calmness of the village elders in the remotest parts of Nepal.

2. I realised appreciating what you already have leads to more happiness than craving for the things you don't have.

3. I saw people living a life on purpose and having a great sense of fulfilment compared in general to ourselves in the West.

4. I noticed the personal power and presence of people who seem to have so little, yet had so much.

5. I saw generosity and abundance and this was so inspiring compared to the mentality of scarcity that I had frequently encountered previously.

6. I observed how the care we experienced from the Nepalese porters for us as a team, instilled similar feelings from us in response.

7. I understood the value of emotional intelligence and our ability to connect with people when we all speak different languages and came from a completely different cultures.

8. We had total belief and trust in our appointed leader, and this was powerful.

Most of all, I will always remember being in the presence of six owners of the VC, who were prepared to lay their life down for their values and beliefs and the organisation they belonged to.

Lessons from Business

Assistant Commissioner Bob Quick,
the Copper who cared deeply for his people

I was fortunate to work with Bob Quick who is highly respected as an exceptional senior policeman. He was known affectionately by his police officers as the "Copper's Copper". This was the finest accolade they could give a man who had reached the higher ranks of the police. I worked with Bob when he was Chief Constable of Surry Police and led a team that made it the top performing force. I also knew him when he was Assistant Commissioner in London's Metropolitan Police in charge of Counter Terrorism.

Bob was a role model of integrity and lived by his strong values and beliefs. As a consequence, he was able to motivate, encourage and inspire his officers so that they became an example to other forces. He was also a leader who was continually open to challenge and feedback and made a point of developing the talent of other leaders, and consequently many of his officers went on to other top jobs. His insistence on maintaining his integrity, doing the right thing and being a leader of honour and trustworthiness eventually cost him his job when he came up against others who would stop at little to succeed. Sometimes the price of inspiring leadership is very high.

Bob and I were thinking about the decline in respect for and faith in, those at the top of public life generally. We agreed that this is quite dangerous as it undermines democracy and our society in the end. I asked Bob his experience and view on inspiring leadership and he said:

"Inspiring leadership has a lot to do with authenticity. Leaders who are honest within themselves convey a sincerity of belief and a consistency of conduct that others identify and trust. We continually underestimate how quickly people identify incongruence between words and behaviour, insincerity or a 'synthetic' persona. In a society where trust in our leaders is declining quickly in key elements of public life it is very important that we understand and address the dissonance between what the public see and what they expect and deserve."

MQ -The Mufti Club

In the midst of the early 2001 recession, gloom and waves of redundancies, I decided to create some positive cheer. I connected the ex-forces officers and leaders in PwC Consulting to make a networking club, named "The Mufti Club" (an Indian word for civilian attire worn by officers when off-duty). I founded the club to bring together leaders with a similar sense of morals, values and beliefs. It proved to be a rave success. Once each quarter, I organised meetings for over 100 leaders from all parts of the firm across Europe. Our after-dinner guest speakers shared their own experiences of leadership in both the military and business. The dinner venues were places like the Army and Navy club, or the RAF club and guests were initially ex-officers from the Army, Navy, Air Force and management consultants who were currently working on projects in the Ministry of Defence.

The events quickly proved very popular and provided a sense of camaraderie. The culture of PwC's Mufti Club was one of panache, style and fun. A similar feel can be found in many top quality clubs. I pulled together a successful alumni knowing that all the members had already been through a tough selection process to join the military with the resultant bonds formed from mutual, shared hardships. The success of the

Mufti Club and eventually its associated network proved to me that there is a genuine thirst for high-quality leadership instruction and constant lifelong learning from the experience of successful leaders in organisations. There is also a dearth of stylish opportunities to connect people who work together. We found that there is great merit in a foundation of shared adventure and leadership development for building trust amongst comparative strangers. Open clubs are also a great way of sharing business leads and opportunities with people who share your sense of MQ.

Adjusting to change according to your moral compass - "Monday"

The most successful leaders are able to handle change according to their moral compasses. In PwC, we were about to have a seismic shift because the new US Government SEC regulations (Securities and Exchange Commission) meant that PwC would be forced to sell off its massive, successful and highly profitable management consulting arm. The Partners knew this change had to be made and as leaders had to cope with a huge amount of uncertainty, about the very future and existence of their own organisation. At the same time, these partners had to encourage those who followed them to hold their nerve. They needed to extol others to give their discretionary life energy and enthusiasm to an organisation that might not exist a few weeks later.

To cope with the paradox of being fully open and authentic on the one hand, whilst needing to maintain confidentiality and secrecy is always a tough balance. It is a challenge to moral intelligence. My preference has always been to be more open and sharing with the teams I have led, and to take them into my confidence. I have found this display of trust to be more authentic. In return, my teams have always repaid the confidence which I have placed in them. The agony of leadership is that there are often highly sensitive pieces of information which you cannot share with those you lead, however severe the implication may be for them. Such was the situation with Winston Churchill when he knew as a result of cracking the enigma code that specific ships were going to be sunk and certain cities bombed, yet he chose not to warn those who were going to die. In that way he protected the code-breaker's information for larger more strategic decisions which helped win the war. Which values and beliefs do you hold most important in such situations?

Recently, I was talking to a friend in another management consultancy who found himself in an invidious moral position as leader. He knew that all the members of his team and himself were going to be made redundant in the next two months. Yet his organisation insisted that he deceive his team and fabricate the truth. He had to sign a legal document that confirmed that he would not let his colleagues (whom he had recruited and led for the last eight years) know. Unsurprisingly he found this inauthentic, dishonest and incongruent behaviour highly stressful. This is not unusual and is often what organisations insist we do as leaders, or else we face the consequences of legal action for telling the truth.

For six months, PwC's consultants had been briefed by our newly appointed CEO that we would be demerged and established through a stock market IPO, as a separate company with 30,000 employees and an exciting new brand name which would soon be unveiled. After much anticipation and a drum roll, we were disappointed and underwhelmed to be told that the new brand name would be "Monday". Unbeknown to the employees, however, the leaders had later struck a last-minute deal in 2002 and utterly changed the game plan. The good news was that we wouldn't be called "Monday". This removed a source of ridicule and humour for our clients and competitors alike. However, the bad news was that we had been sold to IBM for $3.5 billion. This was considerably less than the $18 billion offered by HP two years earlier. The moral dilemma for the leaders was how much knowledge they could share with their employees, when the information was market sensitive.

Honesty and openness with your people – acquisition by IBM Business Consulting

There are many important leadership lessons associated with the integration, acquisition and merger of anything from a small team to a complete organisation. Sadly, they seem to be easily forgotten and need to be continually re-learned. The first lesson is to take all (or as many as you can) of your people with you mentally and emotionally. You must ensure that you win the "battle of hearts and minds". There needs to be a fair balance between what is done **by** you as the employee as opposed to what is done **to** you, in order to ensure high levels of employee engagement.

The importance of honest and open communication, MQ and high levels of trust in the leadership cannot be understated. With the demerger of PwC Consulting and its establishment as a stand-alone business called Monday, the communication and thorough consultation by the leadership with the employees had been excellent. With the exception of the ridiculous name, my peers and I were fully engaged and were very excited about the future. We were prepared to throw our efforts behind the new firm Monday. It had been structured in such a way that we felt we co-owned it, and so we would give a huge amount of discretionary energy to help it succeed. We knew and trusted our leaders and the decisions they made on our behalf. Our beliefs and ambitions seemed aligned.

The last-minute IBM announcement of the acquisition of PwC Consulting is worthy of an MBA case study, but sadly for many of the wrong reasons. Firstly, many employees felt betrayed by the PwC leaders who sold us to IBM. We were committed to setting up a new company on our own, which they had promised for the previous six months. Perhaps the full truth will never be revealed. For many employees, it appeared that the deal was secretive, furtive, rushed and done to us without consultation, rather than by us. The rhetoric from the IBM leadership contained too much spin and insufficient credibility for us fully to trust them. We were told that this would be "a great fit of two very similar cultures". We soon found this not to be true, and consequently for many staff this lacked MQ and our energy, goodwill and huge discretionary effort evaporated overnight. Our PwC Consulting business was merged with a comparatively small part of IBM and our unique character vanished.

MQ, Ethics, integrity, trust and bullying

I have been impressed by the work of Roger Steare, the corporate philosopher, on measuring and assessing people's ethics. It is important to have rules and regulations, however there is much more to this complex area. Roger's "ethicability" Master classes are in great demand and he says: "Corrupt politicians. Unsafe cars. Financial meltdown. Climate change. The greatest challenges we face today are crises of ethics. What are our moral values? How do we decide what's right and find the courage to do it? How do we display leadership with integrity? How do we nurture cultures where doing the right thing becomes part of our organisational DNA?

Ethics is no longer optional, it is absolutely critical to the sustainability and success of our businesses, our public-sector services and every other institution and enterprise. In the UK the new Bribery Act 2010 places a specific legal requirement on Boards of UK Companies to show leadership and take all reasonable steps' to embed the right cultures and behaviour to mitigate the risk of bribery, corruption and fraud. Failure to do so will result in enforcement actions, prosecutions, significant fines and custodial sentences for directors and executives who fail to take these steps to mitigate any corruption."

The finest inspiring leaders I know have a very strong moral compass and behave ethically with integrity and trustworthiness. The paradox is that humans find it easy to spot hypocrisy in others, but are often blind to it in themselves. How do you think you personally would measure up to the test of your ethics, and how would your leadership team perform?

It is a well-known business saying that "what you measure is what you get". What are you measuring in your organisation, and how are you rewarding your leaders? If the only measure you truly focus on is constantly growing profitable revenue, then you will get some very unhealthy behaviour developing amongst your employees. The greatest challenge for the corporate firms which I support is that they exist to "maximise shareholder value", yet this should not mean they abandon their own personal values and ethics. Examples include WorldCom, Enron and Greece's entry into the EU, where people hid results, distorted figures and were economical with the truth in order to get the rewards, profits and bonuses which they so desperately craved.

In coaching situations, where I work with executives who have been accused of bullying behaviour, I frequently discover that their behaviour emerges because they are desperate to achieve the profits and results which the organisation craves. Consequently, they go to almost any lengths to realise those results and end up treating people as objects. Each individual, however, is fully accountable and responsible for their own behaviour and they cannot blame the organisation alone if it has lost its moral compass. It is the leader who is to blame for lacking personal integrity.

Leadership by example
Brigadier John Griffin
Royal Signals, SAS & Group 4

One inspiring leader who stands out in my memory as someone with high integrity, value and beliefs (MQ) is John Griffin the Commanding Officer of 2nd Division Signal Regiment. I learned much as a young Captain when I was his Adjutant, since I was responsible for discipline, standards and maintaining values in the Regiment. My role was to carry out instructions on his behalf. John Griffin was a man who espoused humble excellence and the RMAS motto "serve to lead". He is a wise, highly intelligent, quietly spoken, energetic and driven man. Before he arrived to command, he had already earned great respect across The Royal Corps of Signals. He achieved the rare accolade of passing the rigorous SAS selection and becoming a fully-fledged SAS troop commander. The fact that I learned about John's three tours with the Special Forces from others and not from John, demonstrated his modesty. He would never boast about his considerable achievements but said recently when I interviewed him:

"I just tried to lead in a way that was right, without any great analysis, perhaps just a set of principles, values and examples that I had absorbed from my upbringing, training and experience of leading and being led. And whatever failures I admitted to publicly I can assure you there were many more doubts and perceived failures that I did not own up to."

He was equally clear that he was not a hero: "A soldier is not a hero for joining up to go on operations that might be dangerous, but he **is** when they break cover under effective enemy fire to rescue a wounded colleague. I was sometimes in the way of danger and aware that I would be, but had the chance to weigh risks and make contingency plans. I hope I showed courage in carrying out my duty but mercifully perhaps, while in the Army I never had to make "the hero's decision" described above. Funnily enough the only time I did something that might qualify against my standards of being a hero, was after I left the Army!"

As a leader, he wanted to combine his love for challenge and physical fitness with putting something back into the community. He teamed up with the local York chocolate firm Nestlé and created "Race the Sun". This grew into an annual charity fundraising event involving teams from all over the north of England in an epic competition involving canoeing, cycling, running, orienteering and hiking around the North York Moors.

John was also a leader who developed other leaders by passing on the best lessons, values and standards from his own experience, to young officers. As a result, we had to take part in realistic training operations. An example of the sort of task he set was to complete a close target reconnaissance on a potential terrorist house. We individually had to make the reconnaissance without being spotted, return and present our plans to a diverse collection of battle hardened cynical old soldiers. Presenting to such a hostile knowledgeable audience put us on our mettle and since then, I have never feared making business presentations. There were many other innovative and unusual changes that John instigated as a leader, which unwittingly made him a legend in his own lifetime. I am sure that as a result of his strong values and beliefs he became the Signal Officer in Chief for the whole of the Army. He maintained and demanded very high standards, especially when it concerned the welfare of the people he was responsible for, and he often did battle with the system, to his own detriment and yet to the benefit of his soldiers.

The relationship between the Signal Regiment and the 2nd Division Headquarters staff officers was sometimes difficult. John said: "In the first part of the tour, some of the key senior figures in the HQ had a bad tempered, bullying and directive style of leadership. This is typical of authoritarian types who believe subordinates should obey, and do not themselves ever question their superiors. This is highlighted in the book *On the Psychology of Military Incompetence* by Professor Norman Dixon. As you have observed, the tone set at the top is likely to set the tone for the organisation. So some of the more junior HQ staff thought they could get away with bullying the Regiment and be backed up by their seniors: which they often were. Towards the end of my time, and with General Sir Michael Rose's new leadership, the atmosphere became totally different and became really positive."

On military operations, the staff expected signalmen to do quite menial tasks for them and some treated these soldiers almost as servants. John would challenge such pompous officers, ensuring they were provided with a good service, yet also ensuring that they treated everyone with respect, regardless of their rank or position. These experiences have stayed with me. It is with sadness that I have found that leaders often do not protect the interests of those they lead in the military or in business. Do not, however, confuse this principle of MQ with "blind loyalty" which is corrosive. Leaders have to be fair and balanced and need courage to tackle poor performance, or lack of integrity. As John's Adjutant, I gained great experience by witnessing some difficult situations where he had to apply his integrity and true wisdom to resolve some almost impossible problems.

John was human and therefore at times made mistakes, usually due to the limited information that he had at the time when he was required to make decisions. He did not dither, or vacillate, yet he was quick to acknowledge when he had been either unfair, or blatantly wrong. His moral compass was clear for all to see. He would then publicly apologise and rectify the situation. This strengthened, rather than weakened his position as a leader and empowered, rather than emasculated, his junior leaders. Sadly I meet far too few leaders who are prepared to model that kind of vulnerable, yet courageous behaviour and instead worry about saving face and propping up their own ego.

John had numerous "courageous conversations" with poor performers. He outlined the facts, asked the intention behind their actions and if they were aware of the consequences of what they had done. He then summarised what he understood to be their point of view, expressed how he felt about what they had done, the consequences and the behaviour that he expected them to model in future as leaders. The atmosphere in the room was, at these times, coldly professional. He spoke quietly but intensely, making every word count, he listened very carefully and used the power of silence to incredible effect. I began to appreciate the efficacy of these firm conversations, when I saw how people left his office feeling that they had been properly understood and yet were thoroughly clear about the mistake they had made. I identified this as a difficult, but important skill to develop.

First, I respected the way John appreciated and highlighted their talents, natural strengths and what they had done that had worked especially well. Then, I saw the way that he made inquiries to understand the person's intention using a positive "appreciative" framework and to hear what they thought could have gone even better and the consequences of their actions. Most importantly he was never afraid of frank and courageous conversations, if it was still necessary. This method of guiding people, using first appreciative inquiry to pick up successes and then not avoiding challenging conversations, was for me tough love and was itself inspiring.

It is important to mention the support system that inspiring leaders naturally accumulate around themselves. These may be mentors, executive coaches, colleagues from previous roles, friends or family members. John did this and was especially well supported by his wife Marion who was quick to create humour, joking that: "Behind every great man is an amazed woman". Another quality that John modelled and expected all his officers to do also, was to lead by example and this was illustrated powerfully on the legendary Regimental March. The regiment needed to be able to deploy onto operations at very short notice. So, to practise, with only one hour's warning, first thing on Monday morning, John gave me the order to have the whole Regiment of seven hundred people on the Parade Square, smartly equipped and ready to deploy.

In other regiments, what always followed this sort of parade was traditional "Army bullshit". Officers would inspect the smartness of the uniform, highly polished boots and tidy rucksacks. This is what members of the regiment had prepared for. Instead, John was looking for practical signs that people had the right equipment, so they could do their job. Then, he instructed the officers to take the lead at the head of each of their units. He put himself at the head of his Regiment and took us on a mix of running and marching over a ten mile course, ending in a timed assault course. Throughout the run and the march, our Commanding Officer seemed to be everywhere, running up and down the ranks, encouraging officers and men alike. The best male and female officers, including I'm proud to say my wife with her troop, led by example from the front and encouraged those they led.

At the end of what became known as "The Great Strensall Death March", there was a small yet significant group of officers and NCOs who were immediately called to a private meeting with the Commanding Officer. John had not expected some officers and seniors to wilt, and did not want to show them up. There were lessons to be learned about values and standards. John Griffin left them in no doubt as to the potential consequences of their poor fitness and inability to lead when "the chips were down". He personally organised and took part in a "get well programme" for all these leaders, so he had confidence that they could all lead both in peace and war and could earn the respect that their rank required. John was guided by MQ, standards and values he personally held despite the resistance.

John said: "It was I guess a bit of a cathartic moment, albeit not without humour. I remember Staff Sergeant Smith coming on that parade in fancy dress (a big yellow chicken) and running up and down collecting money for charity. I guess my main aim stemmed from my belief that it was my duty to ensure we were all ready for operations and that war is tough so train hard – fight easy. The greatest disservice we could have done our officers and soldiers was to see them go to war unfit and under-prepared. So in the end, a few ruffled feathers in peace had to be worth success and saved lives on operations." It is not surprising to note that John Griffin made an easy transition from senior military officer to senior leader in Group Four as Operations Director for the Private Finance Initiative Consortium at GCHQ Cheltenham.

John concluded: "Personally I have always been riveted by leadership, effective and ineffective, and tried to learn from myself and others. I considered leadership the core skill for my chosen profession, which has to be paired with management skills and sometimes specialist professional skills in order to be fit to exercise what the Army calls Command."

4 Key Points:

- MQ highlights the importance of your own integrity, values and beliefs. It focuses on your irreproachability, character and discernment.

- MQ is: "being guided by one's moral compass. In its simplest form, this will direct us to do what is right and not just what is correct as we navigate through life."

- We all make mistakes; the key is to rectify our errors quickly, genuinely apologise and get back onto travelling according to our own "True North".

- There were many testing times in the military and business where I had to struggle to hold true to my personal beliefs and values. The price and consequences were often high.

4 Questions:

1. What are you measuring in your organisation, and how are you rewarding your leaders?

2. Do you hold true to your own values as well as "maximising shareholder value"?

3. How do you think you personally would measure up to the test of your ethics and how would your leadership team perform?

4. Which values and beliefs do you hold most important in situations where your organisation expects you to withhold information and distort the truth?

Speaking to inspire other leaders

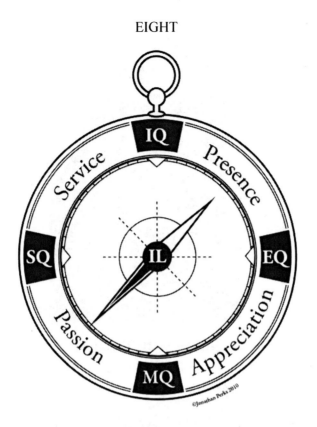

EIGHT

Passion - Love & Inspiration

"To love someone deeply gives you strength. Being loved by someone deeply gives you courage."

Lao Tzu

Leading with Passion
Katherine Tulpa
CEO, Association for Coaching (AC)

I have known Katherine Tulpa for seven years and watched her as she has worked with four organisations to increase their size and develop their offering. She devotes herself with passion to the profession of coaching and supporting other CEOs. I experienced her expertise at first hand when she helped Penna's board and executive coaching team become a successful and respected force in the coaching world. Simultaneously she ran her own business, Urban Calm, which was created to support stressed executives and she founded the Association for Coaching (AC). This is an independent non-profit organisation which now has thousands of members around the world. The Association for Coaching promotes best practice in this field and raises awareness and standards across the Coaching industry, while providing value added benefits to its members – whether they are professional Coaches or Organisations involved in Coaching. As CEO of the AC Katherine devotes hours of her personal time in support of the association and has received many awards for her passion and selfless dedication to the profession of coaching. One of her colleagues on the Global Board is Darren Robson who is respected as an innovative entrepreneur and for his considerable work with charities and Corporate Social Responsibility (CSR). He captured some of Katherine's qualities as follows:

"Katherine epitomises inspiring leadership. She is mentally agile, has the highest integrity and is extremely bright. She is emotionally self-aware and focuses on other people's needs and development. Some years ago she saw my potential and has coached and mentored me, and many others, to success. By setting up Wisdom 8 and the AC she has established a legacy far beyond her lifetime in service of the coaching profession. She has all eight of the qualities of inspiring leadership and you can sense Katherine's presence in a room which is usually preceded by her signature walk; the stomp. She radiates her passion even on early morning calls. Finally her sense of service to clients is highly inspiring."

Passion has inspired my teams and has enabled me to push through even in the darkest hours to great successes. It has therefore become the sixth principle of inspiring leadership. It is far easier to achieve things about which you and those you lead are passionate.

Definition of Passion

By defining passion in leadership, I'm combining the love of leading others with the ability to inspire people to achieve outstanding results. Passionate leaders are committed and emotionally excited about achieving a specific objective or fulfilling a calling. Jonathan Byrnes[27] has written about the requirement for passion; "Most importantly, to be a great leader, you need to find what you really like. That's where the passion, commitment, and integrity come from. In my experience, the most important underlying factor in leadership is whether a person has searched out and found a great match between what's in his or her heart, which is what he or she really enjoys, and the work situation. When thinking about the definition of leaders; 'people who leave their footprints in their areas of passion', It's easy to focus on the first part, how to leave footprints. But the real power comes from the second, working in your area of passion."

Inspiration is the generation and transfer of energy from the leader to the led, so they in turn are enthused by that passion to achieve the most challenging tasks. As the business leader Sir John Harvey-Jones once said: "How do you know you have won? When the energy is coming the other way and when your people are visibly growing individually and as a group." When a leader is doing the job they are passionate about, inspiring others happens naturally and amazing results can be achieved. As Ralph Waldo Emerson said: "Our chief want is someone who will inspire us to be what we know we could be." Passionate leaders arouse and stimulate the emotions and ignite the thinking of others. Passion, love and inspiration can be found in both introverted, quietly determined leaders as well as the louder and more excitable extroverts.

Consequences for leaders who lack passion

It is hard to get excited about achieving an objective for a leader who lacks enthusiasm for the outcome themselves. If your heart is not in what you're doing, then you will not transfer the required energy to your followers for them to achieve the results you seek. Most people have something in their lives in which they are really interested and about which they can speak with excitement and passion. If a leader is unable to transmit this enthusiasm to others, then he is destined to achieve a mediocre and lacklustre performance. President Dwight D. Eisenhower was perceptive when he said: "Leadership is the art of getting someone else to do something you want done, because he wants to do it." If your team members are not convinced by your powers of passion and inspiration, then you are setting yourself up for failure.

Some managers with whom I have worked act as drains rather than radiators, and demoralise rather than impassion their colleagues. In the book *Harry Potter and the prisoner of Azkaban*, there are some evil hooded spirits who are greatly feared called Dementors. They suck the very soul and energy out of their victims. I have watched some managers act like Dementors, speaking over others at length in a monotone, and utterly failing to make a personal connection that excites or energises those around them. Without passion, inspiration and a love of what they do, these managers are highly unlikely to progress further in their careers. They will certainly not achieve the results they seek, other than by bullying, threatening and cajoling. They become the leaders who push from behind rather than excite and encourage by example from the front.

How can passion help you as a leader?

Firstly, ensure that you are doing a job you love. Raw energy, enthusiasm and drive enable people to overcome many obstacles. With passion, whether a quiet confidence, or an excited vibrancy, you can transmit your energy directly to those around you. Tired cynics in any team may be reluctant and hang back; however the vast majority will find it hard to resist the power of attraction that such a leader can create. In moments of crisis and stressful situations when morale is low, and people are frightened and depressed, passion and inspiration are needed more than ever.

As well as motivating others with your own passion, it is worth discovering what makes other people tick. What truly inspires them? A leader who genuinely cares would naturally make a point of finding out all he can about the people he leads. If this is done over a period of time people are able to reveal something about themselves and by opening up and talking about their own interests, hobbies, friends and family, understanding of people's motivation increases. I have found it unusual to have a silent response when I ask people what they are really interested in.

Lessons from the Military

Passion for leading others well, Airmobile Company Commander

My work as an instructor at Sandhurst taught me some tough lessons about the ineffectiveness of brutal styles of management. More importantly, I was introduced to a different way of leading which would later evolve into this philosophy of inspiring leadership. What became apparent to me at that time was that it was important to have an authentic interest in caring for those you lead. Once I had realised this I thoroughly enjoyed the aspects of my role as an infantry platoon commander at Sandhurst.

While at Sandhurst, I orchestrated a complex transfer to a front-line Yorkshire infantry regiment called The Green Howards. This happened when I had served for ten years in the Royal Corps of Signals, and turned out to be midway through my career as an Army Officer. By making this move, I was seen as a bit of a maverick. About 95% of officers remain in the same regiment throughout their whole career to the age of 55 when officers are considered to be too old to fight in wars, and are forced to retire. The Green Howards were first formed 1688 and this close-knit Battalion of 650 people was commanded at that time by Lieutenant Colonel Richard Dannatt.

In this regiment, the finest leaders developed an ability to inspire, motivate, challenge and discipline with apparent languidity and ease. Officers were expected to have enthusiasm for the task without being overtly excitable. This accepted leadership style, where officers led without appearing to try too hard, could be likened to a swan gliding effortlessly across a lake. Meanwhile, they were paddling like mad under the surface. It was a very modest and typically understated English-gentleman style of leadership. The outward appearance that officers cultivated was that of the casual amateur, whilst the leadership that was actually demonstrated was that of a professional. At the time that I joined this small Yorkshire battalion, it contained a disproportionate number of high-flying and very talented leaders.

During my lifetime, this one small battalion has produced three Heads of the Army, about ten Generals and a large number of Brigadiers. I'm still curious as to what it was that attracted talented people to this one battalion and exactly what special ingredient existed to enable so many of them to develop into such high ranking leaders. My hypothesis is that success encouraged further success. Powerful leaders, like Field Marshal the Lord

Inge, took care to foster leadership talent in others and ensure that talented people were spotted and given every opportunity to succeed. He had a passion for excellence and maintained high standards in all he did. During my first year in the Battalion, I noticed that all officers attempted to acquire the overtly nonchalant relaxed attitude to their career prospects, whilst secretly angling for promotion behind the scenes. When officers appeared to be too intense, too serious, ambitious and over-eager, their behaviour was publicly derided by other officers. It was more appropriate to play a more subtle and less openly ambitious game. I learned to be more relaxed.

Openness and authenticity

This culture seemed to be common in several cavalry and infantry regiments, but it was not the culture I noticed in the Royal Corps of Signals. Looking back, it is quite amusing to see the level of acting and inauthentic behaviour that accompanied this apparent languidity across the Army. The fact that military families live and work in close proximity to each other can be beneficial to the development of camaraderie but it also has consequences that are not necessarily good. Close bonds can be formed on many levels. However, in the military, the consequences of not fitting in socially were "career limiting". Fortunately in business, you can choose where you wish to live and with whom you wish to socialise.

Many successful people crave success, reward and promotion, yet publicly protest to be utterly relaxed about whatever happens. It is a theme that has emerged from interviews with both Generals and CEOs. The advice I received early on in my career was to do each job that you get to the best of your abilities and if you do a truly excellent job of leading your team, then the rewards naturally follow. This advice is hard to follow and at times I, like many other leaders, have been an over-anxious, over-achiever. Had I been able to become more relaxed and at ease as a young officer, I might have had even more fun and enjoyment in my first few years in the Army. Focusing on the destination alone fritters away our lives. I have now genuinely become more relaxed and consequently I enjoy myself much more en route. I aspire to live by the motto, "life is a journey; travel it well".

In spite of the slight disconnect between my leadership style and that of some other officers, all was not lost. I was fortunate to have been spotted by Richard Dannatt who was the commanding officer of the Regiment at that time. He channelled my passion and enthusiasm. At the age of 28, he allowed me to command the prestigious and ground-breaking "airmobile screen company". This company contained a unique mix of equipment, vehicles and specialists. He empowered me, gave me independence and let me employ the innovative ideas of my most able and talented NCOs and junior officers. We consequently trialled a new war-fighting concept, and were able to be slightly radical as we developed our role.

We were equipped with the SAS' light strike vehicles with anti-tank rocket launchers, cut-down Land Rovers with machine guns and all-terrain, dune-buggy vehicles with mortars. We were rather a motley, yet highly professional crew looking like a team out of the film *Mad Max*. Our airmobile forces were lightly equipped and highly mobile troops, designed to be transported deep into enemy territory. All our vehicles and large weapons were flown in before the start of the battle, both underneath and within a fleet of helicopters. It was exciting, frenetic, chaotic and mad. On reflection I think now that our life expectancy in wartime would have been very short, as we were likely to have "gone out in a blaze of glory" against a mass of Soviet armour and artillery, but we were full of enthusiasm for our new role.

A German General once remarked, "There are four types of leaders:

1. Lazy and stupid leaders

2. Hard-working and stupid leaders

3. Hard-working and bright leaders

4. Lazy and bright leaders

Take the second type and get rid of them immediately, for they are a liability to your organisation and will needlessly waste time and resources. Take the fourth type and promote them to the highest ranks. They will find the quickest and easiest way to achieve success with the least effort." During my time in The Green Howards as an airmobile company commander, I worked with officers from all four of those categories. Richard Dannatt took a leaf out that German General's book by picking officers from within the Battalion who could get jobs done quickly and then have fun. He knew how to appreciate and inspire his officers.

Wisdom and fast decision-making

What also impressed me at this time in my career was the speed of decision-making that was evident in leaders like Richard Dannatt. In the midst of some of our most stressful and high tempo airmobile operations, instead of the traditional operation orders which normally might stretch from between twenty to forty pages, we had a simple diagram with only two pages of orders. On that basis, a Brigade of 3,000 officers and soldiers would deploy on highly complex operations. The skill of any leader is to communicate, as simply, clearly and succinctly as possible. The selection of each word in these orders mattered. Specific words and phrases would trigger a whole series of well-rehearsed moves just like a finely honed football or rugby team. This need for a common understanding of a set of standard procedures is invaluable in both the military and business, where short response times are needed to ensure a high-quality outcome.

As an entrepreneur some years later, I found the first two years in any new start-up business were especially chaotic, uncertain, hand to mouth, reactive experiences. The first phase of a start-up relies on the drive, passion and inspiration of the leader. Then the leader needs to find some energetic, hard-working and talented supporters. It is only when processes, systems and operating procedures, similar in concept to those in the military, are developed, that businesses can step up to the next level of size and complexity. It is almost as if you need one kind of maverick, fast-paced leader to get things started. At that stage you need quite another type of person to take the business further. Someone who is better at developing systems, processes and stabilising the structure is ideal. This second type of leader is more able to manage the paradox of needing to grow the business and yet also to keep a steady-state of weekly operations. Reuven Bar-On shared from his experience: "There are four different types of leaders that work optimally in the four different seasons or periods of the organisation's life cycle: start-up ('spring'), the quick and steep ascent ('summer'), plateau ('autumn') and the dip before potential death ('winter')." The key is to bring in the right leader at the right time.

I learned many lessons from this airmobile command. I also was able to empower others as well as being able to develop my ability to make decisions rapidly, based on growing wisdom from my previous experiences. I likened my team members to a family of Golden Eagles. Eagles have the freedom to leave the high mountain eyrie and hunt freely in their own patch of sky above the mountains, swooping down to catch their prey and return each year to a nest to rear another family. Allowing individuals the freedom to develop their skills and ideas within a supportive team environment made our team even stronger. I personally flourish and do my best work in environments of autonomy and appreciation, where my boss believes in me and expects me to do well. I expect others enjoy a similar level of trust. I started to develop and apply "expectation theory" from that moment. This theory is the absolute belief by the leader that your team members can achieve excellence if they are given the freedom to do so.

Destructive criticism erodes passion and inspiration

I have come across various occasions where people have created enemies without intending to do so. In the airmobile role, our "sexy company" as the TV film crew called us revelled in the action and fun we were having. Unfortunately that triggered envy and bitterness in one or two of our peers. Perhaps leaders with too much passion and inspiration trigger jealousy. I believe now that enthusiasm and passion can create a negative reaction when others have not developed that same feeling for their own role. Eventually, I decided simply to get on with life and not worry too much about other's jealous comments. As the saying goes: "You can please some of the people some of the time, but you can't please all of the people all of the time."

I find back-stabbing unpalatable, especially when it is personal. If people are not happy with a leader they work for or with, it is always, in my view, better to discuss issues openly with the person concerned. I know from experience that to do that takes courage and can sometimes negatively impact on your career. Frequently, this sort of difficulty arises when there is a clash of values or beliefs. The outcome of the discussion depends on how strongly people are prepared to stand up for their values. I have chosen to leave organisations, rather than being forced to work in an environment which conflicted with my life purpose and what I believe to be the way business should be conducted.

Balancing passion and logic, After Action Reviews (AAR)

One of the disciplines I learned during my time as a Company Commander was to balance passion with logic and reasoning. I spent time after events with my teams analysing what actually happened during our active operations. I have done this after training events and continue to do this after business sales calls to date. Having identified what we learned from these events, we took action to improve our performance next time. In the military we called these sessions "After Action Reviews (AAR)" and whether it was on return from anti-terrorist operations, airmobile operations, training sessions or peacekeeping operations we focused on answering two questions:

1. WWW. What went well?

2. EBI. What would have been even better if ...?

As officers, we were trained to take the view that if at first you don't succeed, then we should study and model the actions of the enemy, and learn from their success. Each member of the team, regardless of rank and status, explained to everyone else what they personally had done well and what would have made their performance even better. These were very frank and honest exchanges and they had the additional benefit of bonding teams and creating very high levels of trust. In business, while the consequences are not life threatening, poor performance can bring a CEO down. From experience, I know that organisations can thrive or shrivel depending on the level of honesty, trust and openness between board members and leaders. Team off-site events can be used to build openness and trust akin to those you get in high performing military teams using AARs.

Lessons from Business

The business need for passion and inspiration

PwC Consulting was a strongly people-focused business, with elements of passion and inspiration underpinning many leaders within the organisation. IBM, as one of the world's top brands, is highly successful by anyone's standards, but it had a very different culture. As a result of its origins this culture was naturally more focused on technology, systems and processes. PwC Consulting had strong leaders at most levels, with minimalist processes and a high degree of empowerment. Delegation and trust enabled consultants to do what was necessary to delight our customers. PwC consultants were comparatively passionate, free-spirited and relatively unwilling to follow rules and procedures, which they considered unnecessary and of limited value to the clients they served.

IBM had a very strong culture which appeared to rely more heavily on compliance with process, structures and systems into which people had to fit. An example of this reliance on transactions and process, rather than relationships, emerged in the second week after IBM had acquired PwC Consulting. My PwC colleague Keith was described by IBM HR in the USA in a brief e-mail as "a delinquent". While factually this was correct, according to the IBM definition of the word, since he was five hours late in submitting his monthly timesheet, such a term is highly offensive to someone in the UK. Moreover, it was unlikely to endear Keith to his new IBM employer, especially after he had been working unrelentingly for twelve hours a day, on a key three month crucial client project.

IBM was proud of the record speed with which it had integrated PwC Consulting and encouraged us to adopt their processes, systems and new structure. What was sad was the way in which the focus was on management, rather than passion and inspirational leadership. This clash of cultures resulted in the erosion of discretionary energy from ex PwC consultants. The unfamiliar IBM management style, combined with insufficient consultation meant that some leaders in IBM unwittingly created organisational terrorists.

Passion killers who forget the people in mergers and acquisitions

The majority of my PwC Consulting colleagues were motivated, entrepreneurial, self-starters. Our job was to act as advisors to big companies on challenging issues, such as mergers and acquisitions and to support, challenge and inspire the client's managers and leaders. It was frustrating to see so much of the practical and pragmatic leadership advice that we would give as consultants to our own clients in similar circumstances, being ignored by some of the leaders we worked with in IBM. We became angry at the comparatively ineffective leadership we were experiencing and the way that our PwC Consulting culture was swiftly and clumsily replaced by the more dominant IBM way. As my old Sergeant Major said to me, when times were tough and the soldiers were deeply unhappy: "If you can't take a joke, you shouldn't have joined. You volunteered; and if you don't like it, you know you can always leave." At first I personally tried to tough it out, in the naïve aspiration that I could change "the way things are done around here ".

I have seen this dilemma repeated by many of my current leadership coaching clients. Some leaders are recruited into very big organisations, with an impressive global reach and high profile brands. These people usually begin their job with a huge amount of passion and energy, but find they are wearing themselves down emotionally. They become exhausted like waves breaking repeatedly and ineffectually against a harbour wall. This is what was happening to me. Had I been able to use some psychometric tool that assesses self-awareness at that time, I would have recognised earlier that IBM was not a culture where my particular skills, talents and passions were best employed. Any battle between an organisation and an individual is a one-sided fight. The individual nearly always loses, when pitched against a big global company.

Every organisation has its own unique culture, established initially by the founders. It then gains a momentum and a life of its own, as the organisation grows and evolves. I made my own choice to leave and go to work for a company where there was a better personal and cultural fit. Have you ever asked yourself how well matched you are to your own organisation's culture?

The search for passion - Science Applications International Corporation (SAIC)

A very talented and respected friend of mine from PwC Consulting, who had left IBM two months previously asked me to join SAIC, just as I had come to the realisation that I would have to leave IBM. SAIC was unknown to me at that time. In my haste to move away from the discomfort of the acquisition, I did not apply all of my own principles to the transition. In particular, I did not fully research specifically how my strengths and talents could best be used in SAIC and whether the reality of the job would match the rhetoric of the head-hunter's sales pitch. I now understand more about what was going on for me and others in a similar situation in psychological terms. When working in a stressful environment, the tendency is to fight, which I did by being difficult and argumentative, or flee, which I also did by moving to another organisation. Being under stress, I failed to do my "due diligence" as to the style of leadership I would find in SAIC consulting.

SAIC was a massive US owned company with multi billion annual revenues, thousands of employees globally and was a leading provider of technical services and solutions. Like IBM, it was another highly successful and profitable business. My colleagues and I were hired to create a new, entrepreneurial management consulting part of the business in the UK. I aspired to start their first ever executive coaching business as a key component of this. Everyone makes mistakes in life. The optional yet crucial part of this process is to learn from them. Joining SAIC was my choice and the mistake was completely my responsibility. My first lesson was a reminder that it is important for me personally to work for leaders to whom I can easily relate, and who inspire me with their passion, warmth and openness. I need to be able to respect both their character and competence to trust and commit to following them.

Executive coaching was still a comparatively new profession at that time. During my job interview, my future boss had expressed enthusiasm about using me to set up a coaching business. I quickly learned that in reality, it was of little interest to SAIC. Management consulting revenue and profit was what SAIC wanted, and my leadership coaching was never properly supported. I know with the wisdom of hindsight, that for me to feel fulfilled, the kind of work I do needs to be the primary or as a minimum, the secondary, focus of the organisation I am working for. I want to be working on something that matters and to be with people who are passionate about what they do. I find it demotivating and disempowering if my profession or service line is a minor element, which does not sit easily with the main purpose of the organisation. Working in a company with a well communicated focus, clear priorities and ones that are in complete alignment with my life purpose is deeply affirming for me. I found this was missing for me in SAIC.

I also began to realise that it is important that leaders have a clear written and verbal success contract with their boss. In this contract, both sides agree what success will look like and what the outcomes will be. They must agree how success will be measured and specifically how it will be rewarded. Apart from the standard contract of employment, I realised I had not gained sufficient clarity on my psychological contract in SAIC. Finally, I was reminded that all leaders should trust their intuition. If a new job or situation seems to be "too good to be true", as this role did, then it probably is unsustainable.

On the upside, there were a number of beneficial outcomes from my seven months in SAIC. I learned about the challenges of launching an entrepreneurial executive coaching business and I identified those who were, in my opinion, the best UK coaches in our very young profession. I was able to make the transition from being a consultant to becoming a fully qualified coach within the financial security of a well-paid job. In addition, I was able to learn from, review and reflect on a wide variety of experiences acquired by consulting to the public and private sector clients, in this my third global professional service firm. I also felt comfortable that by the time I left, I had more than met my side of the bargain by bringing in considerable amounts of profitable consulting revenue. I had also delighted clients in helping them solve complex, people-based issues and maintained the professionalism and reputation of my employer.

Leadership by example
Stefan Barden
CEO Northern Foods

Stefan Barden, the CEO of Northern Foods has a particular passion for leading his organisations and his people. His values are totally in line with his role. He has an impressive leadership pedigree: a first class engineering degree from Leeds University, early development years as a leader in Unilever and an MBA from Warwick Business School. He has had the finest consultancy experience with McKinsey and Company Inc; senior leadership roles with Iceland Frozen Foods; and experience as MD of Heinz UK and Ireland. On meeting Stefan, you immediately become aware of his intelligence, passion, sense of energy and a drive to achieve significant results.

It is a powerful combination to find a leader with high IQ and also strong EQ. Stefan has those skills, and he is fascinated by the technical detail of business and also is interested to know what motivates his colleagues to succeed. He has an incisive way of distilling and identifying the key aspects of any issue, and instinctively knows what will lead to success. He uses a vast range of consultant business tools to make sense of complexity. His ability to absorb masses of information and constantly learn about successful leadership approaches means he is far more effective than many of his business peers. He is an early adopter and once he has learned specific coaching tools, he rapidly puts them into effect.

Another successful aspect of his leadership style emerged, when I facilitated meetings with his Executive Board and top teams. He is very clear when communicating his intention and is able to overcome inflexible resistance. He sets the direction for his business and knows where his True North is. He also uses a coaching and mentoring style when developing his leaders and considering succession planning. He acts as a powerful mentor to others and shares his thought processes while teaching people to use business tools that add value. Indeed, added value is a key word; he will frequently ask himself and others "where do you add value to the business?" This leads to some tough conversations about performance and he is not shy about having courageous conversations with his Managing Directors and Service Directors. For CEOs of stock market listed PLCs, skill is needed to manage main board Chairmen, Non-Executive Directors and financial analysts. Stefan makes a particular point of spending a lot of time persuading and winning over such stakeholders.

One final observation of Stefan is that leadership skills and acumen are even more important when times get tough and people look to you for calmness and reassurance. At those moments, his sense of focus, drive for high business performance and motivation pays handsomely.

4 Key Points:

- Passion has driven and inspired my teams and me in the darkest hours to the greatest successes.

- Inspiration is the generation and transfer of energy from the leader to the led, so they are enthused by that passion to achieve the most challenging tasks.

- Use After Action Reviews (AARs) to identify WWW and EBI – what went well and what would make things even better.

- Mergers and acquisitions have to be handled with sensitivity to maintain the passion and inspiration of the employees. This is when inspiring leadership adds most value.

4 Questions:

1. Have you ever asked yourself how well matched you are to your own organisation's culture?

2. What are you passionate about?

3. How will you unlock the passions of your team members?

4. Who was the most passionate and inspiring leader that you loved working for and how did they add the most value?

Multi-national Leadership

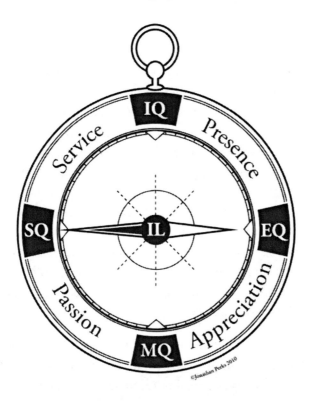

NINE

SQ - Spiritual Intelligence, Meaning & Purpose

"I've come to believe that each of us has a personal calling that's as unique as a fingerprint - and that the best way to succeed is to discover what you love and then find a way to offer it to others in the form of service, working hard, and also allowing the energy of the universe to lead you."

Oprah Winfrey

Creating my own sense of meaning and purpose

Spiritual intelligence has become very important to me in the last few years. I know personally that there is a vast difference between the levels of happiness I felt when I did not have a clear understanding of either my life purpose or what made meaning for me at work, and how I feel now. It is as if I had been standing on one bank of a fast flowing river. Earlier in my life it was foggy, and I could only see partly across the river and was unable to find a way across. Gradually as I created sense out of my life it felt as if I could see the stepping stones. Finally the sun came out and I could see the far bank in all its glory. In my early years in the Army I focused on doing the most daring, varied and interesting jobs I could. Then I became focused on promotion and attaining position and status. I expended little energy on clarifying my life purpose, nurturing a good attitude and focusing on my behaviour. On reflection, I think my inspiring leadership compass was spinning around in all directions. I simply moved from one exciting job to another.

I was forced to spend time thinking about what I really wanted to do after I left the Army and this enabled me to clarify my life meaning and purpose. Even then I was probably too focused on company brands and the positions within organisations where I wished to work. With the help of a leadership coach, I identified my own SQ and it was as if the jigsaw pieces of my working life fell into place. After that coaching, I began to move patiently from stepping stone to stepping stone across onto the far bank of the river. My course of action has become much clearer now I have criteria against which I can benchmark what I am prepared to do, and what I won't do. I liken this change to the description by Earl Nightingale[28] about a ship leaving port with a clear destination. If you set off with no clear destination, you will drift around the oceans being surprised when you crash into things and run aground. Without a clear destination to aim for, you are highly unlikely to ever make it into any harbour, other than by chance.

I have been inspired by Viktor Frankl[29] and his book *Man's search for meaning*. Based on his horrendous experiences while surviving three Nazi concentration camps, he concluded that the philosopher Friedrich Nietzsche had it right: "He who has a 'why' to live for, can bear with almost any 'how'." My fascination with why leaders do what they do and how people make meaning for themselves and those who follow them, has made SQ my 7th principal of inspiring leadership.

Definition of Spiritual Intelligence

SQ is an area of considerable interest and research at the moment. According to Zohar and Marshall,[30] SQ is "how we access our deepest meanings, purposes, and highest motivations". Spiritual intelligence is described by Tony Buzan[31] as "awareness of the world and your place in it". Within inspiring leadership, I define purpose as the object towards which you strive, or for which you exist. It is your life calling, aim or goal. Your life purpose is that which you are in service of, and it is as much about the journey as the final destination. It helps you answer the really big questions of life such as, "who am I, what is my identity?" and "why am I here on this planet?" The motivational speaker Wayne Dyer delivered some sage advice on the topic of purpose: "When I chased after money, I never had enough. When I lived my life on purpose and focused on giving of myself to everything that arrived into my life, then I was prosperous."

A few years ago, in Penna Consulting, we conducted some interesting research into what creates meaning and purpose in the workplace[32]. We carried out a survey amongst almost 1,765 UK employees based on earlier research by Roffey Park[33] and found that 70% of employees are looking for more "meaning at work". The strength of the relationship between someone's job and personal identity, seems to grow the further you rise up in an organisation. In my coaching, I have seen CEOs and Managing Directors lose their sense of meaning and purpose, or what I refer to as "True North", when they get made redundant from an organisation. We found from our survey that if firms put more effort into creating greater alignment of meaning between the Company and its people then 55% of employees said they would be more motivated, 42% would be more loyal and 32% would take more pride in their work.

The Penna research into "Meaning at Work", published in October 2005, indicates that in this "Knowledge Era" where capital resides within the individual, the ability of organisations to attract, retain and engage talented workers, would increasingly benefit from greater alignment of individual values to "corporate meaning". Penna set out to establish the definition of "meaning at work", how organisations create it and what impact it has on the individuals and the organisation.

The Penna findings concluded that "meaning" is created at the interaction of three sources – the individual, the organisation and society. At the individual level, meaning is about "a sense of self" – identity and an alignment of personal and organisational values. Approximately 1 in 5 employees said that their job plays a vital role in their view of who they are. At the organisational level, meaning comes from the sense of community created by work, the opportunity to interact with others, to contribute to, and take pride in the organisation's success. Twelve percent of the respondents put work ahead of family or social life as their primary source of community. Thirdly, meaning at work is created by an organisation's ability and desire to contribute to society in a positive way. This explains the attractiveness of working for eco-friendly organisations, and those philanthropic companies led by individuals with reputations for doing good deeds. The interaction of these three factors creates "Meaning at Work".

In Professors Reuven Bar-On and Michael Rock's ongoing research into SQ, they define it as "the ability to lead a more meaningful and fulfilling life, for ourselves and others. The process of becoming more spiritual involves first being aware of what we perceive to be fundamentally important for us and others. It then entails cultivating that which we view as important, utilising it to live a more meaningful life, as well as dedicating much of our time and energy to it. Eventually, there is an attempt to balance one's spirituality with other important aspects of our life to achieve a more fulfilling existence".

Consequences of a lack of SQ for leaders

In all the leadership coaching work I do, SQ is consistently the area which senior leaders and people in general have ignored and now wish to identify. The pattern I have observed is that between the ages of about 40 to 55, many people that I coach begin to have more of an awareness of their mortality. This may be because a close friend or relation becomes terminally ill and dies. It could also be that for successful senior leaders, the financial rewards for their success mean that their basic needs are already met. Concerns such as funding their pension, their children's education through university, or paying off their mortgage are generally already in hand. People are therefore considering what to do next in their lives. It is also the age at which their parents become older, more infirm and are in greater need their support. This mid-life period is when people start to question their life purpose and meaning, and often wonder why they should continue to do what they do. Leaders who try to avoid any discussions of SQ tend to be people who are perceived by their followers to be lacking direction and are less authentic, consistent and inspiring as role models. Henry David Thoreau, in his book *Walden* warns of the danger of a lack of SQ: "The mass of men lead lives of quiet desperation."

In my opinion, a low level of SQ for leaders is closely connected to the pace at which they live their lives. Without an awareness of the world and their place in it, the temptation is to continue to keep busy. It is almost as if we are too frightened to stop and look at ourselves in the mirror and ask "why am I doing all this?" Living life at top speed without stopping to question our intention can lead to disaster. I've been asked recently to help a number of leaders who have gone past this breakpoint. The consequences are severe and the symptoms of losing direction are too often shown by: heavy drinking, broken and dysfunctional family relationships, poor health, weight issues and even clinical depression.

A failure to address issues of SQ can lead to a loss of perspective and proportion. The result may be a tendency for even the most capable people to be drifting rudderless on the ocean of their lives with no harbour in sight. I asked one particular leader, who was struggling to cope with his life both at work and at home: "What is your life purpose?" He was completely at a loss for a reply and eventually lamely offered the suggestion: "To pay off my mortgage?" My firm reply was that there has to be more to life than that! Fortunately there is.

How can SQ help you as a leader?

There are rich rewards for those who are prepared to find answers to the awkward questions I have just mentioned. These are the key life-changing questions that don't go away. As a leader once you become clear and succinct about your meaning and purpose, the different parts of your life begin to fall into place. The benefits to you as an individual are that you will feel a greater sense of inner peace. No amount of frantic activity, or ever increasing amounts of money and material possessions, can give you a similar level of sustainable satisfaction. What accompanies this calm feeling is a more laser-like focus on the few things that really matter in life. This includes an improved ability to identify key factors that help most, when leading a high performing team to achieve successful business results.

When a leader is resolute in their life purpose and meaning, they are calmer, more grounded and balanced than people who have not paid attention to their SQ. For the cynics amongst you, I would like to remind you that I am a pragmatic Yorkshireman, with a background in both the military and business. This is not "fluffy stuff". I've had the pleasure of working with leaders with high SQ in both the military and business. It is clear to us all that some people have "got their act together" more than others. When leaders with considerable SQ speak, it is obvious that their inspiring leadership compass is steady, and there is no doubt in their mind where their True North is pointing. Having a strong sense of purpose and sticking firmly to it can be a challenging and difficult road to travel requiring courage to maintain. People have to work hard to develop a deeper respect for their purpose and integrity than they have for being popular. Stephen Green,[34] in his excellent book *Good Value - Choosing a Better Life in Business* asks: "By what star does that inner person navigate and would they even know when it is off course?"

Lessons from the Military

A clear meaning and purpose - 22 SAS

I once went on a special visit, when I worked for the head of the Army (CGS), to Hereford in Wales to see the elite British Special Air Service Regiment. We visited 22 SAS to hear about their operations in various parts of the world, especially the first Iraq war and Northern Ireland. The SAS Commanding Officer was an impressive leader and gave us an insightful commentary on what his troops were doing. This was delivered with the air of a leader who was calm, relaxed and fully in control. He had an intensity of eye contact, a succinct delivery combined with a brooding personal power and presence. He was also a leader with a very specific purpose and mission. The experience he had accumulated on previous Special Forces and infantry tours gave him wisdom beyond his years.

He showed us his men undergoing intense and very tough training for operations. We travelled with him in a vehicle which was used in the simulated assault on a terrorist house where negotiation had finally broken down. In the simulation, the hostages were to be executed in thirty minutes time by their terrorist captives. The purpose was clear. An SAS trooper used a ladder from the roof of our Range Rover to throw stun grenades and entered the building through an upper window. An officer bellowed "house clear" and we were safe to go in. The General and I were positioned on seats within the "killing room" as if we were the hostages, with five lifelike terrorist dummies armed with machine guns set up around the room. We were given explicit instructions not to move a muscle until we were tapped on the shoulder by an SAS trooper who had declared "room clear".

We were then left utterly alone and a long eerie silence descended. The lights suddenly went out; a smoke grenade was thrown into the room and red laser beams flicked about us. Within seconds these beams passed across our bodies and onto the faces of the terrorist dummies, followed by a dozen muffled shots from the black clothed troopers who had broken into the room. The lights came back on; we were given the "all safe" tap on the shoulder and permitted to move again. When I saw the bullet holes in the various terrorist targets next to me I realised that I had been the closest I ever wished to be, to death. I have a deep admiration for those who are selected to become Special Forces officers and soldiers.

After this terrifying experience the General and I were driven at break neck speed in high performance cars on twisty narrow lanes and roads. The expert drivers suddenly spun us around in "T turns and J turns" as they extracted us from unexpected simulated terrorist roadblocks. Our final destination was a massive conference room where we were given a full briefing on the latest SAS operations. My old friend David Hudson, who had powered with consummate ease through the same Para selection course as me, gave a riveting account of a highly ferocious gun battle he and his troop had had with terrorists. We heard an incredible account by an NCO who hobbled into the room. His horrific battlefield injuries exacerbated by the torture he received after his capture ensured that he would never walk properly again. He gave us the full account of exactly what had recently happened in the SAS operations in the first Gulf War. Some of this incredible tale of daring and heroism has now been included in the famous book *Bravo Two Zero*.

These men had an unwavering sense of purpose combined with fitness and courage that helped them survive many crisis situations. While publicly they may not have admitted that they were scared, frightened or uncertain of what to do, that was often how they felt. The qualities of inspiring leadership seemed to run through everything we experienced and heard about that day. The high level of trust and mutual respect that they held for each other combined with the wisdom they had gained from their experiences were vital to their success. In addition they demonstrated a passion for their job; they were humble and yet excelled at what they did.

Officers and soldiers like these fully lived the motto of: "Serve to lead". Many of these heroic people were prepared to sacrifice their own lives to save their colleagues. They had carried injured friends over long distances to escape the enemy. They showed inspiring levels of care and compassion amongst the bloodshed and violence in war. The NCO we spoke to had himself been captured by the Iraqis and put through unbearable torture for many weeks, hence his permanent disfigurement and hobbling gait. Inspiring leadership can be truly uplifting in even the most extreme conditions.

A clear sense of life purpose - Warrior Company Commander

High performing teams are galvanised by a clear sense of purpose, direction and a common set of objectives. Our impending deployment to Bosnia on my later posting gave urgency and an edge to the training and the live-firing that we were doing in the Green Howards with our Warriors. We had to select and re-train the best Green Howard infantry foot-soldiers to become drivers, gunners and vehicle commanders of the complex, expensive twenty-five tonne Warrior armoured fighting vehicles. Through ignorance, we unwittingly sometimes gave roles to individuals for which they were poorly suited. I think the Army could usefully have applied some simple psychometric tests at that time, to ensure greater success and a lower attrition rate during the training.

A two-month deployment to the Canadian prairie in the heat of summer followed this conversion training and provided us with a combination of simulated battles and live-firing attacks. Our impending deployment on peacekeeping operations in Bosnia gave a clear sense of meaning and purpose to everything that we did. All leaders were fully tested on their ability to cope with stress, pressure and became proficient at fast decision-making.

We were required to operate at times wearing respirators and full NBC (nuclear, biological and chemical) over-suits. We drove with all the hatches closed in the turret of our armoured vehicle with outside temperatures well above forty degrees, bouncing across rough prairie. I was trying to encode and decode radio messages, attempting to navigate across featureless terrain while keeping tabs on the movement of my thirteen other armoured vehicles. I simultaneously gave and received orders about the movement of the enemy. At any time, we were expecting to meet the enemy, and then I was also required to manually load the

30mm cannon and give commands to my gunner to fire as we continued travelling at top speed. Both the friendly forces and the enemy formation had laser transmitters and sensors fitted to all vehicles and our helmets. This meant that as we operated weapons systems, we could either "kill or be killed" at which point we were removed from the operation.

Attempting to make sensible decisions in such a high tempo, high stress and sleep-deprived situation was extremely challenging. Very few leaders made the right decisions all of the time. Our success or failure was highly public. In the simulated battles, we had to "live or die" by our decisions. There were many moments in the turret of my warrior when I bounced around, feeling hot, drenched in sweat and more than slightly confused about what was going on. I was conscious that everyone else in the company was relying on me to make the correct decision. That was real pressure! When I made questionable decisions, there were a lot of people who cursed me.

I learnt from this experience of leading an armoured infantry company, that there is a fine balance between intuition, and more considered, cost-benefit analysis style decision-making. There are appropriate times to use each. Some people consider that the most effective problem solving involves the ability to steadily and rationally weigh the pros and cons of a variety of options, and then consider the costs and benefits of each, before selecting the most appropriate. I agree but I also know that in achieving your purpose there can be a requirement for highly impulsive, reactive decision-making, based on wisdom, gut-feelings and intuition. This is essentially immediate problem solving under pressure. This is required from emergency hospital staff, firemen, police, fighter pilots as well as front-line combat soldiers. And it's great training for those corporate leaders working under extreme pressure!

Remaining on purpose and the least-worst option

When there was time, as officers we had also been trained to conduct a full, detailed and written analysis of the critical situations we faced. These involved identifying the purpose of our boss and, in turn, their boss. We reviewed the wider political, military, social and technical context that we were operating in. We also considered what the competition was doing and the impact of various factors such as terrain, weather and the location and availability of our friendly forces. From this, we would deduce the various options open to us, weigh the pros and cons and then recommend the best option, which would lead to the detailed plan of action. At times, it could be agonising trying to decide what exactly the right option to take was. I wondered whether my decision would eventually turn out to be correct. Often none of the available options were ideal, and therefore I had to choose the "least-worst option". Key to this was always basing my decision on the purpose outlined by the leader.

I realised the impracticality of such a detailed analysis in some high tempo situations. For example it was inappropriate when I was bouncing around in the turret of my warrior fighting vehicle. I had less than sixty seconds to make a decision and so I had no choice but to use a combination of fast decision-making plus innate intuition to select the wisest course of action to take. I gave commands, and the whole company would alter course at speed to attack the enemy from a different flank. The tempo of an advance is maintained if you can continue at the same pace yet rapidly alter course; this is vital in business leadership too. Reflecting on this simulation exercise, I realise that as leaders, army officers were processing huge amounts of information in a very short space of time. We were able to do this as a result of well-practised and finely honed training, the knowledge and experience that we had gathered and frequent use of our intuition. We always connected everything we did to our purpose or "mission".

Personally, I also realised I had finally become more in tune with my feelings and emotions (gut feeling) and followed the decisions that simply felt right. These days, as a leadership coach, I treat my intuition with great respect. When combined with experience, I find it serves me well. When I make mistakes and look back to analyse what went wrong, it is often that I have overridden my intuition and should not have trusted what was being said. It is often hard to analyse your decisions retrospectively using cost-benefit problem solving techniques. It can sometimes be hard to explain to others the logic and reasoning that made up the component parts of an intuitive decision that was made under pressure of time.

Highs from live-firing in Canada

The finale of our highly focused preparation for Bosnia was to conduct a live-firing company attack across the Canadian prairies. Our fervent hope was that we were going to manage to keep the peace between the Bosnian Serbs, Croats and Bosnian Muslims and nothing like this would ever be required. Then again, the lessons from Afghanistan taught us that we had to prepare for the unexpected.

This sort of live firing event has to be seen and experienced to be believed, and is a paradox of experiences; it was thrilling yet scary, invigorating yet energy sapping. In business is that there are similar moments during to negotiation of big deals, pitches to win new business and the completion of business-critical projects. Sometimes leaders and their teams, such as lawyers and investment bankers, work through the night and push on despite their exhaustion. These situations may involve hostile takeovers, mergers, acquisitions or large IT delivery programmes that are about to "go-live". There is real pressure, conflict, stress, unrealistic deadlines and lots at stake. This is when the most inspiring leaders are in their element.

When things go well for leaders, psychologists describe the moment as being "in the flow", or "in the zone". While I've had my share of disasters, yet leading in Canada was one of those superb "in the flow" successful moments, which I found utterly exhilarating. I learnt from this exercise in Canada that experience and thorough preparation allow a leader to cope with very demanding and complex situations for long periods of time. By the end of that day I was utterly exhausted, since I had been living on nothing but adrenaline!

Making a positive impact in the world

My life purpose is: "Inspiring leaders by supporting and challenging them so together we make a positive impact in the world". Consequently one of the most rewarding aspects of the UN peacekeeping task was the help we were able to give to shattered communities in Bosnia, allowing them a return to some kind of normality. I valued our work in helping to protect the Royal Engineers as they laid replacement water pipes, and provided electricity to the mountain villages affected by the war between Croats, Muslims and Serbs. We supported charities from the UK, which brought in desks and stationery for the town's primary school. While things would never be the same as before, within six months it was satisfying to see an element of normality returning and the market re-opening. I find that many inspiring leaders in the workplace look for ways that they and their teams can make a positive difference in communities and other charities. In that manner through their corporate social responsibility they add meaning and purpose to what they do, and to the lives of those less fortunate than themselves.

Each situation that I experienced in Bosnia required a different leadership style. Leadership often requires dealing with a variety of conflicting situations. I found myself choosing to be tough, gentle, decisive, or to pause for thought, depending which was most appropriate to the context in which I found myself. As in previous crises there were many occasions when I really was not sure what to do, and I had many anxious moments hoping that I had made the right decisions. The basic principles of inspiring leadership, in particular serving to lead, making wise decisions and using every aspect of our emotional intelligence, were relevant. At all times I was able to check my decisions against the mission to ensure I was in line with it (SQ). I constantly ask myself: "Am I living my life on purpose and where am I adding real value?"

Lessons from Business

Sense of purpose and playing the bigger game

To be an inspiring leader requires a depth of self-reflection, wisdom and philosophical curiosity. It is fundamentally important to decide what your purpose on this planet is, and what you are in service of. Ask yourself what legacy you intend to create both in your lifetime and after your death. I sometimes ask executives to write their own obituary. I ask them to focus first on what others may write about them if they were to die in the next week. Then they write a second obituary about how they would like to be remembered if they were to die five years in the future. It is often a difficult and poignant exercise and reveals some glaring gaps which people immediately want to address. The obituaries I have read in newspapers never talk about the material possessions accumulated. Instead they focus on how people related to each other and talk about the bigger game a person played, by serving others and making a difference during their time on the planet.

Recently, as our mother Tricia slowly passed away, I spent a lot of time with both my brothers Graeme and David around her hospital bed. Those days, whilst we put our working lives on hold, were poignant and special ones which I will always treasure. Our conversations ranged far and wide from the appreciation of our wives and children, to reminiscing about growing up with our unorthodox mother and how we got through the good and bad times. I laughed with David, who is now an artist and a teacher; at the inspirational words he had painted as graffiti on his bedroom wall when he was in a rebellious teenager phase. He had written "happiness is contagious; be a carrier!" These conversations highlighted for me a few simple yet paradoxically complex and profound philosophical questions. These questions involve SQ and elements of EQ such as success and happiness. They are the questions that quietly tap at your window and won't go away:

1. What is happiness?

2. If happiness is a journey rather than a destination, how do you travel the road well?

3. We know that sustained happiness comes from within us, rather than from material possessions, but how do you begin to build it?

4. If accumulating wealth allows you to do the things that matter, how much is enough?

5. What are the things that matter most to your own ongoing happiness?

6. What does success mean to you?

7. How can you personally measure success?

8. Where do you add value at work and in your life?

9. What is your life purpose; what difference can you make to other people?

I would encourage you to spend some time reflecting on these questions, since they are profound and may influence how you shape the rest of your life.

Using SQ to fine tune your business and life purpose

I am deeply indebted to Katherine Tulpa, Penna's first Senior Master Coach and Georgina Woudstra, an extremely talented coach and serial entrepreneur. They helped me set up what became a highly successful Board and Executive Coaching business within Penna Plc. Together, we created the brand, values, beliefs, identity and life purpose for our new team and our clients. These two talented leaders have since set up their own very successful coaching business called Wisdom 8 and remain some of Europe's top CEO Coaches.

In the start-up phase, the aim of Penna's coaching team became clear. We established a working environment that suited us all. We identified the behaviour we aspired to model and were looking for, in the coaches we invited to join our expanding team. We began to build up the specific skills and capabilities that Penna's board and executive coaching business needed, through careful selection of these coaches. Some of these capabilities came from the experience and coaching qualifications that our coaching associates already had, whilst others came from the courses we ran ourselves. The added benefit of these internal courses was that we created cohesion and camaraderie within the team and generated a shared set of values and beliefs.

The "team away-days" became a wonderful tool for building and reinforcing a sense of meaning and purpose. Over the last few years, we have held a number of off-site team away-days both for our clients, and separately, for our own coaching team. In every case, these events have had a significant positive impact on participants by generating greater respect, mutual understanding and forward momentum, to improve the business. These events also highlight differences between team members and allow people to express their views on the best way forward. Sometimes they show who truly adds value, and who needs to add more. We always made space in our schedule to allow creative ideas to be expressed by every member of the team. We learned an enormous amount about our individual strengths and talents and where our passions lay during these events.

When setting up our new coaching business, we developed a culture of openness, abundance and continual development of enhanced methods of coaching. We focused on developing leaders and were constantly learning about our profession ourselves. The team was highly creative and innovative; there was never a shortage of new ideas and suggestions. My challenge as the leader of this top quality team, containing other leaders, was to maintain a clear focus and sense of purpose. There was a danger that we might have dissipated our energy, by beginning work enthusiastically on a collection of new initiatives, none of which might ever have been finished. I had to develop more impulse control (something I was not especially skilled at) as well as use my assertiveness. I defended my decisions in a non-destructive way and by giving my team clear goals we often implemented fully some of the excellent suggestions that we generated.

Two of the principles of inspiring leadership, SQ and MQ were critical foundations for our success. By single-mindedly focusing on my own values and beliefs, my personal identity and my life purpose, everything became much clearer in my mind. Success components fell into place for the coaching business that I was creating with my talented team. As a leader, it was essential that I did this work with the support of someone I completely trusted, and I received this support through my own deeply experienced ICF Master Certified Coach, Carolyn Free-Pearce. I learned from feedback generated by psychometric testing and from this personal coaching and reflection. Hence, I was able to define my life purpose in a way that was sufficiently distilled to truly energise me every day.

**Carolyn Free-Pearce,
Executive Coach**

One tip I wish to share with you is that I keep a small spiral notebook, which fits in the inside pocket of my suit. In it I write down my life purpose, plus my goals for the year and the key tasks I intend to achieve each day. I'm a great fan and heavy user of my i-phone, yet also find a small spiral notebook to be invaluable. I constantly refer to this notebook throughout the day and use it as both a reminder and filter, to focus my mind on the things that matter most to me personally, and that help me be successful in the work I do with clients, and the way I build teams.

Once you have clearly defined your own life purpose and your sense of meaning, values and beliefs then you will find that you attract people with a similar calling. Together you can jointly achieve that shared outcome. Equally by the "law of attraction", there will be people who are not interested in working with you or your team. Instead they are likely to be attracted to others who share their different life purpose and interests. The paradox of inspiring leadership is that the most effective teams share similar attitudes, purpose and goals. At the same time they can contain a diversity of personality types, background, gender, ethnicity and upbringing.

We all have to learn how to judge an appropriate level of disclosure of information about ourselves as leaders. This is especially true when giving speeches, attending team meetings and in the first introductions to new acquaintances. How expressive a person is depends primarily on their personality preferences. I tend to be quite relaxed and am comfortable about sharing a lot of personal information. I have however, learned to temper this trait, depending on the level of comfort of other people with my self-disclosure. Some people prefer to guard their emotions, give very little away and wait to see what the other person does first. Only when they feel safe will they then make a gradual and selective disclosure of their personality, beliefs, attitudes, background and other personal details. Under the right circumstances as a speaker, I have found that an appropriate level of personal disclosure creates a more open and safe team environment. People often enjoy feeling a connection with someone else's life story because we can say to ourselves: "Yes, me too!"

The purpose of the leader

A common theme in the best teams which I have worked with is that much depends upon the careful selection of the leader. You can have the finest collection of individuals, yet when it has a weak leader with a large ego and fragile self-confidence, the team invariably underperforms. It remains a loosely grouped collection of capable individuals, rather than becoming an integrated, efficient team. The job of the leader is to deal in change, set a compelling vision and to align everyone behind its implementation. Leaders with high levels of SQ empower those they lead by creating meaning in what they do. This releases everyone's energy in service of something bigger than themselves. To be truly authentic, a leader needs humility and they have to be both strong and yet prepared to admit when they are wrong or don't know something. Such a leader is of inestimable value to organisations.

The best leaders use strongly held personal values and beliefs to create a clear purpose and sense of meaning in the work place. They can then define the reason as to why their organisation exists. Inspiring leaders generate a common purpose and espouse it with an infectious passion. The team's sense of purpose and meaning initially comes from the leader.

They must genuinely care about the organisation's raison d'être with an intense energy and a burning desire to fulfil its purpose. Without a clear, aligned sense of direction, a team will drift back into individualism. "Those who stand for nothing, fall for everything."

Intent

A clear mission or intent, communicated with clarity, is what all team members need from their leader. A focus for the team combined with an unambiguous intent behind the various projects is a powerful recipe for success. Team members need an answer to the question: "Exactly what do you want me to do and what does success look like?" To communicate succinctly the expected outcome and specifically how success will be measured is vital. "Intent and purpose" are two words which are very closely linked. For me the first provides a tactical day-to-day aim and focus, whilst the second gives the overarching strategy and reason for the team to exist.

Creating meaning and purpose at work

I've been involved in research carried out by Penna and have spoken at conferences about what creates meaning and purpose for people in their work. As a result of the research that Gallup did, we now know that "people join good organisations, but leave poor managers". SQ raises three fundamental questions:

1. What is your life purpose?

2. What makes meaning for you?

3. How can you create a sense of meaning and purpose for the people you lead?

I can usually tell when I'm coaching whether those three questions have been addressed. Where they have, people have a greater sense of calmness, purpose, focus and energy. Equally when I'm with leaders and groups who have never paused to consider aspects of their spirituality, I sometimes detect a sense of superficiality, busyness without direction, fear, anxiety and stress. When a leader has a sense of life purpose and sense of spirituality, they also have a healthy amount of self-regard and self-esteem, which may or may not come from a religious faith. By spirituality I mean the creation of personal meaning and purpose. Penna's research was focused on finding and creating greater "meaning at work". From it, we found that there were some common requirements for people to be energised relating to themselves as individuals, the organisation and society:

The individual requires:

- A sense of "self" – and the space to be oneself

- Balance between work and non-work life

- Harmony between personal values and those of the organisation in which they work

Within an organisation, there is a requirement for:

A sense of community at work – the opportunity to feel part of something bigger than themselves

- The opportunity to interact with others

- The opportunity to contribute to the organisation's success

- A manager or leader who helps create meaning for them individually

- In society people like to feel they:

- Have an opportunity to contribute to society

- Work for an organisation with a strong sense of corporate responsibility

What is now apparent to me is that when someone's job aligns with their individual purpose, these people give far more discretionary life energy to what they do. The result is they become happier, more contented individuals, who act as a positive influence on their colleagues. This also encourages high levels of integrity and trust to develop, and consequently people feel more able to challenge unhealthy behaviour openly.

Leading from the front
General Sir Richard Dannatt

One of the greatest mentors and leaders that I have worked for is General Sir Richard Dannatt. He is one of the military role models who still remains an inspiration for me, since he is someone who unconsciously lives the values of inspiring leadership. His recent book on his own experience and leadership views is compulsive reading and is titled: *Leading from the Front*. I first worked with him when I was a 28 year old Major commanding an airmobile company, and he was a Lieutenant Colonel and the Commanding Officer of the 1st Battalion the Green Howards. In the last twenty years, he has risen through all the most demanding leadership roles to become Head of the British Army, before moving into a second career as a high profile military advisor, author and inspiring leadership speaker.

Richard retains his humble excellence irrespective of his personal bravery and achievements. Inspite of his frenetic work schedule, he still has an ability to connect intimately with people he meets and be genuinely interested in his team and work tirelessly to help them succeed. He is a man who cared deeply for those he led. Not many jobs require people to die alongside those they lead; he has been close to death on a number of occasions. He saw two of his men die beside him as victims to a hidden IRA sniper. He survived a potentially lethal car crash and had a minor stroke.

He gained international respect recently when he publicly made a stand against the British Government to fight for more resources for soldiers who were dying in Afghanistan. Such a spirited stance was one based on high integrity, strong values and beliefs, and the trust which he had built as part of the psychological contract. He championed the creation of the Military Covenant with the soldiers across the whole of the Army. This highlighted that while a soldier is required to be prepared to die in service of their country they had a right for certain kinds of support from the country in return. Due to his stand, Army officers and soldiers are held in very high regard in the United Kingdom; this is not true in many other countries.

General Dannatt made a point of connecting deeply on a personal level with everyone when he met them. He and his wife Pippa are able to chat with people from any walk of life. They are good at keeping in touch with a vast range of friends and contacts around the country. He is unusual in that he has "the double blue" of both a high IQ and a very well developed emotional intelligence (EQ). He is a man who has lived his life on purpose (SQ) and has strong personal values and a strong faith (MQ). In many ways, he is the fully integrated inspiring leader since he has an intensity of quiet presence, appreciates those who are talented and do good work, is passionate about his calling and serves to lead.

4 Key Points:

- SQ is about: "How we access our deepest meanings, purposes, and highest motivations".

- Consider how Friedrich Nietzsche's quote resonates with you: "He who has a 'why' to live for, can bear with almost any 'how'."

- In my military experience, having a clear intent, mission and purpose gave unquestionable focus.

- Penna Consulting's research into what creates meaning and purpose at work is worth studying.

4 Questions:

1. Where do you add value at work and in your life?

2. What is your life purpose?

3. What difference can you make to other people?

4. How will you create greater meaning and purpose for the people you are honoured to lead?

Managing Director

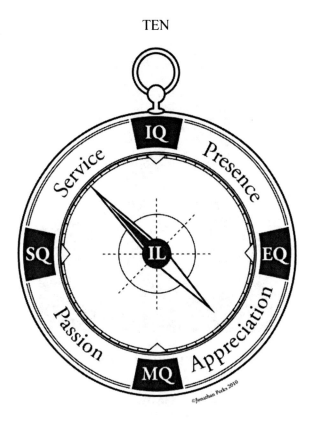

TEN

Service - Serve to Lead

"The best way to find yourself is to lose yourself in the service of others."

Mohandas K. Gandhi

Serving others
John Hackett
HSBC

John Hackett is responsible for 12,000 people in HSBC as the UK's regional head of service delivery operations. In many ways he exhibits the qualities of inspiring leadership. He has 26 years' service with the Midland Bank and HSBC. In his early years, before becoming a branch manager, he learned many of his leadership skills as an officer in the Territorial Army. He recognises the Army Officers' motto of "serving to lead" and aspires to lead by personal example. He has always followed the philosophy of servant leadership. When rising up through the bank, having begun his career as a bank clerk, service was his watchword. He got the job done, without complaint, however humble or trivial his task was.

In his words: "Service is about doing things for other people and going the extra mile for them. Often tasks are menial or unpleasant but somebody has to do them. I turned my hand to whatever was required from opening up the office very early for a customer, to closing very late, to distributing the morning post and cleaning dog mess off the front steps." When working with him and eight of his colleagues in a virtual, global project team, I noticed how effective he is in a team situation and in serving others.

John lives a life on purpose and spends time with his wife every year in January setting up personal and professional goals for the next one, five and ten years. He constantly sets out to answer the question: "How can I be of service?" In addition to a very demanding day job, John serves others by growing leaders more widely. As a mentor for HSBC's aspiring leaders' programme, he found himself with colleagues on a service project in the Brazilian jungle. When talking with locals they were helping, he found they lived on less than $200 a year. In a wonderful challenge to our manic lifestyle and distorted priorities, the locals considered that John and the other Westerners were poor compared to them, since they spent so little time building relationships with their own families and instead spent too long at work. This was a similar message to the one I received in Nepal.

As a small example of John's inspiring leadership style, he makes a point of finding someone to appreciate and compliment once each day for the way they serve their customers. He began a programme called "casting starfish". Junior managers recommended to John the staff that had produced exceptional service for others. He and his managers then made a point of speaking to those nominated employees, to thank them for their service. Firstly, the member of staff (who then wore a small golden starfish badge) came away feeling valued and more motivated. Secondly, the managers themselves were lifted and enthused by the interaction with a member of staff. All were able to see the difference that people can make by providing exceptional service to colleagues or customers. John based the service initiative on the star fish story by Loren Eisley[35] which I retell here in one of its various permutations:

"One day a man was walking along the beach when he noticed a boy picking something up and gently throwing it into the ocean. Approaching the boy, he asked, 'What are you doing?'

The youth replied, "Throwing starfish back into the ocean. The surf is up and the tide is going out. If I don't throw them back, they'll die.'

'Son,' the man said, 'don't you realise there are miles and miles of beach and hundreds of starfish? You can't make a difference!'

After listening politely, the boy bent down, picked up another starfish, and threw it back into the surf. Then, smiling at the man, he said...
'I made a difference for that one'. "

The 8th principle of inspiring leadership is drawn from my training on the RMAS motto of "serve to lead" but also from my mother's accounts of my father's sense of service to the pilots he led and the country he served and died for. Finally it is inspired by my powerful drive to help serve others as individuals, in teams and organisations in order to make a difference.

Definition of Service

For the first twenty years of my working life, I was trained to follow the motto "serve to lead" after joining the Royal Military Academy Sandhurst in the UK. RMAS issues all officer cadets with a little red book called *Serve to Lead (An Anthology)*. It contains inspiring tips on how to lead well. Service is giving of yourself to over-deliver, in the way you lead teams, and in the support you provide customers, so they know you really care and genuinely put them first. Field Marshal the Lord Slim[36] captured this Army motto of service well:

"Unselfishness, as far as you are concerned, means simply this - you will put first the honour and interests of your country and your regiment; next you will put the safety, well-being and comfort of your men; and last – and last all the time – you will put your own interest, your own safety, your own comfort."

In the Army, I was taught to tend to the comfort of those I led before my own needs. I was also reminded that a leader should "go there first" and not ask others to do things they had not, or would not do themselves. General Sir John Hackett[37] (no family connection to John in HSBC) encouraged people to be servant leaders with the following advice:

"I said that leadership was concerned with getting people to do things. What I meant was getting them 'to do things willingly'. What then must there be to a leader if he is to secure this willing acceptance of what he wants? He must be able to offer to those under him what they need. First of all, they need direction in the execution of a common enterprise. But they have other needs and these of course will vary. It may be courage when they are afraid. It may be perception when they are muddled and confused. He must give them this. But above all, he must be able to take upon himself some part of their trouble and so help to secure their release from a burden which can be intolerable. He must be the possessor of qualities which are relevant to the task with which his men are concerned; skills and qualities which they respect. Even at the lowest level of military leadership, the leader may not have all the relevant skills. It does not matter: what the group wants is a leader not a paragon.

He must be able to manage fear, first in himself for if he cannot, then his leadership must begin to fail: but in others also, for otherwise they may collapse. He must also be able to manage failure as well as success, for failure is seldom final and the man helped on from one failure may well fail no more. The personal qualities required are not found everywhere. A few people are born with them but too few for the Army, as for any other enterprise where leadership is wanted. Men who might be leaders have therefore to be sought out, and then trained and helped to form the habit of acting as the leader should."

Consequences of a lack of service in leaders

When leaders are not imbued with the values and attitudes of serving to lead, they can appear to be selfish. Seeking to pursue their own interests before those of others, chasing personal promotion at all costs can lead to an erosion of others' trust in them. It also turns the organisation into a toxic and unhelpfully political environment. The symptoms of this sort of behaviour are manifest in e-mails copied openly (or secretly) to a large number of other people, especially bosses. Leaders with this selfish approach can indirectly generate a number of "organisational terrorists". The erosion of service to the organisation, customers and the team will result in a mindset of "everyone for themselves".

A lack of a service ethos also results in a splintered and fragmented team, where backbiting and point scoring behaviour emerges. It becomes an unsafe environment where people don't feel they can have honest or open conversations. Instead people meet in clandestine ways. Not only do followers criticise the selfish leader, but they begin to heap criticism upon the whole organisation. They start to withdraw their discretionary energy and unofficially "work to rule". If a leader has strong intuition, they will know that something is wrong. They will sense that their team members are unhappy yet may not be able to bring the problem into the open. Ultimately, as in far too many teams, interactions cease to be relationship-based and leadership becomes purely transactional.

How can service help you as a leader?

Leading by example does not mean that you do every job yourself and fail to delegate anything. It is completely the opposite. You need, on occasion, to demonstrate that you have at some time in your career completed similar roles to those being done by your subordinates. Equally important you need to prove occasionally that you are prepared to do the most demeaning or unpopular tasks, which is helpful. Lao Tzu (Father of Taoism) spoke of the way a leader serves his team by inspiring them to achieve greatness: "The bad leader is he whom the people despise; the good leader is he whom the people praise; the great leader is he of whom the people say 'we did it ourselves'." Serving others is all about putting the team and the organisation before many of your own needs and is especially important if you want your team to follow you willingly. While developing this approach I would add the caveat that you should be mindful not to become a rescuer who sees everyone else as victims, and don't completely ignore your own basic needs.

In business, you will not be required to die in the service of those you lead. However, we should be prepared to lose our jobs by standing up for our values at critical moments and acting with integrity. When it comes to it, few leaders are genuinely prepared to do that. Some people call these moments "crucible moments" and they shape the way a leader develops in response to these major events and decisions. I have previously described a couple of personal crucible moments in my life such as the Para training and live-firing warrior company attacks in Canada. Both were about serving and leading others when I was struggling to survive myself. The Nobel Peace prize theologian Albert Schweitzer said: "I don't know what your destiny will be, but one thing I know: the only ones among you who will be truly happy are those who have sought and found how to serve."

When your team knows that you are motivated by a sense of service they follow your example. Service is an attitude of mind and is one route to happiness. A genuine attitude of service to customers and clients is always apparent. Sadly, it is an attitude that is not as prevalent as it could be and is therefore highly prized. Such exceptional service is the route to repeat business, referrals and long-term profitable relationships.

Lessons from the Military

The Royal Military Academy Sandhurst

When I joined the British Army as an Officer Cadet in 1980, you couldn't find a more macho and masculine environment, especially at its world renowned leadership development centre: the Royal Military Academy at Sandhurst (RMAS). It was here at the age of eighteen that I spent almost two years studying the theory, art and practice of leadership. This was a gift that I have always valued. Even amongst the best global brands that I work with, no company comes close to this level of investment and commitment. Indeed in my twenty years as an officer, I calculated that the British Army invested hundreds of thousand pounds specifically on my continued training and leadership development. I'm sure the cynics among you would ask "is it worth it?" I believe it is. The price of leadership incompetence and ignorance is too high to pay. On military operations, you cannot put a price on the loss of one man's life and the consequences of indecision. Military operations demand a particular style of leadership, and this has to be learned. Some aspects of military leadership are too extreme to translate into civilian situations. There are many military qualities, however, which have become foundations of the inspiring leadership model.

I'm sure that it was a deliberate caricature, and rather tongue-in-cheek, when my Non Commissioned Officer (NCO) instructor met me at the front door to New College at RMAS. He took the suitcase from my mother and told me: "Say goodbye now lad, I'm your mother now!" However, everything did change for me. When I went through the "de-civilianisation process", I received quite a shock. My rigorous training was vastly different to the gentle, thoughtful, kind upbringing that I was used to. The theory was that in order to bond a diverse group of civilians together and weld them into a tightly knit team of budding junior leaders, they first have to have a common enemy. That enemy was to be our Captain and the NCO instructors. To survive in that environment and on harsh operations around the world, I had to learn to be robust and override certain feelings and emotions. It was only later, as I started to bring up two daughters, and then again as I re-trained to become a leadership coach, that I started to rediscover and employ my "soft power" effectively. These softer skills with an appropriate use of my military "hard power" make a much more powerful combination when used in leadership roles. Today, I coach the best business leaders to combine both hard and soft power.

Serve to lead

As an officer, it is expected that you would not ask those you lead to do anything that you are not capable of doing yourself. Often, you are expected to lead by example and go first into the most threatening situations. This is probably the most dangerous position to be in and requires a huge amount of courage. As a leader, you usually have greater knowledge of the facts and have done some sort of analysis of the situation. That means that you understand far more about the risks involved than the people you are leading. When on active operations in dangerous parts of the world, as an officer you have to share the same hardships as those you lead. There is no place for arrogance or superiority. As a military leader you have to be with your soldiers on operations or in the field of battle. Sharing every experience and genuinely looking after your soldiers while maintaining the ability to lead, is a true test of leadership skills. Serving to lead is also vital to excellent leadership in business.

When you receive your Queen's commission as a British Army officer, the psychological contract is that you may well have to die leading those for whom you are responsible. With the exception of the police and firemen, none of the businesses I work with expect that of their employees. However, in business, the daily casualties are those who are made redundant. In order to keep profits up and costs down especially in times of recession, some leaders (such as CFOs) also tend to want to "sweat their assets" more than usual. It can be harsh for those who give their all for their firm to find themselves being made redundant.

Service in senior leadership roles: Army Staff College

I realise why the Armed Forces have a well-earned reputation for some of the best leadership training in the world. Whether soldiers, SAS leaders, staff officers or Generals, the wisdom of the decisions people make have a profound effect on the welfare and lives of the many other people we serve. I feel that much of my Army experience has been of service and value to society. In particular, we focussed on serving others on peacekeeping operations, supporting the civil community, being on counter terrorism operations and training other leaders to make a difference in the world.

I worked hard to be selected for the Army Staff College at Camberley. In 1994 a diverse selection of 180 officers gathered at the Army Staff College to be trained as to the ethos of service. While the majority were from various army Regiments and Corps, we also had officers from many other nations as well as the Navy and RAF. These two years of intense leadership training were often referred to as "the junior General's course". Undoubtedly, the course was excellent preparation for the majority of senior leadership roles in both the military and business. The first year focused heavily on making us into technical staff officers in service to politicians. We learnt about the complexity of procurement of new equipment and weapons systems. This didn't play to my talents, and I can't say I found this year exciting. Nor was procurement something I wished to do more of in the future. It's often just as useful to know which career paths you don't wish to pursue, as it is to identify which ones do excite you. Throughout our staff college training the importance of being in service to our country, to our government and to the people we lead, was strongly reinforced.

Special leadership qualities

Looking back at the photographs of the Army Staff College course, I realise that I was working with a very talented and impressive peer group. Many have risen to the top levels in the British Army, or their own armed forces (for those who were from overseas nations). In addition, a large number have also been successful in business. I have thought about the qualities that marked out the more capable leaders and realise that they tended to have an unshakable and powerful self-confidence combined with modesty. They have an ability to listen intently, summarise and succinctly pinpoint issues and options, and recommend the best approach to take. The best leaders have strong values, beliefs and integrity and are able to connect with a variety of different people. They invariably have a powerful personal presence and often "look the part".

Being intelligent with a sharp mind is never enough on its own. Officers whose main skill is high IQ were sometimes referred to in a deprecating manner as NANS (not allowed near soldiers). People like this were more usefully employed in difficult, theoretical and technical staff officer roles. The best and brightest leaders also need strong interpersonal skills and well developed emotional intelligence. The secret to success is to be in service to something and someone larger than you. Serving to lead others; your country, your company and your team is what marks out the finest inspiring leaders.

Lessons from Business

Service - Recruiting and leading an army of giants

I have benefited enormously from my time working in different businesses after I left the Army, particularly from my six years in Penna Consulting. Before I set up my own global leadership coaching practice, I was exposed to alternative perspectives and leadership techniques. I recruited, led and managed a large and diverse collection of some of the finest executive coaches across Europe. I deliberately set out to surround myself with an army of giants. These were individuals who were impressive leaders in their own right and who were each metaphorically a couple of inches taller than me in the skills they possessed. I therefore created my own paradox; on the one hand, I wanted leadership coaches in my team who were highly independent, entrepreneurial self-starters. They were required to sell, design and deliver high quality coaching, and delight clients. Yet on the other hand, I needed these people to be collaborative, generous spirited and to work together as a "best team" on the larger tenders and proposal work, without a clash of egos. This combination is hard to achieve and very difficult to find.

The clients that we coached were CEOs, executive board members, Partners, Managing Directors and leaders of UK Government Departments and the world's top global brands. My challenge was that in wishing to lead and shape the development of this loose collection of free spirits, I had to recognise that any one of them had an equal capability, right and ambition to be the Managing Director instead of me. Being a leader amongst leaders who themselves develop and coach other leaders is a similar challenge to that of being an officer leading a large group of fellow officers. It is clear when the decisions you make are good and when they are mediocre and there is little tolerance for failing. The antidote is to apply the qualities of inspiring leadership. This involves always aspiring to serve to lead, being fully present with colleagues, appreciating their talents and committing yourself with total passion.

By aiming to live the values of inspiring leadership myself, both in the way I led the team and coached clients, I realised I was setting myself very high expectations. It is emotionally draining when you open yourself up to scrutiny from your peers. In leadership development, consulting and executive coaching businesses, you must match, or surpass the standards of serving others that you espouse for your clients. I am conscious that I could have been a better servant leader and made wiser decisions, however I was determined not to face mutterings of hypocrisy. Rather, I tried to lead by example in a way that advertised and marketed the difference we could make when acting as trusted advisors and catalysts for our client's change. That is why serving to lead and humble excellence became such an apt philosophy for Penna's board and executive coaching team. We wished to live by Gandhi's philosophy and "be the change you want to see in the world".

During my time as a Managing Director at Penna, the pragmatist in me knew that as an inspiring leader, I had to utilise all my skills and take greater accountability, especially in recruiting, managing and serving some of the top coaches in Europe. I had to overcome a number of challenges and the spirit of service to both the team and our clients was paramount.

Serving to lead
Major General John Stokoe
Royal Signals and BT

Major General John Stokoe CB CBE was a senior army officer up until 1999, managing change programmes and creating and implementing army-wide policy in the Ministry of Defence. He then took up a command role with one hundred thousand soldiers worldwide. On leaving the armed forces, he became Managing Director of a business unit in Amey Support Services and in 2003 joined Lend Lease Corporation as Director of Corporate Affairs and Marketing for the UK, Europe and the Middle East. He became Director of Defence and Security with the BT Group in 2006 and is now the Vice President/Managing Director BT National Government Division.

John has an energy, passion and sense of fun about him. This is combined with a talent for using his personal power and presence to inspire and warmly relate with those he meets. He achieved the unusual feat of being promoted all the way from private soldier (Signalman) to Major General. Yet he still maintains a wonderful sense of modesty and is a great example of the paradox of humble excellence. Such humility is an important aspect of serving to lead. His personal example of servant leadership became legendary on an escape and evasion exercise. As the commanding officer, he insisted on being treated in exactly the same way as every other member of the Regiment. Consequently, he was put through the same three days of intense physical depravation on limited food and water, lack of sleep and was kept in a barbed wire camp. During this time he had a recurrence of an earlier attack of malaria, and the doctor recommended him to be returned to camp. This he refused. It would have been against his strong leadership values and beliefs to make his Regiment undertake training that he had not personally experienced, and he was determined to go through the same hardships as his men. Instead, all he asked for was a plastic bin bag so he could sweat-out his illness and remain in the barbed wire forest camp with those he led.

He then led his men with considerable skill and courage, on foot for over 120 miles. This distance was travelled while he was escaping and evading from the Hunter Force that was determined to capture such a prestigious Commanding Officer. There were many close shaves and tense moments. He made it all the way to the border with his three colleagues and helped them swim across a lake at night to safety on the far side. He was then deliberately betrayed by me (as exercise controller) to ensure that he was captured by local partisans. He was also put through the mandatory interrogation training like all his other "prone to capture" EW soldiers. Despite the fact that he was weakened by the malaria, he still refused to give anything away whilst under interrogation. He looked for the good in others, was always immaculately turned out, led by personal example and remains a man of the highest values and integrity. He was powerful model to us all of leading by example, serving to lead and inspiring leadership.

When I recently asked John what was his leadership philosophy, he said these words: "To me, leadership is a very personal matter: it cannot be taught, though principles can be imparted; it cannot be assumed with the mantle of authority invested by position. It is an affair of the heart. At the heart of the way I operate, both now in business and when I was a serving soldier, are the very people for whom I am responsible and on whom the organisation depends for success. Knowing them, their strengths and weaknesses, their desires and fears, is fundamental to enabling them to give of their best. Deep down all individuals want to do well - and the environment to do just that is created by leaders who know, respect and encourage their people."

4 Key Points:

- Service is giving of yourself to over-deliver, in the way you lead teams, and in the support you provide customers, so they know you really care and genuinely put them first.

- A lack of a service ethos results in a splintered and fragmented team, with backbiting and individuals seeking to score points over each other.

- As an army officer, or business leader it is expected that you would not ask those you lead to do anything that you are not capable of doing yourself. Often you are expected to lead by example and go first into the most threatening situations.

- Excellent service in business is one of the biggest differentiators and ensures greater repeat business and loyal clients. They buy you and everything you stand for; you don't need to sell.

4 Questions:

1. In whose life have you made a difference?

2. What does a sense of service and sacrifice mean to you?

3. How will you serve your team more and so lead them with humility?

4. Who is your best role-model of serving to lead other people?

The winning team that set the Cyprus Walkabout record

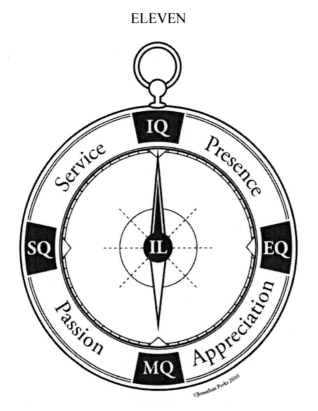

ELEVEN

The Integrated Inspiring Leader - Conclusion

"If you don't design your own life plan, chances are you'll fall into someone else's plan. And guess what they have planned for you? Not much."

Jim Rohn: American entrepreneur, author, and motivational speaker

Bringing it all together

If we could bring together all 8 principles that I have discussed, then we would become more integrated inspiring leaders. Integration of all qualities would also mean that we could bring an attitude of inspiring leadership to all parts of our lives and avoid compartmentalising it. The reality, however, is that we are imperfect humans who frequently make mistakes and fall short again and again. Luckily, most of us don't give up, since we are fuelled by hope for a more ideal world, and aspire to make a difference by the way we lead.

The dangers of complacency

If we do not continually work towards being more fully integrated as leaders, we develop shortcomings in too many of the 8 principles. We are then in danger of "dis-integrating" and becoming a manager who is mistrusted. Other people will only follow such managers, because they have to comply rather than because they willingly commit themselves. In the 1987 film *Wall Street*, Michael Douglas played the ambitious character Gordon Gecko who epitomised the dis-integrated leader. His mantra was "greed is good", sadly his amoral, ruthless and uncaring approach exists in some business managers I come across today. These people leave a wake of destruction and emotionally broken people behind them. I believe there has to be a more sustainable way of inspiring other people according to a pragmatic set of principles. This is the reason why this book on inspiring leadership was written.

Reflection

While writing this book, I sought to balance the stories and lessons from my time in the military and business. Understandably, I have a far greater wealth of material to draw upon from my military experiences. However, I also came to the stark realisation that I have also found a shortage of integrated inspiring leaders in business.

Why is that, I wondered? It is my view that the military invests a huge amount of money, time and resources training leaders to ensure they are fit to lead in the most challenging of circumstances. In contrast, most businesses spend very little time, money and resources on training and developing leaders. Their focus is too often on the short-term need to make ever more profit by increasing sales, cutting costs and pushing up share price. Very little is invested in the long-term growth and future of the people who help sustainable business growth. Some leaders who focus almost purely on financial data know only, as Oscar Wilde said: "The price of everything and the value of nothing." They think training and development coaching is too expensive. However if they think such education is expensive, they should consider the cost of ignorance! As a consequence of such reluctance to invest in the development of future leaders, those promoted into positions of responsibility are sometimes ill prepared. People don't cope well with the stresses and strains of leading a diverse and complex group without preparation for the challenge of leadership. Everyone suffers in the long term; leaders, employees, clients and business profitability. This critical situation therefore strengthens my resolve to fulfil my own life purpose.

Lessons in navigating through life- Cyprus Mountain Marathon

The following story shows how it is possible to combine the 8 principles of inspiring leadership in an integrated manner. As a young officer, I hankered after more challenging leadership opportunities and so accepted an invitation to spend time with one of the British Army's most prestigious Regiments, the Scots Guards. I spent two amazing years as Platoon Commander with the 2nd Battalion Scots Guards, just after they had returned from the 1982 Falklands War. There were many harsh and tough leadership lessons that they had learnt and which they willingly taught me. I had a very steep learning curve as a twenty-two year old officer leading Guardsmen who, unlike me, had already been into battle. They had seen fear, hatred and faced terror, death and mutilation. With the memories of war on their minds both the Commanding Officers that I served with kept the readiness of the Battalion high, so that we were ready should the Scots Guards be required to go on active duty again. Their favourite saying, forged from wartime experience, was "be prepared for the unexpected". This motto has served me well throughout my life as a leader in the Army and in business.

Appreciating those you lead

I believed even at that time, that when people care for each other, almost any loose collection of diverse individuals could be made into a successful team. I developed a "little black book" in which I kept details of every one of my Guardsmen. I was genuinely interested in them and learnt about their wives, found out their children's names, which football teams they followed, what other interests they had, and what their personal talents, strengths and areas for development were. I was initially teased about this book by the other Guards Platoon Commanders. I learnt later it was because they felt that I was showing them up. They felt others may deduce that they did not care enough about their own Guardsmen, nor appreciate what motivated and inspired them. Eventually, discreetly other Scots Guards officers started to build up their own little black books and showed authentic interest and appreciation for the Guardsmen they led.

One conversation that I witnessed had a lasting impact on me. Early one morning, a Guardsman timidly approached his Platoon Commander. In a stuttering voice, he sought advice about what he should do now that he had just learned that his girlfriend in Scotland was pregnant. The officer concerned was a wealthy, well-connected member of the English aristocracy. Sadly, he lacked an appreciation of his men and had minimal emotional intelligence. Unfortunately his reply to the anxious Guardsman, who had taken a considerable amount of courage to raise the topic, was blunt. He said: "Don't bother me with your trivia, can't you see I'm busy!" The consequence of this act of uncaring leadership was that all the Guardsmen ostracised him and were quietly reluctant to follow him ever again. Other officers found it hard to relate to his way of mistreating those he led. Shortly afterwards the officer was posted to another job and then left the Army. What a tragedy that in those days there was no benchmarking, or emotional and social intelligence development, nor any executive coaches to help improve the leadership qualities of some of these highly trained yet misguided and potentially capable officers.

Intelligence and wisdom

While with the Scots Guards, I also learnt a tough personal lesson about the consequences of arrogance. We were embarking on the prestigious annual inter-platoon competition, and the organisers intended to make it brutal and challenging, to match their recent experiences in the Falklands War. At the time, I considered myself to be a very fit runner. Even in the midday heat of 40°C in Cyprus, where we were based, I thought I would find the forced march and subsequent platoon tasks easily within my capability. I was wrong. The 10-mile march was done at a very fast pace. We ran and speed marched with a very heavy load of personal equipment up and down hills, to the summit of a small mountain. I kept the platoon's morale and humour high for the first 5 miles. Then as my radio operator struggled, I offered to carry his radio. In a moment of further madness, I also decided to carry the machine gun for another struggling Guardsman.

Loaded down with this extra kit, it was not long before I was struck mute and unable to inspire myself, let alone thirty other Scots Guardsmen. My wise platoon sergeant, a veteran of the war, had the equipment redistributed and whispered quietly in my ear: "Please don't do anything stupid like that again, sir. The Guardsmen need officers to keep their energy for thinking straight and making the right leadership decisions, when they are all exhausted and can't think for themselves." Sure enough on completing the march, I was given a series of stretching, intellectually demanding problems to solve. I realised just how inexperienced I was and that I really had not mastered my profession as an infantry leader.

I was determined to become a more skilled leader and to fully study the science and complexity of my job. I realised I had not fully embedded my own essential principles of leadership. From that day forward, I aimed to become a leader who could bring out the finest qualities in those who followed me. I also realised that I had to acquire wisdom not only from my own experiences but also to listen to the advice of other mentors while I had little experience to fall back on.

The Challenge, the Cyprus Walkabout

My next challenge in Cyprus was to run a double mountain marathon. The misnamed "Cyprus Walkabout" is the highlight of the sporting year on the Island and comprises two mountain marathons rolled into one. Taking place in the relative cool of October, it is a rugged two-day orienteering ordeal covering a total of 70 miles up the 6,000 foot high Mount Troodos and back down to Episkopi. Military competitors from all parts of the world still vie to take part. As an extreme sport, it always attracts a very strong field of the world's fittest mountain marathon runners. On the two successive years I competed in this competition, it undoubtedly provided one of the most challenging tests of physical endurance, mental strength and team spirit for members of the Scots Guards and rivals from other nations. The competition was designed to test navigational skills and route selection under intense physical and mental pressure. It also taught me many lessons as a leader which I have applied and taught to others throughout my life.

Serving to lead – meeting the task, team and individual needs

I have been brought up since my training at RMA Sandhurst on the leadership theory of John Adair. This highlights the importance of balancing the three competing needs of the task, team and individual. So in preparing to win the walkabout competition, I had a clear task with specific objectives. We built up a team of thirty of the toughest and fittest men in the 2nd Battalion Scots Guards, supported by excellent administration from the battalion. We trained hard and also partied hard together, and so built very strong bonds and a sense of camaraderie. There was nothing I asked of my team that I wouldn't do myself too.

The majority of soldiers in the team had returned from fighting in the Falklands War. There were also men who had served in the Foreign Legion, the Guards Parachute Pathfinder Platoon and in the SAS. They willingly shared their invaluable experiences, and their professionalism permeated our team. I learned from them about the tougher side of life. Some of the team had been brought up by violent, abusive fathers, had lived amongst the meths drinkers and drug addicts in Glasgow, had been to jail, and had failed many times in their lives. These soldiers had seen limb-less men screaming with agony on the battlefield, friends shot down before their eyes, had themselves bayoneted the enemy in the freezing cold, wet and dark. They had watched officers freeze-up in moments of indecision on the battlefield. They had pushed themselves way beyond the point of utter exhaustion. Also they had felt the complete range of emotions from despair and fear to the ecstasy of victory. How could I match that?

As a young officer being amongst such men put me on a very steep learning curve. The experience made me realise the importance of getting to know the strengths and weaknesses of each individual member of the team. As a result, I made a point of building intimacy and trust with each soldier in turn. I listened a lot and asked questions to try to get an understanding of their hopes, fears, feelings and aspirations. Sometimes I got it right, and at other times I got it wrong. I always learned from my mistakes and aimed to be a better leader on the next occasion. I travelled an emotional roller coaster. Sometimes I felt doubt and anxiety over how I should best lead such a hardened group, and at other times I savoured the elation from our successes. Serving to lead others means earning the right to lead by looking after the team and the individuals in it.

Sponsorship and support

At the time in this Battalion, I was fortunate to be amongst a very high calibre group of officers. They would continue to undertake a wide variety of challenging leadership roles throughout their lives. In the first year, the Scots Guards Commanding Officer (later to become Major General Michael Scott CB CBE DSO) gave us the task of getting as many teams as we could to finish in the top 10 of the competition. In the first year, our team was managed by a bright, dynamic and maverick officer called Lieutenant Colonel Tim Spicer. He later became famous in 1997 with his company Sandline when his employees were hired by the government of Papua New Guinea to put down a rebellion on secessionist Bougainville Island.

In the second year, our new Commanding Officer (later to become Major General Sir Iain Mackay-Dick KCVO MBE) put me in position as both a mountain marathon runner but also to take over the leadership of the team with an even more specific mission. We were now to win the competition and get as many Scots Guards teams in the top 10 of the 92 competing teams from around the world. He ensured that we focus on nothing other than our training on the mountain for three months. We were excused from all duties and were not distracted by any of the usual menial tasks which are the scourge of life in barracks. The importance of this sort of strong sponsorship by talented, well-connected and influential leaders has stuck with me and is very relevant to business life as well. The best sponsors help you overcome obstacles and get your team what they need to succeed. This allows you to focus purely on the things that matter and not be distracted by trivia. I see the importance of this today in the global project teams that I coach.

Plan the whole route- strategy and tactics

The ability to see the bigger picture became an essential skill. At the start of the event, each 3-man team rushed forward to the master map with our unmarked map to copy the Day 1 route with its 12 checkpoints. While this had to be done at speed, one error in transposing information could lose us the race, as we would have flailed around looking in the wrong spot for the checkpoint. Success from then on required strategy: to have an overview of the whole route from start to finish and being clear on the final destination. We also needed to decide on our tactics: focusing in minute detail on the routes we wanted to take and being aware of the presence of other competitors between our current location and the next checkpoint. In business, it is also crucial for the leader to keep an eye on the overall goal and to ensure that the work being done is "on purpose" and meaningful (SQ). Others can then put all their energy into the task, knowing their efforts are adding to the end result.

When times were at their toughest and we were exhausted, the most we could do was to focus on putting one foot in front of the other, as we ran up yet another part of the mountain. I constantly visualised the finish line and the end goal in order to encourage myself and team to keep us all going through these bleak moments. The knack was to be able to step back and see the wood not just the trees. As a leader then and now, there is something motivational about that responsibility which I find keeps me going when my body cries out "give up!"

Team selection

Time and effort spent in team selection is never wasted. Hiring decisions made in haste lead to numerous problems later on. These can be costly in terms of diminished team performance plus the unnecessary expenditure of time, emotion and finance. The efforts that Tim Spicer expended in the first year promoting the Cyprus walkabout internally within the Battalion were invaluable. It meant that in the second year there were a huge number of applicants who wished to be selected for the squad from which we would choose our final eight teams. The three simple rules of selection we used were:

1. Can they do the job (skills, capabilities and fitness for the role)?

2. Will they do the job (motivation and attitude)?

3. Do they fit in (rapport and team building)?

In business, it is also wise to have a rigorous and clear selection procedure. You should include psychological profiles to highlight emotional and social intelligence (EQ), personality and motivation. Then follow it with a number of team interviews and presentations by candidates. It also pays to have a six-month probation period, which is firmly enforced. Then if either side feels they haven't met the criteria for selection, then they should make a clean break immediately. Personally, I find having courageous conversations about poor performance to be tough. I have sometimes lacked the hard edge needed to sack someone during their probation period, because I never feel I've had sufficient time to see people perform to the best of their ability. Usually at that stage, the dilemma is that we have formed a strong bond of friendship.

Usually I requested, and was always granted more time for people to get fully up to speed in their new role. There are benefits to giving new employees time to settle in and prove their true talents, skills and capabilities. In more complex jobs, this period of getting up to speed can take between 12 and 18 months. I am still learning to have the courage to make the tough decisions to remove new hires early that are clearly unsuited to their role.

Emotional literacy to understand the fastest and slowest team members

As any team leader knows, you cannot have a team made up of individual gladiators who never work together. When people have such high levels of talent, self-assurance, independence and assertiveness, these sought-after qualities can almost become a weakness for a team. It is challenging when the superstars consider themselves to be so good that they should be the leader rather than you! The emotional and social intelligence qualities needed in this situation are a mix of listening skills, being able to read other people's emotions and a robustness to prevent you as the leader being steamrollered. Issues have to be dealt with assertively and quickly, to prevent disgruntled team members becoming "organisational terrorists" and undermining discipline and morale. When I focused on the needs of individuals in the team, rather than worrying about my own performance as a leader, I was more successful in connecting and motivating the team.

The weakest point in any chain is the link where it will snap when under strain. This was true of our eight 3-man running teams. It was always the slowest person we had to watch, encourage and cajole, since the time didn't stop until the last man finally crossed the finish line. In squad training it quickly became apparent who were the slow runners and who would not be able to sustain the pace for the full two days of mountain marathons. I had to remain highly flexible and cope with changes. Sometimes, the gladiatorial running stars had bad days too. People were consequently reassigned from the running squad into the back-up and reserve squads.

Whilst we trained the teams for the competition, we matched fast runners with good navigators. Navigation could have been a critical vulnerability and fast runners would have gone to a lot of places quickly, but not necessarily the right checkpoints! Taking these lessons further into business, I have aimed to match up people so they can advance with similar speed and not be held back and frustrated by less capable people. Everybody has a specific talent. The skill as a leader is having the emotional literacy to recognise individual talents and understand rapidly changing situations. You should identify exactly what people are good at and which values and beliefs drive them, then give them lots of opportunity to practise and excel at what they love doing. That produces the best results.

Fitness for the job and sustained training

Very few people can turn up and succeed in a two-day double mountain marathon competition without having undergone a sustained fitness training program. We learnt in our first year that it paid to train intensely and prepare in intricate detail for this significant event. The only exception I remember was a remarkable cavalry officer called Tom who appeared to be able to party and drink alcohol through the night and then run up the mountain effortlessly the very next day. He eventually ended up in the SAS. My own personality preference is for last-minute activity, but I realise that in so many ways advance preparation pays off. As a leader in business it is wise to rehearse thoroughly before public speaking, to plan strategy meetings and scenario plan before difficult, emotionally charged disciplinary, or performance interviews. It is important to ask yourself and those you lead: "Are you fit enough to sustain your performance in this job? If not, what are you going to do in order to ensure that you are?"

In addition to maintaining and sustaining your own physical and mental fitness to do well in your role, the other benefit is that you avoid illness, or injury. This may otherwise remove you from your work and overload colleagues, who will have to cover for you as well as doing their own job. When you do injure yourself, after the initial frustration, it is worth taking time for a full recovery. This can be an opportunity to reflect on your performance, your job and how you will quickly get back up to speed when you return. As an integrated inspiring leader you should therefore always nominate reserves and have a clear succession plan in which individuals are identified. Then, everyone is fully aware of who is lined up to replace you and the leaders below you.

MQ - Knowing True North

I have talked earlier in this book about discovering and expressing to others where your "True North" compass needle points. This is your guide and is derived from your personal integrity, standards and clear values. It should sustain you through your many setbacks and moments of temptation. Being clear on what beliefs and values guide you, regardless of where you are, who you're with, or in which organisation you are working, is highly reassuring to you as a leader, as well as to the people who follow you.

Throughout the walkabout race, it was essential to be clear where the physical True North was on the map. This is because there were many difficult challenges such as deep ravines, or moving through the thick scrub in which we could get seriously lost and head off in completely the wrong direction. This would lose precious time and potentially the chance of winning the race. The best navigators in orienteering races, and in life, can immediately point in the direction of True North. They rarely ever need to look down at the map or compass needle. They innately know what the right direction is, or how to behave.

Everyone loses their way on occasion in their job and life, and we forget to follow our True North. Those are moments to learn about the consequences of not living our lives on purpose and according to the high level of integrity, values and beliefs we aspire to follow. The issue is not the fact we have a problem or make a mistake, because we all do. Instead, it is the manner in which we rectify it and learn from our errors that differentiates truly effective leaders from the average managers.

Map and compass - "the map is not the territory"

The maps that we had of the Troodos Mountains in Cyprus were ten to fifteen years out of date. They missed out many of the smaller tracks, footpaths and even the rather obvious brand-new four-lane motorway across the mountainside. Therefore, we spent a number of weeks scouring back and forth across the mountain. We found what was missing from the map, recorded it on our master map and made that the closest fit we could to our experience of reality. We had to remember that the old map was just a two-dimensional representation of the ground and was far removed from what we would actually find.

Knowing that "the map is not the territory" we come to the realisation that everyone experiences the world differently. This is a direct result of their different belief systems, mental filters and prejudices. We must accept that our own belief systems distort how we see the world. We see it according to our own outdated mental map. When we realise this, we can become more open to others' perspectives and are better at understanding that others are not wrong, they just see things differently from us. If we are not too arrogant, or dogmatic, then we might more easily question our own view and have the humility to admit that our map may be wrong. With this healthier attitude, we would be far more accepting and less judgmental of others as a leader. By accepting that the map is not the territory, we could become more successful and more broad-minded as leaders. The challenge as leaders is to know when we are wrong, or when we need to press ahead according to our internal True North.

MQ & Integrity - don't win at any price

In seeking to win and be the best, I learned some very hard lessons from mistakes. My biggest one occurred in the Cyprus road marathon. Our Scots Guards team was using it as preparation for the mountain marathon, and I was desperate to perform well. I trained continually and obsessively nearly every day. I ran mile after mile on the mountain roads and on the coastal roads for four months. My training routine became focused on achieving a very fast marathon time of 2 hours and 45 minutes. When the race day came, I was revved up and totally absorbed in achieving my goal. My girlfriend was a jockey on the Nicosia racetrack and met me at the start of the marathon and produced a smarty-like pill just before I ran off. She convinced me it was harmless and since it helped the horses run fast, it might help me too. Without a moment's thought, I popped it in my mouth. That was a big mistake. As planned, I ran the first 10 miles in 60 minutes and the second 10 in a further 60 minutes. The final 6 miles seemed like an epic struggle down a never ending road with a large chain anchor dragging behind my legs.

My body was closing down on me. My vision narrowed onto the finish line and I could hardly see, walk or speak. I was in turmoil as then I lying in 4'h place and getting slower and slower and the crowd screaming at me to keep going. At times in business, I have been haunted by a similar feeling. That sensation of knowing I must keep going to achieve the goal, yet feeling overwhelmed, anxious, exhausted and never able to reach the finish line when it is so close. I passed out four-hundred yards short of the finish line and collapsed until I was helped to my feet by two kind competitors. Like good Samaritans, they lifted me up and helped me to slowly weave my way to the finish line. It seemed to last an eternity and every part of my body was failing on me. I marched in a drunken weaving manner to force my legs forward and literally fell across the finish line in 6th place in 2 hours and 56 minutes.

The medics looked very anxious and lifted me into an ambulance and rushed me to hospital. I was delirious when the doctor later proscribed an acute case of heat exhaustion from the Cyprus sun and the effects of the lethal pill. I will never know what was in my girlfriend's innocent-looking pink pill. My agonies were not over yet. Meanwhile our little military ambulance broke down on route for thirty minutes and the temperature inside its claustrophobic metal box rocketed. I cramped up, had acute spasms and was violently ill as I passed in and out of consciousness. The doctors reassuringly told me later that I nearly died.

Three days later I was allowed out of hospital to recover slowly. The leadership lesson for me was clear and unforgettable. I was told by a business leader "anything is possible if you are prepared to pay the price and live with the consequences!" However, I vowed to be wiser and learnt from my near death experience that nothing is worth winning at any price, especially if you have to break the rules.

Learning from your mistakes

When you are the leader responsible for the team and are lost, exhausted and under pressure, it is vitally important that you don't press on. Instead, it is better to admit your mistake and retrace your steps to the place you last knew you where you were. Then, use your compass and map to start out again. Sadly very few leaders do this, and their pride prevents them from confessing when they are lost and out of their depth. I always admire leaders who admit when they don't know the answer and humbly seek the views from those they lead. It is always startling when the best answer comes from an unexpected quarter. In the Korean War, the American pilots outmanoeuvred the adversaries by using the "OODA loop" - they Observed the situation, Orientated themselves, Decided and swiftly Acted and then they immediately observed again, before returning around this decision-action cycle to beat their opposition. Using a similar technique to adjust to the continuously changing business environment means you will develop the flexibility to out-manoeuvre your competitors.

The classic navigational error is to get lost and then mentally force-fit the map to what you are actually experiencing on the ground. You can delude yourself for a couple of hours. The deception goes something like this: "If only I could just bend the track shown on the map, then it would be pretty similar to the one I am running on now." You convince yourself that perhaps "they forgot to include this small hill and river." There comes a time when you have to stop yourself, recalibrate and ask "who am I trying to fool?"

Don't follow me, I'm lost too

There were moments on the mountain when we caught up with other teams, or they caught up with us. It is always very tempting to follow somebody else, especially when you are under pressure or lost. You think that they look more confident, seem to know where they are going and probably can map read better than you. The easy option is to mentally switch off and follow someone else for a while. This is a mistake and can lead you badly off course. Eventually, you end up without a clue as to where you are. I remember in one orienteering event in my early days of navigation and after breathlessly racing after an opponent for a couple of checkpoints, I got close enough to see a badge on their back which warned me: "Don't follow me-I'm lost too!"

I have learnt from bitter experience, both in the military and business, that it is far wiser to follow your own counsel. Choose your own route, move at a slower pace and be certain of the direction in which you're heading. This is more courageous than blindly rushing after everybody else, in a headlong dash to you know not where. Often it pays to be different and to trust your own judgment. Many people are completely lost both physically and morally and are far too busy driving fast in their manic rush through life. They don't make time to stop and re-energise themselves and consequently can unexpectedly and dramatically run out of juice.

Sustainability for the long journey, eat, sleep and rest

When travelling at speed relentlessly for hours and undertaking two marathons over two days, the punishment on the body is enormous. Consequently you need to build your strength beforehand and be fully rested, whilst being at the peak of your own fitness. We work in such manic, stress-filled business environments. It can be seen as a badge of honour at work to be far too busy to stop to spend time with your friends, or see your family as they grow up. In the three months training for the mountain marathon, I made a point of ensuring that the team had a balanced regime in which they ate and drank well. We mostly drank water and juices rather than alcohol until after the race. We built in time so the team rested, relaxed, had time off with their families and had fun. On the night before the run, we went out for big team dinner of pasta and filled ourselves with soft drinks, in order to cope with the heat in the mountains on the following two days. After the competition, we gave ourselves a day to rest, recover and hobble about since our feet were fairly sore.

Presence, personal power and tough love

There is an old saying that "the darkest hour is just before the dawn". A bad situation often seems worse just before it improves. This was most apt for us at the very end of Day one of the mountain marathon. The three of us in my team were utterly exhausted. Although we had the good news from the last checkpoint that we might have been in the lead, we were totally spent. We just wanted to walk up the final two miles to the summit. At that moment, I knew that as the leader I had to step forward and do something to keep us going. I call it tough love, yet for a further fifteen minutes I could only just stagger on myself, choosing to take the easy option and avoid the difficult confrontation. Somehow the sense of responsibility and accountability as the leader enabled me to dredge up additional energy from the depths of my being. This was all about personal power, leadership presence and not shrinking from my responsibility. I started shouting encouragement and physically pulling the other two by the front of their shirts. This meant that we all broke into a stumbling run, until we crossed the finish line that day. I'm sure my team thought I was mad and perhaps I was!

Often in business there are similar challenges where everyone is stumbling along. It is only you as leader who have the full responsibility and you must realise that you need to have the personal courage to step forward. You should lead by example frequently in order to raise the pace and encourage everybody to follow you. The impact of your example of servant leadership should never be underestimated. It can fundamentally change situations in battle and in business. You can't pay a surrogate to go in your stead, run in your place, or inspire others by merely parroting your words. It is your own personal charisma, presence and example that make all the difference.

Service - go the extra mile for success

It pays always to be prepared to go further than you planned in serving the people you lead and the clients you work with. It is incredibly powerful when others know you will go the extra mile for them. Both in the Cyprus walkabout and in training for the airborne forces selection, I found you have to be prepared for unexpected surprises which mean you have to keep going, just when you thought you had finished. This attitude makes the difference between coming first or second, between victory and defeat. In our first year in the walkabout competition, my team came third and the remaining Scots Guards teams in a variety of other positions in the top 40. In the second year we trained particularly hard and focused on developing the attitude of going an extra mile and never giving up.

A similar stamina lesson was driven home on the Airborne Para selection course. The instructors made us complete a demanding 8-mile march with full kit and heavy rucksacks. As we staggered into barracks, the group was strung out over quite a distance. We were relieved to know that we were going to shower and go home. It was our single-minded obsession and kept us going. The instructor had other plans. He turned us around, and to our shock we had to run out of camp again to repeat the course. He said since some members of the squad had not kept up, that we would all do it again as punishment. He goaded us: "In war if one member of your team fails gentlemen, then you all fail!" After the first mile a number of people gave up. That meant that they "failed themselves" immediately and left the course that night. What they were unaware of was that the instructor had planned that we would be turned around after another half mile and returned to camp. The message is that the enemy or any business competitors don't necessarily play fair. They never follow your timings or planned milestones. You have to be prepared for the unexpected and to go beyond what you were mentally prepared to do in order to win.

Savour the success

I will never forget the excitement, exhilaration and feeling of pride on our second day of running down the mountain. Our pulses raced as we entered the final two-mile home stretch to the finish line of the second marathon. We had leapt, jumped and slid down scree slopes and run steadily up other hills. Like a lesson in life, it is bizarre how many hills you have to climb up when you know you are meant to be going down a mountain! From the excitement of the support teams at each check point, we got a powerful feeling that we were capable of seizing first place. That news spurred us on to even greater effort. We knew that the whole of the Battalion were lined up along the final stage of the route. They were ready to greet our eight Scots Guards teams and gathered around the massive banner which read "Cyprus Walkabout - Finish".

We could hear a helicopter above us from which the Commanding Officer was encouraging us. He had a megaphone and was yelling "Come on Perks!" and "Come on the Scots Guards!" We were also strongly motivated by Scots Guards pipers playing their bagpipes besides the dusty track every half mile for the last two miles to the finish. The roar of excitement from the troops, as they realised we were in the lead, helped us to power through the last two miles. It felt like a scene from the film "Chariots of Fire" with the three of us running in slow motion with the hairs on the back of our necks standing up to the sound of the inspirational bagpipe music. We were grinning like maniacs!

The euphoria of achieving everything that we had been asked, and more, made the often painful preparations and every mile of the race fade into insignificance. In a strangely masochistic way, we had all enjoyed the journey from start to finish. It was an experience I will remember with pride to my dying day. We set the still unbeaten world record time. We also have the accolade of achieving first, second and third places and having every single one of our in teams in the top ten. As our teams crossed the line minutes ahead of the competition, the Battalion went absolutely wild. We were rushed by a sea of over 400 euphoric supporters and lifted onto the shoulders of the Scots Guardsmen. They paraded us about the barracks like the winners in an intense Celtic–Rangers Scottish football final.

At the prize giving that night I was handed the winning trophy. It was a life size solid bronze patrol boot on a plinth. I thrust it aloft above my head and immediately was responded to with a huge animal roar from the Battalion that filled the air: "Yes!" We passed the trophy around each team member who kissed it like a scene from winning the Football World Cup. The twenty four members of the team were treated like heroes for months. We could do no wrong, and that night we were immediately taken to the Sergeants Mess where the Regimental Sergeant Major said: "That trophy looks heavy sir. Let me take it off your hands and put it here in our Trophy Cabinet." There it stayed all year while he treated us all to many rounds of drinks and games to celebrate.

We went out to celebrate the next night in quieter style and really acknowledge what an incredible victory we had achieved. In life and in business, it is far too easy for any of us to push on after each of our successes to the next challenge. Far too rarely do we stop to savour the good feelings that result. High achievers are too often obsessively driven to accumulate goal after goal like some life-long check list to be ticked off. Remember to be in the moment, celebrate, acknowledge your considerable achievements and reward yourself. After all you have strived so hard, for so long to get where you are now!

SQ - a job you really love

There was one of major contributing factor to our success in the Cyprus mountain marathon and indeed other orienteering competitions throughout my time in the Army. That was the fact that I love the combination of the intellectual challenge of navigation, high levels of fitness, leading team members and competing either to improve my own times or to win against others.

Linking this to my various roles in business, it seems obvious to say that you should always do a job you really love. Sadly over 50% of the senior leaders who I meet don't really love their role, or the work they do.

Personally whenever I find myself doing a job that I don't enjoy, I analyse what factors I could change to ensure that I end up doing something more to my liking. Making a lot of money on its own sounds good, but is never enough for inspiring leaders and it doesn't make you successful. Instead, you must be doing something that gives you a sense of meaning and purpose, something which you are passionate about and that you really love doing in order to become fulfilled. This is the essence of really living your life on purpose.

Applying the 8 principles of inspiring leadership to your life

I am going to conclude this book with some practical pointers on how you might develop and enhance aspects of inspiring leadership in your own job and career. These are a taste of the eight modules and seminars which I intend to give on the topic of inspiring leadership.

1. Acquire wisdom (IQ)

Greater wisdom is accumulated from your own experience, reflection and learning from others. Make a point of gathering around you your "success team" of mentors and coaches who can then share their wisdom, stories and experience. Wisdom can be accumulated from studying and modelling the decision-making processes and behaviours of other inspiring leaders. Learn from them how they developed the ability to analyse a situation and make difficult decisions under pressure. There are several helpful problem-solving processes and techniques which you can learn. Most importantly, you need to listen to your intuition, gut feeling or sixth sense. Conduct after action reviews (AARs) to learn from every experience, whether good or bad. Select the best leaders in your organisation, and find ways to work with them and learn from them. Equally identify the worst leaders, and actively avoid them. Use them as a reminder of the consequences of poor leadership. After every experience, always ask yourself: "What have I learnt, and what action will I take?"

2. Enhance your personal power and presence.

The other seven principles of inspiring leadership all contribute to a strong level of personal power. The ability to be authentically yourself and to have complete alignment between what you think, what you say and what you do, is the most genuine way of enhancing your personal power. Some of the best leaders I know have very high levels of personal power due to the fact that they know themselves well. They are genuinely curious about other people, listen well, summarise what they hear and are quietly assertive. The ability to be totally attentive to another person undoubtedly develops high levels of presence, which in turn builds trustworthiness. Genuinely looking the part of an inspiring leader is quite important. It is only sustained by a strong sense of being grounded, ego-less, calm and very clear about exactly who you are, what you stand for and what you will not accept.

3. Develop your emotional and social intelligence (EQ)

There is great value in measuring and developing your emotional and social intelligence as a leader. Complete a questionnaire, like the EQ-i, to benchmark and understand your own level of EQ now. Then, work with your coach to develop the areas which will make the most significant difference in your work and your life as a whole. Read and study about the topic and seek out other inspiring leaders, who have developed high levels of emotional intelligence, and learn from them about the ways they have done this in a sustainable and enduring way. Start by enhancing your self-regard combined with developing your emotional self-awareness. Follow these by developing high levels of empathy and happiness, and you will stand out as a leader.

4. Build an attitude of gratitude and appreciation

Go out and catch your own people "doing things right". Tell them specifically what it is that you value about their contribution. Make your appreciation genuine, immediately after the event and don't make it gushing, or overdo it, since that will negate its value. Appreciate and recognise what you have already that is working well both for you personally as a leader, and for your organisation and team. Inculcate a culture in which you and others seek out and overtly value performance and behaviour that is working well. In every meeting, feedback session, or interview, always end the session with feedback on a single leadership quality that you appreciate about each other. Maintain a genuine attitude of gratitude for what people do for you, wherever you are, and whoever they are. Others will always remember you in a positive way, and you will continue to touch people's lives and make a positive impact in the world.

5. Strengthen your values and beliefs (MQ)

There are various exercises that will help you to identify and prioritise the most fundamental values and beliefs which drive your life. Again, you should use them as a check list when considering new roles, organisations or long-term relationships. Are your values and beliefs fully aligned with the organisation for which you work? Are they also aligned with those with whom you have the closest and most intimate relationships? If so, then you know you will have the most satisfying and fulfilling experiences. Prioritise your values and beliefs so that when you find yourself in conflict, your decision-making is clear and simple. Choose to live your life by a strong set of values especially those that enhance your trustworthiness. Adapt yourself to the situation in which you find yourself, and choose the point at which you will refuse to change your viewpoint based on your own strong values and beliefs or when you are prepared to be flexible. The battle between principle and pragmatism is a long and bitter one. Some people die for their values and beliefs, whilst some make others die for theirs!

6. Increase your passion

Inspiring leadership means that you love and care for those you lead, even if at times their behaviour frustrates you. They, in their turn, may love following you. Sometimes, you will need to display tough love, have courage and challenge unacceptable behaviour. When you insert passion into the way you lead others, then we know from Penna's research that you can create a greater sense of meaning and purpose. This increases productivity by twenty to thirty percent. Put passion, energy, drive and zest into the way you lead others. In that way, you will breathe life, spirit and inspiration into your relationship and the work that they have to do.

Inspiration has to be authentic and come from deep within you. You can't pretend to be inspirational. If you neither love the work you do nor do the work you love, then there are a variety of exercises you can do with a coach to discover your real calling.

7. Discover how to live your life on purpose (SQ)

Be crystal clear about your life purpose and what you want your legacy to be during your lifetime. Even more enduring is to decide what you will leave for posterity. It is rarely financial but often about the quality of your relationships that make a positive difference in the world. This principle requires some careful reflection, high levels of self-awareness and the assistance of a good mentor or coach. This will help you unearth and vocalise succinctly the calling that will give you the most fulfilment. Keep testing, honing and refining your life purpose into a simple sentence which you can use as a litmus test against all life choices you make.

8. Serve others to lead

Happy leaders enjoy giving of themselves and serving others. Being of service to others can also enhance your happiness, provided it is done in a healthy way. The quality of humble excellence is admirable. Leadership by personal example means that you're never too arrogant, or too proud to roll up your sleeves and help out. The principle of serving to lead is far more of an attitude based on a genuine question: "How may I serve you?" As a leader are you "prepared to take the bullet" for those you lead? Are you genuinely abundant and willing to go the extra mile for those you lead in a modest way without fanfares and trumpets? If so you will earn respect, loyalty and trust. Find out what motivates and drives team members, their interests and passions, what success means to them and how they like to be rewarded.

My father's legacy

Some years ago, I had a life-changing insight as a result of some very powerful coaching. As I focused on my own life purpose, I had an imaginary conversation with my long-dead father and said to him: "In your honour, I will make something of my life." I had idolised my father and he had been my inspiration in the darkest and most difficult stages of my life. At those moments, his memory had helped me draw on my deeper mental resources as a leader. One such example was in encouraging my exhausted team to reach the summit of the Mount Troodos on day one of the Cyprus Walkabout. The question that I was now asked by my coach was: "Just how powerful would it be to live your life with inspiration from within yourself, since your father's DNA and his wisdom now resides in you?" I therefore rephrased my leadership mantra to become: "In **my** honour, I will make something of my life."

I am continually inspired by the extract from the book *A return to love* by Marianne Williamson:

Our deepest fear is not that we are inadequate
Our deepest fear is that we are powerful beyond measure.

It is our light, not our darkness, that most frightens us. We
ask ourselves, who am I to be brilliant,
gorgeous, handsome, talented and fabulous?

Actually, who are you not to be?
You are a child of God.

Your playing small does not serve the world.
There is nothing enlightened about shrinking
so that other people won't feel insecure around you.
We are all meant to shine, as children do.

We were born to make manifest the glory of God within us.
It is not just in some of us; it is in everyone.

And, as we let our own light shine, we consciously give
other people permission to do the same.
As we are liberated from our fear,
our presence automatically liberates others.

My request of you

My final request of you is therefore for you to make the most of the unique talents and gifts you have been given and apply them to living your life on purpose. Consider ways of serving others in your life as an inspiring leader, so that you are successful, as a result of being fulfilled by the work you do and the difference you make to the people around you. You can make a positive impact in the world with the smallest and most apparently insignificant acts of courage and kindness. Remember that nothing is insignificant and that everything and everyone matters. It takes your wisdom to add perspective and prioritise the things that matter most. Begin now.

4 Key Points:

- There has to be a new and more effective way of sustainable leadership.

- Think about your personal growth, your fulfilment and life purpose.

- "Just how much is enough?" is a question we should ask ourselves in this age of greed and materialism.

- Tips are provided on how to apply the eight principles of inspiring leadership to your life.

4 Questions:

1. What do you learn from navigating through your own life and career?

2. What is the big question for you that just won't go away?

3. How will you apply at least one of the principles of inspiring leadership to your work and life?

4. What might be the biggest difference this philosophy could make to your life?

The Scots Guards Winning Team, Cyprus Walkabout

EPILOGUE

Reuven Bar-On

(The person who conceptualised the idea of EQ, authored the EQ-i and co-edited The Handbook of Emotional Intelligence and Educating People to Be Emotionally Intelligent)

In writing this book, Jonathan Perks has unequivocally created his *magnum opus* in the field of leadership. *Inspiring Leadership* represents an important source of information that must be read, studied and applied. As such, it will hopefully serve as an invaluable resource for those who work in any aspect of executive coaching and leadership development.

The primary message that emerges from these pages is that the 8 principals of inspiring leadership drive successful leadership. These basic attributes of the inspiring leader are masterfully exemplified in numerous stories that the author shares with the reader relying on three decades of experience in the military and corporate world. His specific conceptualisation of leadership is based on thousands of hours of being a leader, coaching other leaders and coming in contact with a wide variety of both positive and negative role models over the years.

While the individual's emotional and social intelligence ("EQ") is one of the key prerequisites for becoming an inspiring leader, all of the other prerequisites described by the author are also based on this significantly important construct combined with cognitive ("IQ"), moral ("MQ") and spiritual intelligence ("SQ"). Additionally, inspiring leaders must demonstrate the true "presence" of a leader, genuine "appreciation" for those they lead, "passion" for their work, and the capacity to "serve to lead" and lead by example. When all of these attributes combine, they form the eight points of a compass that is designed to point the way and help inspiring leaders stand out as: (i) adept problem solvers and wise decision makers; (ii) possessing a unique and motivating presence; (iii) emotionally and socially intelligent; (iv) appreciating those they lead; (v) being guided by a set of values and beliefs that are non-negotiable; (vi) radiating passion in what they do; (vii) being driven by a sense of meaning and purpose; and (viii) serving others, their organisation and the larger community.

The fundamental importance of Jonathan Perks' message is that *Inspiring Leadership* provides an invaluable compass for coaching designed to help individuals become better leaders and establish a climate that inspires others to do their best, enjoy what they do and enhance the overall effectiveness of their organisation.

I have three wishes regarding the potential impact of this book. First, I would like the readers to not only gain a deeper understanding of how they should lead but to become more inspiring leaders themselves. Second, I would like to see some of the readers be encouraged to research this concept of leadership as well as design effective ways of developing it. Last, I would like to see organisations eventually hire, train and promote inspiring leaders for the numerous reasons described in this book.

It was both effortless and enjoyable to write this epilogue, because Jonathan is a person I admire, respect and am constantly learning from. It was both an honour and a privilege to have been asked to summarise *Inspiring Leadership*; and, more importantly, it is a humbling experience for me to have the author as a friend and colleague.

Recommended Reading

A selection of my favourite books which have influenced and inspired me.

The Three Laws of Performance	Zaffron and Logan
Time To Think	Nancy Kline
Resonant Leadership	Boyatzis & McKee
The Power of Now	Eckhart Tolle
Coaching For Performance	John Whitmore
Non-Violent Communication	Rosenberg
First Break All The Rules	Marcus Buckingham and Curt Coffman
Growing Leaders	Yearout, Miles and Koonce
The Seven Habits	Stephen Covey
The Power of One	Bryce Courtney
Long Walk To Freedom	Nelson Mandela
The Heart of Success	Rob Parsons
Spiritual Capital	Zohar and Marshall
McKinsey's Marvin Bower	Edersheim
Breaking The Rules	Kurt Wright
Drive	Daniel Pink
The 80-20 Principle	Richard Koch

TA Today	Ian Stewart and Vann Joines
The Making of Them	Nick Duffel
The Invitation	Oriah Mountain Dreamer
Chasing Daylight	Eugene O'Kelly
Feel The Fear And Do It Anyway	Susan Jeffers
Clever	Goffee and Jones
Moral Intelligence	Lennick and Kiel
The Winners Bible	Doctor Kerry Spackman
A New Earth	Eckhart Tolle
Why Should Anyone Be Led By You?	Goffee & Jones
Co-active Coaching	Whitworth, Kimsey-House and Sandhal
Executive Coaching - With Backbone & Heart	Mary Beth O'Neill
The Anatomy of Peace	The Arbinger Institute
Success Intelligence	Robert Holden
Our Iceberg Is Melting	John Kotter
What Got You Here Won't Get You There	Marshall Goldsmith
What The Bleep Do We Know?	William Arntz
More Time To Think	Nancy Kline
A Return To Love	Marianne Williamson
Working with Emotional Intelligence	Daniel Goleman
Emotional Capitalists	Martyn Newman

Effective Coaching	Miles Downey
The Speed Of Trust	Stephen Covey
Parkinson's Law	Northcote Parkinson
The Richer Way	Julian Richer
Think And Grow Rich	Napoleon Hill
How To Win Friends And Influence People	Dale Carnegie
Man's Search For Meaning	Victor Frankl
The Prophet	Kahill Gibran
The Secret	Rhonda Byrne
The Psychology of Achievement	Brian Tracy (CD)
Lead the Field	Earl Nightingale (CD)
Coaching for Leadership	Jonathan Passmore
Educating People to Be Emotionally Intelligent	Reuven Bar-On, Kobus Maree & Maurice Elias
EQ-i Leadership User's Guide	Reuven Bar-On
Working with Emotional Intelligence	Daniel Goleman
Primal Leadership	Daniel Goleman, Richard Boyatzis & Annie McKee
The Stress Effect: Why Smart Leaders Make Dumb Decisions	Henry Thompson

References

[1] O'Neill, Mary Beth (2000), *Executive Coaching with Backbone and Heart*, San Francisco: Jossey-Bass Publishers

[2] wordnetweb.princeton.edu/perl/webwn

[3] Gardner, Howard (1983) *Frames of Mind: The Theory of Multiple Intelligences.* New York: Basic Books

[4] Field Marshal The Lord Harding of Petherton, addressing the Senior Division at RMAS when Head of the Army., July 1953. From Serve to Lead (an Anthology)

[5] Dixon, Norman, F (1976) On the Psychology of Military Incompetence, Pimlico

[6] Rock, David (2008), SCARF A brain based Model for collaborating with and influencing others, Neuro Leadership Journal Issue 1 2008.

[7] Bennis, Warren (2010) Still Surprised: a memoir of a life in leadership

[8] http://www.thefreedictionary.com/presence

[9] Fox, George (1658) Quaker faith and practice, 2.18, Warwick Printing Co. Ltd.

[10] Tolle, Eckhart (1997) The Power of Now, a Guide to Spiritual Enlightenment, Namaste publishing, Canada

[11] Perks, Jonathan (2008) Bosses who cannot switch off are at risk of derailment, 28th August, Financial Times

[12] Bar-On, Reuven (2006) The Bar-On model of emotional-social intelligence (ESI), Psicothema, 18, supplement, pp13-25

[13] Bar-On, Reuven (1997) The Bar-On Emotional Quotient Inventory (EQ-i): Technical Manual, Multi-Health Systems Inc., Toronto, Canada.

[14] Goleman, Daniel (1998) Working with emotional intelligence, Bantam Books, New York.

[15] Buckingham, Marcus, and Coffman, C W (1999) First break all the rules: Gallup study into Managers, Simon & Schuster, London.

[16] Perks, Jonathan and Bar-On, Reuven (2010) Coaching for Emotionally Intelligent Leadership chapter within *Leadership Coaching: Working with leaders to develop elite performance* edited by Jonathan Passmore and published by Kogan Page.

[17] Kline, Nancy (1998) Time to Think: Listening to Ignite the Human Mind, Cassell

[18] Hammond, Sue (1996) The Thin Book of Appreciative Inquiry, Thin Book Company Publishing, Plano Texas

[19] Tracy, Brian (1990) The Psychology of Performance, CD by Nightingale Conant

[20] Jane Elliott Health Reporter BBC News, 22 March 2008,http://news.bbc.co.uk/1/hi/health/7304287.stm

[21] Lennick, Doug and Kiel, Fred (2005) Moral Intelligence: Enhancing Business Performance and Leadership Success, Wharton Business Press

[22] Borba, Michele (2002) Building Moral Intelligence, The Seven Essential Virtues that Teach Kids to Do the Right Thing, Jossey-Bass

[23] Dilts, Robert (1990) Changing Belief Systems with NLP, Meta Publications, Capitola, California,

[24] Orwell, George (1945) Animal Farm, London, Penguin Group

[25] Schwarzkopf, Norman (1992) It Doesn't Take a Hero, Bantam

[26] Major General Julian Thompson, Commander, 3 Commando Brigade Falklands 1982, From Serve to Lead (an Anthology)

[27] Byrnes, Jonathan (2005) The Essence of Leadership, Harvard business school article, 9/6/2005

[28] Nightingale , Earl, (2002), Lead the field, CD by Nightingale Conant

[29] Frankl, Viktor (1946), Man's Search for Meaning

[30] Zohar, Diana & Marshall, Ian (2000) SQ: Spiritual Intelligence, the Ultimate Intelligence, Bloomsbury, London

[31] Buzan, Tony (2001) The Power of Spiritual intelligence, HarperCollins Publishers Ltd

[32] Penna Research Report (2005), Meaning at Work Coordinated by Trevor Lambert

[33] Holbeche, Linda and Springett, Nigel (2003) In search of meaning at work, Roffey Park

[34] Green, Stephen (2010) Good value - choosing a better life in business, Penguin Books

[35] Eiseley , Loren (1969) An adaptation from *The Star Thrower* (or "starfish story") *The Unexpected Universe*.

[36] Slim, William (1957) Courage and other Broadcasts, from Serve to Lead (an Anthology)

[37] Hackett, John (1968) C-in-C British Army of the Rhine, Transcript of BBC broadcast Looking for Leadership, from Serve to Lead (an Anthology)

Lightning Source UK Ltd.
Milton Keynes UK
UKOW04f0333111014

239925UK00002B/43/P